Spelling
Games and Activities

GRADE

6

All illustrations and photography, including those from Shutterstock.com, are protected by copyright.

Writing: Monika Davies
Content Editing: Kathleen Jorgensen
Lisa Vitarisi Mathews
Copy Editing: Cindie Farley
Art Direction: Yuki Meyer
Illustration: Bryan Langdo
Dana Regan
Cover Design: Yuki Meyer
Design/Production: Paula Acojido
Yuki Meyer
Jessica Onken

EMC 8276

Congratulations on your purchase of some of the finest teaching materials in the world.

Photocopying the pages in this book is permitted for <u>single-classroom use only</u>. Making photocopies for additional classes or schools is prohibited.

For information about other Evan-Moor products, call 1-800-777-4362, fax 1-800-777-4332, or visit our website, www.evan-moor.com. Entire contents © 2023 Evan-Moor Corporation 10 Harris Court, Suite C-3, Monterey, CA 93940-5773. Printed in USA.

CPSIA: Sheridan Saline, Inc., Saline, MI, USA [10/2023]

Contents

What's in *Spelling Games and Activities* 4

How to Use *Spelling Games and Activities* 7

Spelling Word List 8

Themed Units

Let's Celebrate! 11
Words about parties featuring words with double consonants,
the -**tion** ending, and a schwa sound in unaccented syllables

Heroes 21
Words about heroic qualities featuring words with suffixes,
r-controlled vowels, and words with consonant digraphs

Let's Get in Shape! 31
Words about exercise featuring consonant blends, consonant
digraphs, and silent letters

Family Roots 41
Words about family relations featuring multisyllable words,
words with hard and soft **c** and **g**, and **r**-controlled vowels

Exploration 51
Words about discovery featuring different sounds of **c**, vowel
digraphs, and vowel pairs across syllables

A World of Food 61
Words about international foods with Latin American, Asian,
Middle Eastern, and European roots

Solving Mysteries 71
Words about mysteries featuring **r**-controlled vowels, consonant
digraphs, and words with a schwa sound in unaccented syllables

It Came from Outer Space! 81
Words about space featuring Greek and Latin roots, consonant
blends, and **r**-controlled vowels

Extra Practice Worksheets 91

Spelling Strategies 152

Answer Key 159

What's in *Spelling Games and Activities*

Support for Writing

Spelling skills are essential for children to practice in order to communicate well in writing. Many people rely on technology to fix their spelling, but technology can only guess what the writer means. Spelling must be accurate to be understood. Even though there are many spelling rules and even more exceptions, spelling practice can help students understand those rules and apply them to their writing.

Spelling Games and Activities gives you two ways to help your students practice spelling:

- the engaging themed unit section, which brings together related words in grade-appropriate contexts in fun and interesting ways

- the extra practice worksheets section, which uses words from Evan-Moor's *Building Spelling Skills* series and can be used to enrich those lessons or on its own

8 Themed Units

Spelling Games and Activities offers 8 units of grade-level topics that engage students and provide context for practicing spelling useful words. Each unit introduces 18 theme-related words along with the spelling patterns and rules that are used in those words. The unit continues with fun puzzles, cutouts, and other activities to practice writing and spelling the words, followed by a game or other special activity done as a class or in small groups.

Unit Features

You can assign all the pages in a cohesive unit or choose individual worksheets as needed to support your spelling program or to reinforce words learned in other content areas. Each 10-page unit provides a set of spelling words and related spelling tips, a variety of activity pages, and a game or project with teacher directions.

Unit Overview

An introduction telling students what the unit's words have in common, along with the words themselves

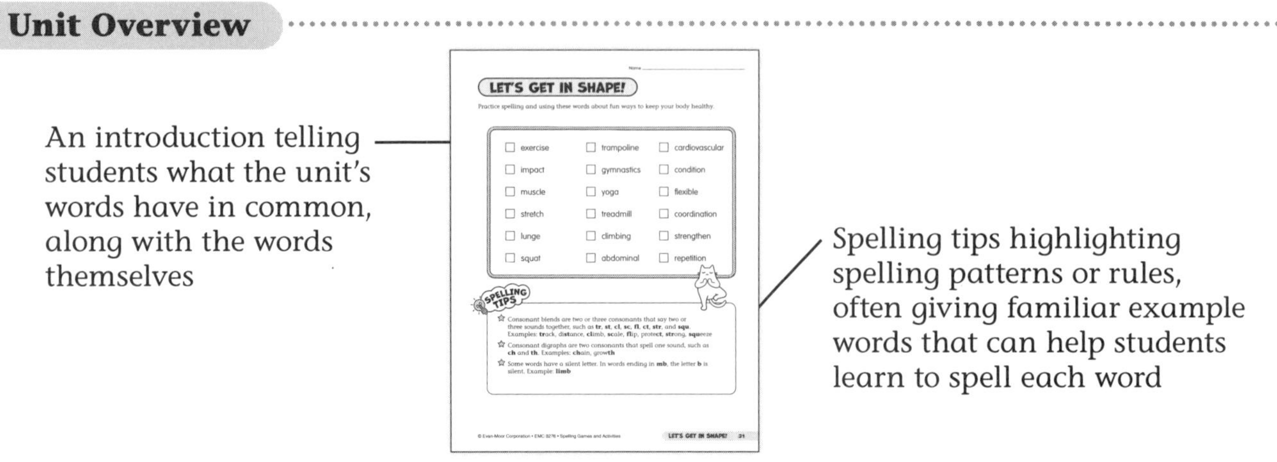

Spelling tips highlighting spelling patterns or rules, often giving familiar example words that can help students learn to spell each word

Spelling Games and Activities • EMC 8276 • © Evan-Moor Corporation

Theme-Based Activity Pages

There are a wide variety of theme-based activities in every theme unit. These are some examples.

Connect similar words

Students analyze words, looking for specific spelling patterns or structures.

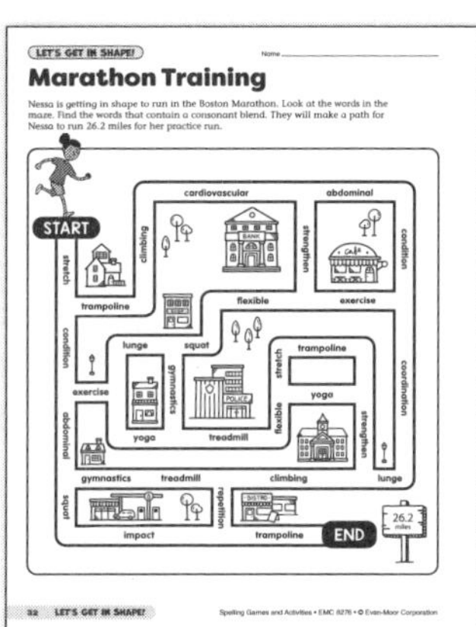

Find and fix misspellings

Students read lists or short texts, identify mistakes, and fix them.

Use sound and meaning clues

Students use clues to figure out the spelling words.

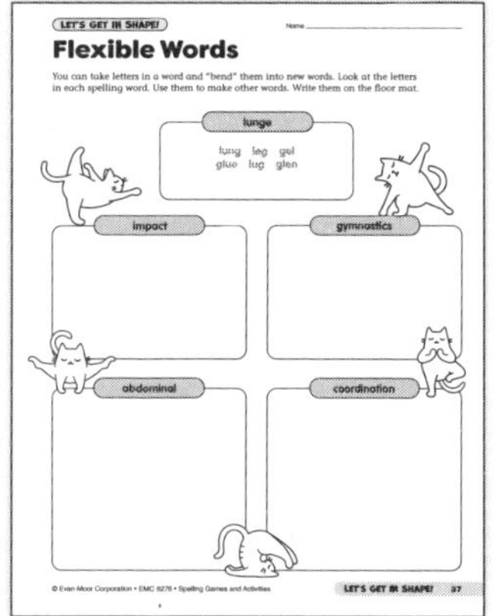

Make words from words

Students use the letters in their spelling words to make other words.

Game, Activity, or Hands-on Center

A fun theme-related game, often a variation of a familiar children's game, lets students practice their words in a small or large group setting.

A page of instructions and materials for the teacher is included, as well as any cards or game boards.

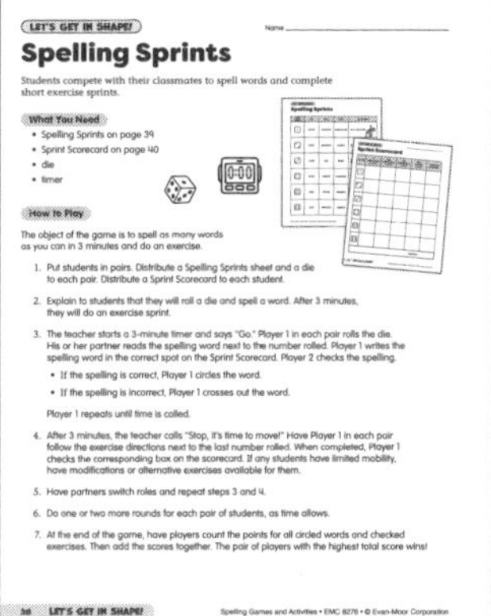

Extra Practice Worksheets

Students apply the same spelling tips from the themed units to sets of words from *Building Spelling Skills*. These pages can be used independently or with any spelling series.

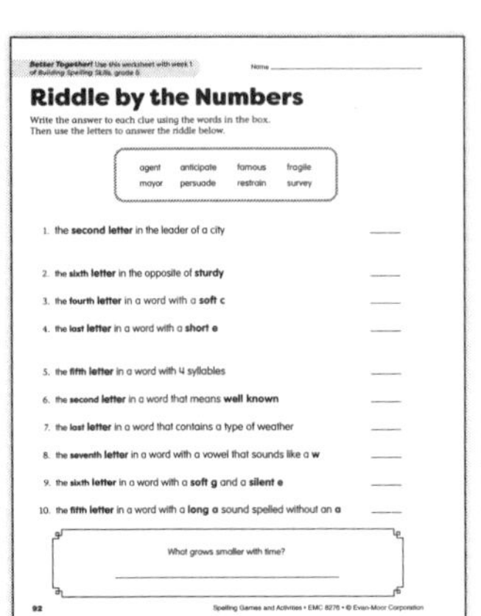

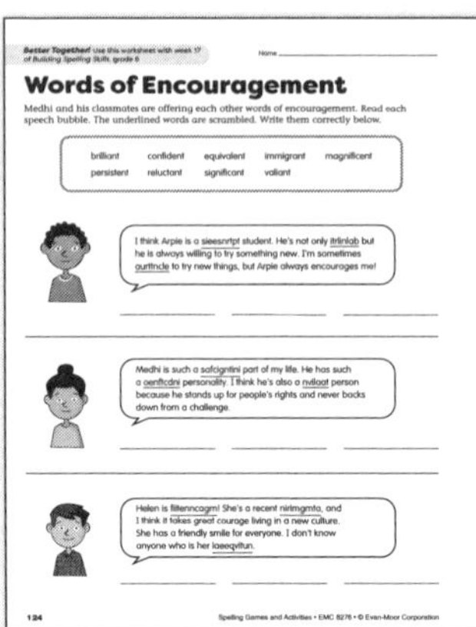

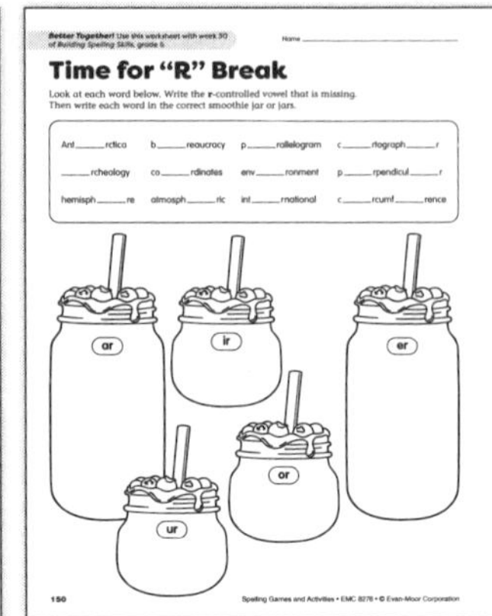

Additional Resources

Spelling Strategies

A variety of useful strategies that help students learn a word's spelling by analyzing sounds and word structures or by using dictionary skills and memory aids

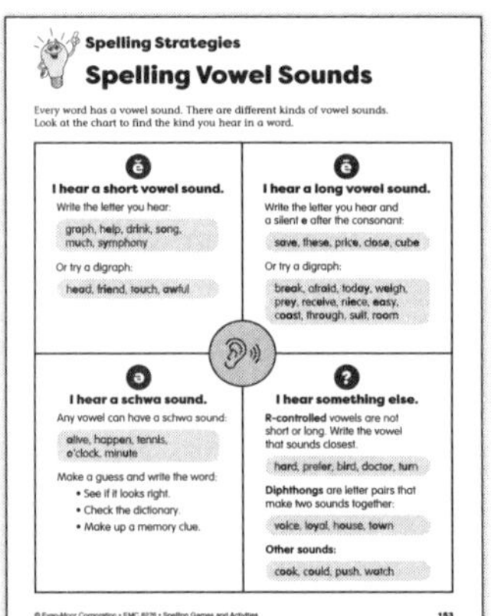

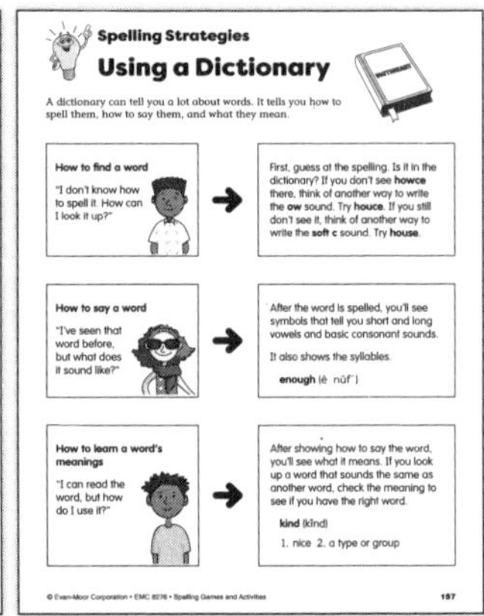

Spelling Word List

Alphabetized glossary of all spelling words in the book

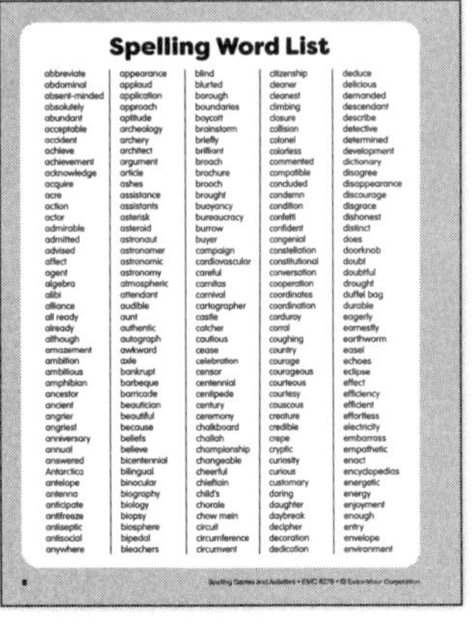

Answer Key

Provided for any page that has student answers. The correct answer or a sample response is shown, unless the question is completely open-ended.

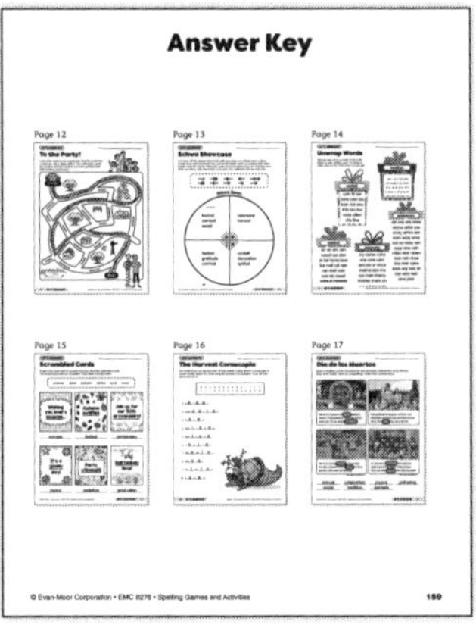

How to Use *Spelling Games and Activities*

Flexible Use

Decide which pages you will use. You can use an entire unit from the themed section, pages focusing on a particular skill, or extra practice pages that apply skills to different words. Then print copies for your students. It is recommended that you include the introduction page that provides helpful spelling tips for the skills you're working on.

Connections to Other Subjects

The units in this book were chosen to represent common experiences of children in sixth grade, along with general grade-level words. These topics may relate to other subjects you are teaching and could augment other lessons. For example, A World of Food and It Came from Outer Space! could be used with a language lesson on word roots. Heroes could be used with a history lesson focusing on civil rights. Exploration and It Came from Outer Space! could extend a science lesson about oceanography or astronomy. Let's Get in Shape! could be used when students must spend recess inside on a rainy day. Use any set of spelling words with a handwriting lesson for extra practice in both.

Extend the Challenge or the Words

If you find an activity or game particularly useful, feel free to use it as a template for other sets of spelling words or other features of the same words. For example, the activity on page 110 asks students to draw a path through words with the **cher** sound. You could change the words and give students the same task. You could also use the same words and have them draw a path through words spelled with a vowel digraph or words with a **long e** sound.

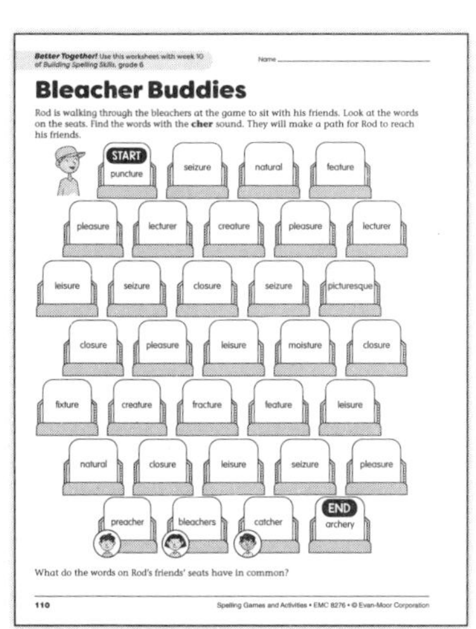

Use the Extra Practice Worksheets

If you want additional practice on specific skills or want students to practice applying skills to a new set of words, use pages from the extra practice section. This section features all the spelling words from Evan-Moor's *Building Spelling Skills* weekly lessons. If you are using *Building Spelling Skills*, you can use these extra practice worksheets to enhance your weekly lessons, giving students more practice with the same words.

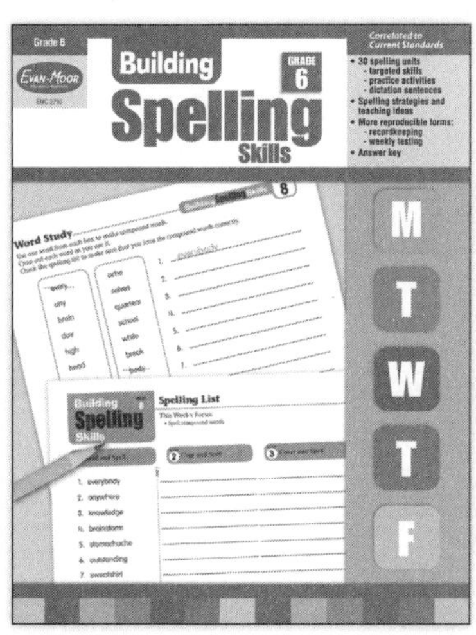

Spelling Word List

abbreviate	appearance	blind	citizenship	deduce
abdominal	applaud	blurted	cleaner	delicious
absent-minded	application	borough	cleanest	demanded
absolutely	approach	boundaries	climbing	descendant
abundant	aptitude	boycott	closure	describe
acceptable	archeology	brainstorm	collision	detective
accident	archery	briefly	colonel	determined
achieve	architect	brilliant	colorless	development
achievement	argument	broach	commented	dictionary
acknowledge	article	brochure	compatible	disagree
acquire	ashes	brooch	concluded	disappearance
acre	assistance	brought	condemn	discourage
action	assistants	buoyancy	condition	disgrace
actor	asterisk	bureaucracy	confetti	dishonest
admirable	asteroid	burrow	confident	distinct
admitted	astronaut	buyer	congenial	does
advised	astronomer	campaign	constellation	doorknob
affect	astronomic	cardiovascular	constitutional	doubt
agent	astronomy	careful	conversation	doubtful
algebra	atmospheric	carnitas	cooperation	drought
alibi	attendant	carnival	coordinates	duffel bag
alliance	audible	cartographer	coordination	durable
all ready	aunt	castle	corduroy	eagerly
already	authentic	catcher	corral	earnestly
although	autograph	cautious	coughing	earthworm
amazement	awkward	cease	country	easel
ambition	axle	celebration	courage	echoes
ambitious	bankrupt	censor	courageous	eclipse
amphibian	barbeque	centennial	courteous	effect
ancestor	barricade	centipede	courtesy	efficiency
ancient	beautician	century	couscous	efficient
angrier	beautiful	ceremony	creature	effortless
angriest	because	chalkboard	credible	electricity
anniversary	beliefs	challah	crepe	embarrass
annual	believe	championship	cryptic	empathetic
answered	bicentennial	changeable	curiosity	enact
Antarctica	bilingual	cheerful	curious	encyclopedias
antelope	binocular	chieftain	customary	energetic
antenna	biography	child's	daring	energy
anticipate	biology	chorale	daughter	enjoyment
antifreeze	biopsy	chow mein	daybreak	enough
antiseptic	biosphere	circuit	decipher	entry
antisocial	bipedal	circumference	decoration	envelope
anywhere	bleachers	circumvent	dedication	environment

 Spelling Games and Activities • EMC 8276 • © Evan-Moor Corporation

© Evan-Moor Corporation • EMC 8276 • Spelling Games and Activities

equality
equivalent
eruption
especially
establish
everybody
evidence
exaggerate
exclaimed
exercise
exhaustion
expedition
experiment
explained
explanation
export
expression
fajitas
famous
fascinating
fasten
favorite
feature
festival
finally
finely
fixture
flexible
fluorescent
fondue
formal
formula
fortitude
fracture
fragile
freighter
frequent
friction
friendlier
friendliest
friendship
frighten
fugitive
galaxy
gathering
genealogy
generation

genuine
geography
geologist
geology
gestured
gesturing
glacier
glimpse
gnarled
goalie
goulash
government
graduation
grammar
graphite
grateful
gratitude
gravitate
gravitational
gravity
grievances
guacamole
gymnastics
halves
harvest
headquarters
heir
hemisphere
heredity
heritage
hesitated
hesitating
high school
hockey
hooray
hostel
hostile
humanitarian
humor
humorless
humorous
ignorant
illegal
imitation
immature
immediate
immediately

immigrant
immigrate
immobile
immortal
impact
impatient
imperfect
import
inability
inanimate
incautious
incident
incite
inconvenient
indelible
independent
inertia
infectious
inhabit
inquire
inquired
inquisitive
insight
insignia
insisted
inspiring
instant
instruments
international
interrupt
intriguing
investigate
investigator
invitation
journeys
joyous
judgment
knowledge
latitude
lecturer
legacy
leisure
lengthen
lineage
lithe
logical
lonelier

loneliest
long-distance
longitude
loose
lose
lovable
loyalty
lunge
luxury
magazine
magician
magnificent
marriage
maternal
mayor
meager
meanwhile
membership
mentioned
menu
meteor
microscope
miniature
misbehave
misdirect
misfortune
misspell
moisture
molecule
moment
mosquitoes
motive
muscle
museum
musician
national
natural
navigation
neither
nominee
nonconformist
nonexistent
nonfiction
nonsense
numerous
obedient
obey

obnoxious
observation
observed
obsolete
obstacle
obstinate
occasion
occurrence
ocean
oceanographer
officer
official
offspring
often
ointment
old-fashioned
once
opinion
opportunity
opposite
optimistic
orchestra
orchestras
ordinary
outstanding
ownership
oxygen
painless
pamphlet
parallelogram
parasol
participant
partnership
passersby
paternal
pathetic
patience
patients
patriotism
peculiar
peninsula
perfectly
permanently
permission
perpendicular
persistent
persuade

persuasion
pharmacies
phenomenon
photograph
physical
physician
picturesque
pique
pitcher
plague
play
pleasant
pleasure
pliable
plight
plumber
pneumonia
poetry
polyhedron
portable
powerless
preacher
precious
predictable
prediction
prescribed
prescribing
principal
principle
profitable
protector
proverb
punctual
puncture
purpose
puzzling
quesadilla
quiche
quietly
radiant
react
reaction
reappear
recede
received
recommend
referee

reformat
rehearse
reign
rein
relationship
relative
reliable
reluctant
remarked
repetition
replied
rescuer
respect
restrain
rewrite
rhombus
ridiculous
rupture
satellite
scented
schedules
schnitzel
scientific
screamed
sculpture
seize
seizure
semiannual
semicircle
semicolon
sensible
sensor
separation
sergeants
shipwreck
shortage
sibling
sighed
signal
signature
significant
similar
sincerely
skied
skiing
sleuth
slight

social
solar
solarium
solstice
solution
spaghetti
sparse
spectacle
spectator
squat
starvation
stationary
stationery
stellar
stethoscope
stomachache
stowaway
straight
strength
strengthen
stretch
studied
studying
stupendous
substances
subterranean
success
successful
succession
sufficient
suffocate
sulfur
support
surely
surname
survey
sushi
suspect
suspicion
sweatshirt
symbol
symmetry
symphony
teamwork
tedious
telescope
temporarily

tempura
terrain
territory
their
themselves
theorem
theory
they're
thieves
thorough
thoughtful
through
thumbprint
tikka masala
tireless
tomatoes
tradition
traitor
trampoline
transact
transform
transport
treadmill
trestle
triad
triathlon
triceps
triplicate
trolley
truancy
trustworthy
turmoil
twice
typhoid
typhoon
uncertain
underage
undercover
underestimate
underneath
unicorn
uniform
unify
union
unique
unit
universe

unlikely
unreliable
unsure
unusual
utilize
vacancy
valiant
valuable
varieties
videotape
vigilant
violation
voluntary
voyager
waist
warning
wasteful
whined
whispered
wholesome
worthy
wrestling
xylophone
yoga
yogurt
zealous

Spelling Games and Activities • EMC 8276 • © Evan-Moor Corporation

LET'S CELEBRATE!

Practice spelling and using these words about parties and the reasons for having them.

- ☐ festival
- ☐ gathering
- ☐ ceremony
- ☐ symbol
- ☐ gratitude
- ☐ social

- ☐ joyous
- ☐ harvest
- ☐ carnival
- ☐ tradition
- ☐ celebration
- ☐ decoration

- ☐ invitation
- ☐ graduation
- ☐ annual
- ☐ anniversary
- ☐ confetti
- ☐ success

SPELLING TIPS

☆ Some words have double consonants after a short vowel.
Examples: a**pp**reciate, we**dd**ing, su**mm**ertime

☆ The -**tion** suffix is pronounced like **shun** and is often used with nouns.
Examples: **action**, **vacation**

☆ Most multisyllable words have a **schwa** sound. The schwa sound is found in unaccented syllables. There is no rule for which vowel to use to spell it.

Name _______________________

To the Party!

Look at the words in the countryside. Find the words that contain the **-al** or **-tion** suffixes. They will make a path for Carolina and her family to reach her grandparents' 50th wedding anniversary.

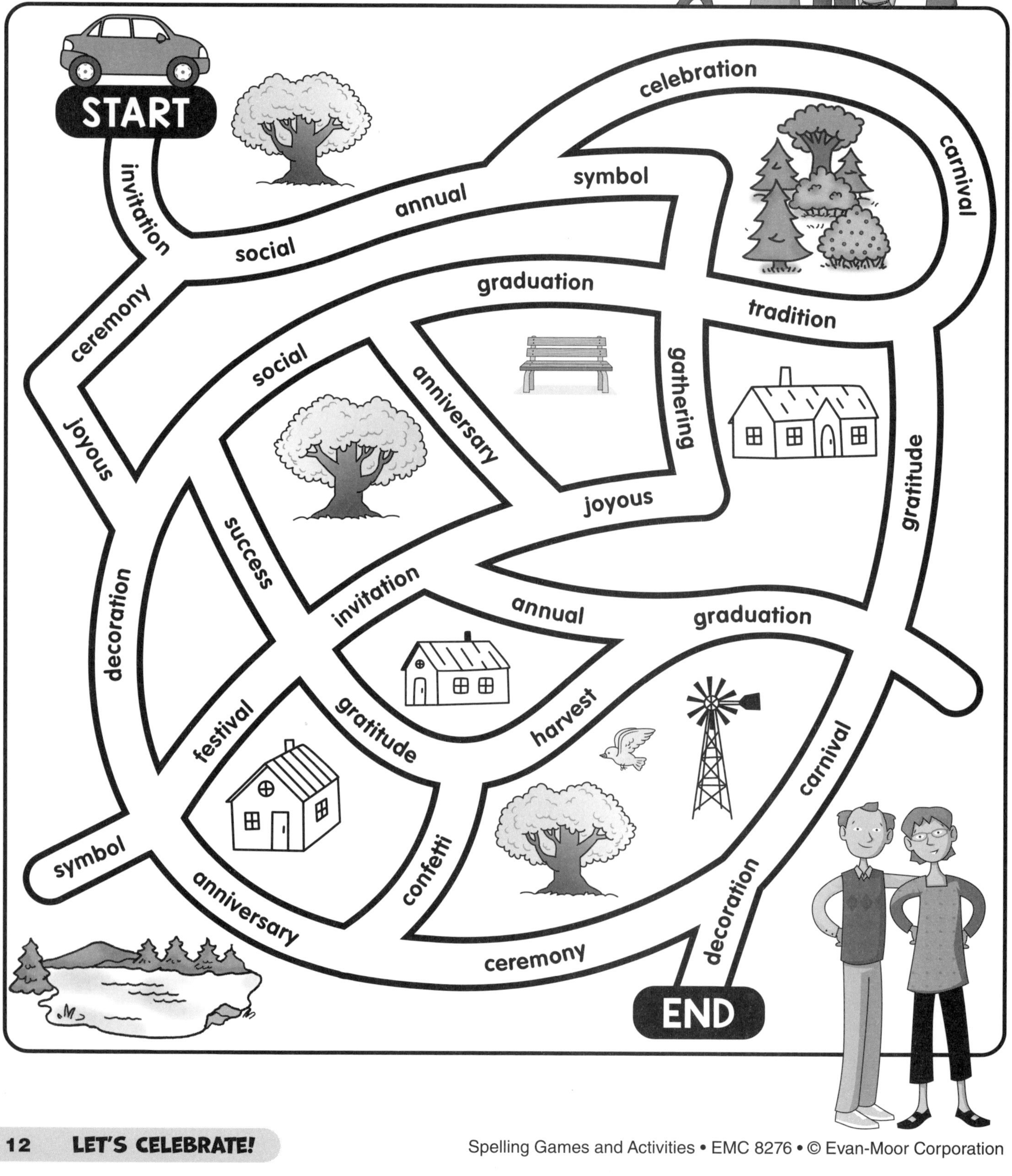

Spelling Games and Activities • EMC 8276 • © Evan-Moor Corporation

Name _______________________

Schwa Showcase

Let's show off the schwas! Most words with more than one syllable have a schwa sound. Read each word in the box and decide which vowels are making each schwa sound. Circle the vowels. Then write each word in its Schwa Zone. If a word has more than one schwa, write the word in each zone. Use a different color for each zone.

| annual | carnival | ceremony | confetti | decoration |
| festival | gratitude | harvest | social | symbol |

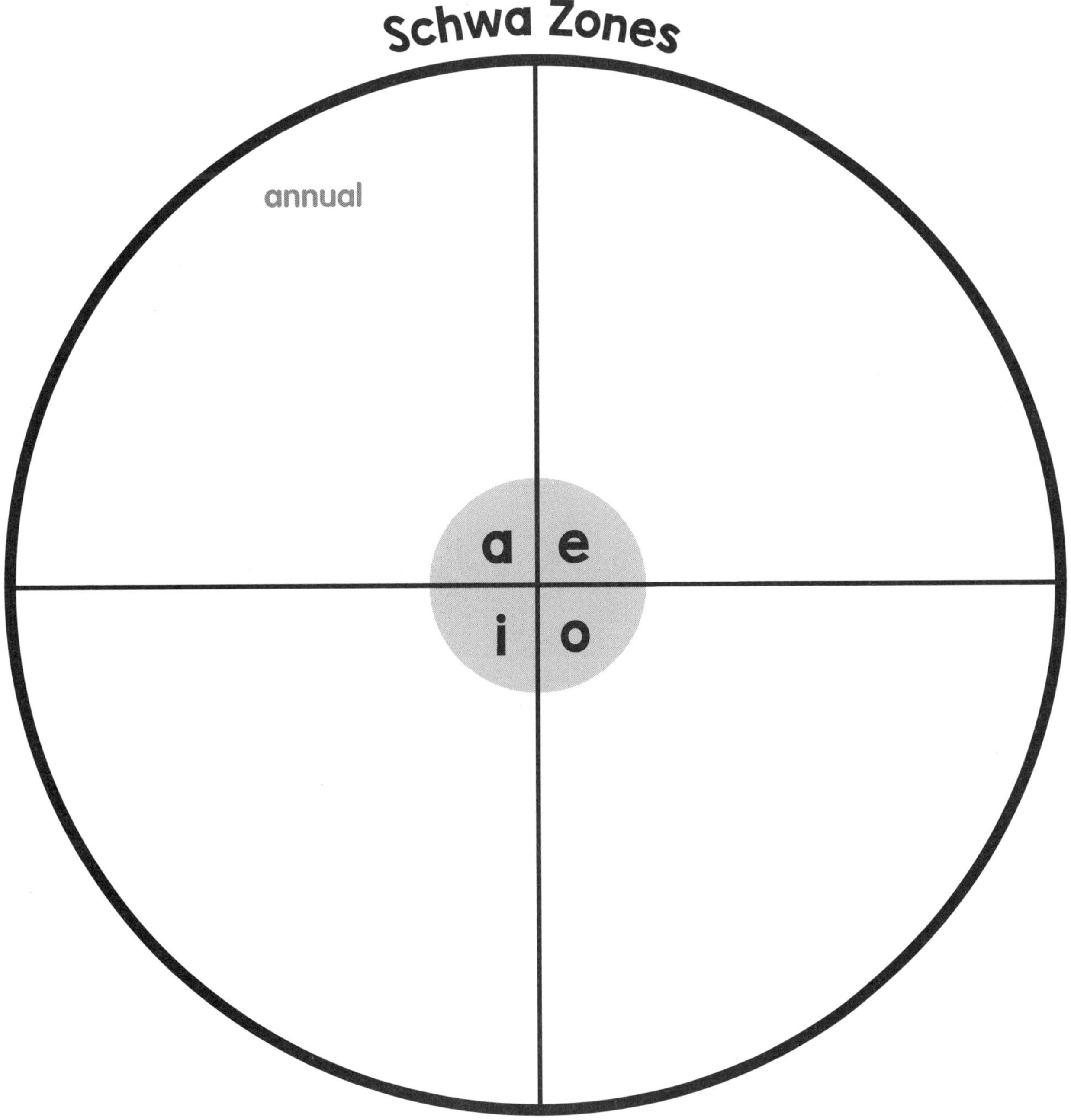

Name ___________

Unwrap Words

Unwrap some party presents! Look at the letters in each spelling word. Use them to make other words. Write them on each gift.

    Spelling Games and Activities • EMC 8276 • © Evan-Moor Corporation

Scrambled Cards

People often send cards for special occasions. Read the celebration cards.
The underlined words are scrambled. Write them correctly below.

> anniversary   festival   graduation   invitation   joyous   success

Name _______________________

The Harvest Cornucopia

The words below are missing some of their vowels! Luckily, there's a cornucopia of vowels nearby. Finish the words using the harvested vowels below. Cross off each one as you use it.

```
a a a a a a a e e e e i i i i
i i i o o o o o o u u u u u
```

1. j_____ y_____ _____ s

2. grad_____ _____ t _____ _____ n

3. h_____ rv _____ st

4. ann_____ v _____ rs _____ ry

5. grat_____ t _____ d _____

6. c_____ rn _____ v _____ l

7. dec_____ rat _____ _____ n

8. ann_____ _____ l

9. inv_____ tat _____ _____ n

10. s _____ cc _____ ss

Spelling Games and Activities • EMC 8276 • © Evan-Moor Corporation

Name ______________________

Día de los Muertos

Javier is making a poster about how he and his family celebrate Día de los Muertos (Day of the Dead). Circle any misspellings. Write them correctly below.

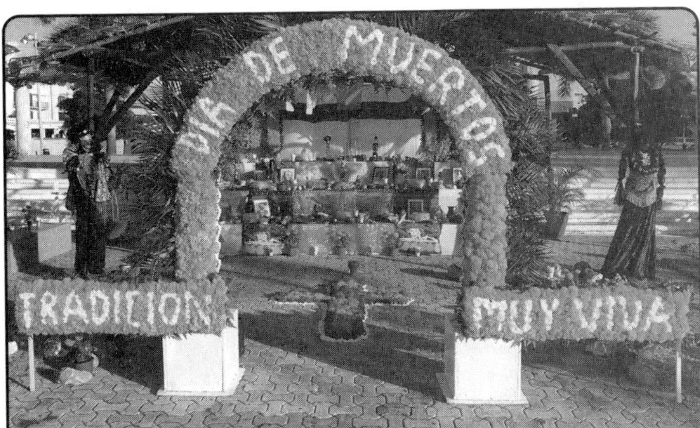

Día de los Muertos is an annyul holiday in Mexico. It takes place on November 1 and 2 every year. It's my favorite celabration!

During Día de los Muertos, we honor and remember our loved ones who have passed away. It is a joyus time, not a sad one.

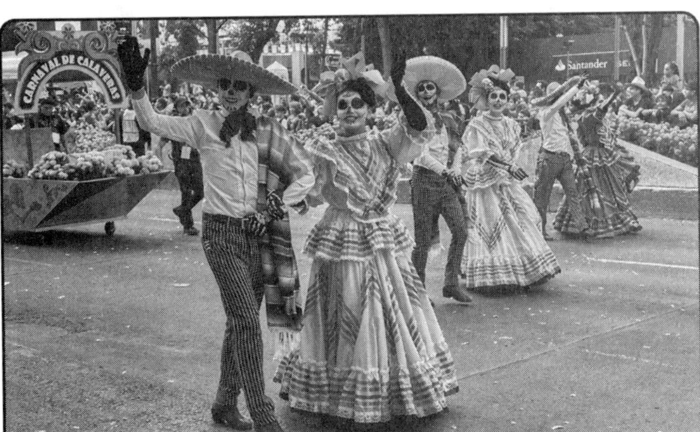

Dina Julayeva / Shutterstock.com

We have a family gathring on these days. It is also a time for us to be soshel. We have parades with music and dancing.

An *ofrenda* is a tradishion that welcomes spirits back to their family. It has pictures, food, and other simbles of the returning spirits.

betto rodrigues / Shutterstock.com

______________ ______________ ______________ ______________

______________ ______________ ______________ ______________

Name _______________________

Triangle Bunting Banner

Students work together to create celebratory bunting banners.

What You Need

- Let's Celebrate spelling words list on page 11
- How to Make a Bunting Banner on page 19
- Bunting Triangles on page 20
- scissors
- glue or tape
- string
- markers
- things to decorate the bunting banner such as dried pasta, beads, buttons, cotton balls, paint, glitter, pom-poms, dried leaves, foil

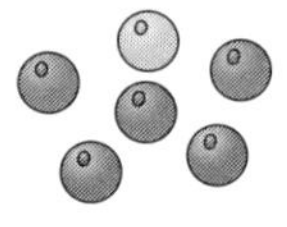

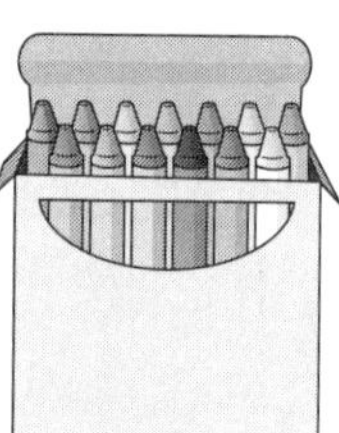

What You Do

1. Put students in pairs. Distribute 1 copy of the spelling words list and How to Make a Bunting Banner to each pair, along with 6 copies of the bunting triangles, scissors, glue or tape, string, markers, and decorating materials.

2. Explain to students that they will create a bunting banner for an upcoming event, such as a graduation ceremony, a holiday party, a seasonal celebration, or an annual tradition (you can decide on the event or have students choose).

3. Help students brainstorm words associated with the chosen celebration. Write their words on the board for students to refer to.

4. Review the banner instructions with the students. If needed, demonstrate how to cut, fold, glue, and write a word on one, and show how the string will go through the top.

5. Have students make their triangles. Tell them to choose 6 words from the spelling words list and 6 celebration words. Have students check each other's spelling before they write. Encourage them to give each other spelling tips as needed. Remind them to write the words big enough to be seen from the middle of the room.

6. Have students decorate their triangles and thread them onto the string. Hang up the bunting banners for the event.

How to Make a Bunting Banner

1. Cut out the diamond shapes. Fold them in half. This creates a triangle.

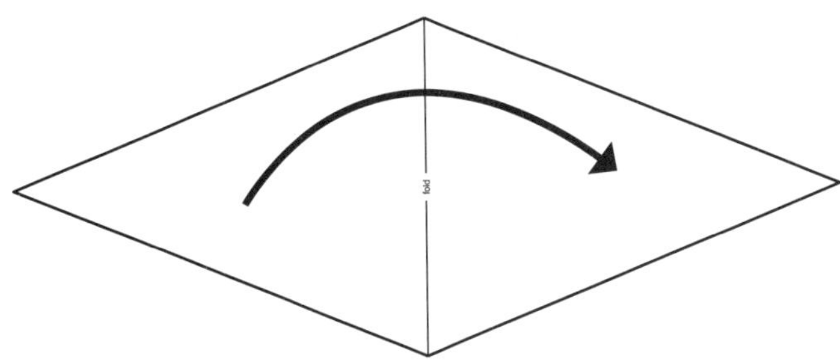

2. Tape or glue the bottom part of your triangle so it stays together. Only the tip should be glued together so that you can thread string through the triangles in step 4.

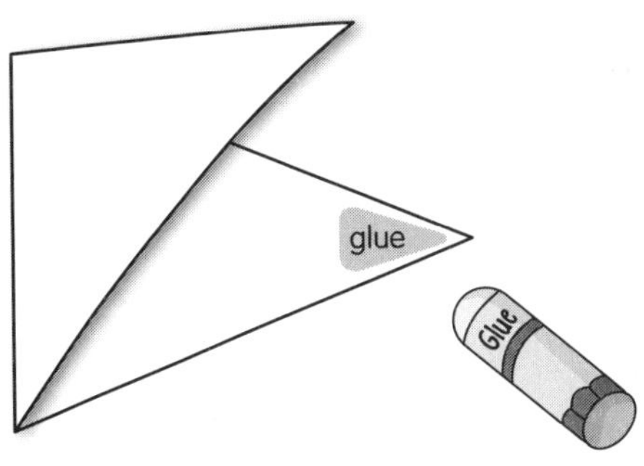

3. Write one word on each triangle. Make sure people can read them at a distance. Then decorate your bunting banner.

4. Thread string through the triangles and hang up your bunting banner. Then celebrate!

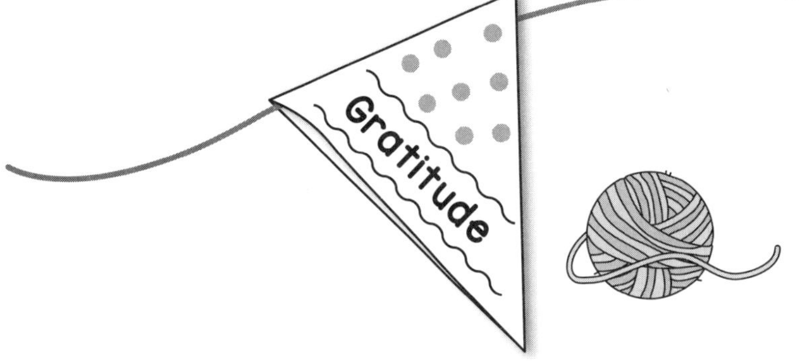

© Evan-Moor Corporation • EMC 8276 • Spelling Games and Activities

Bunting Triangles

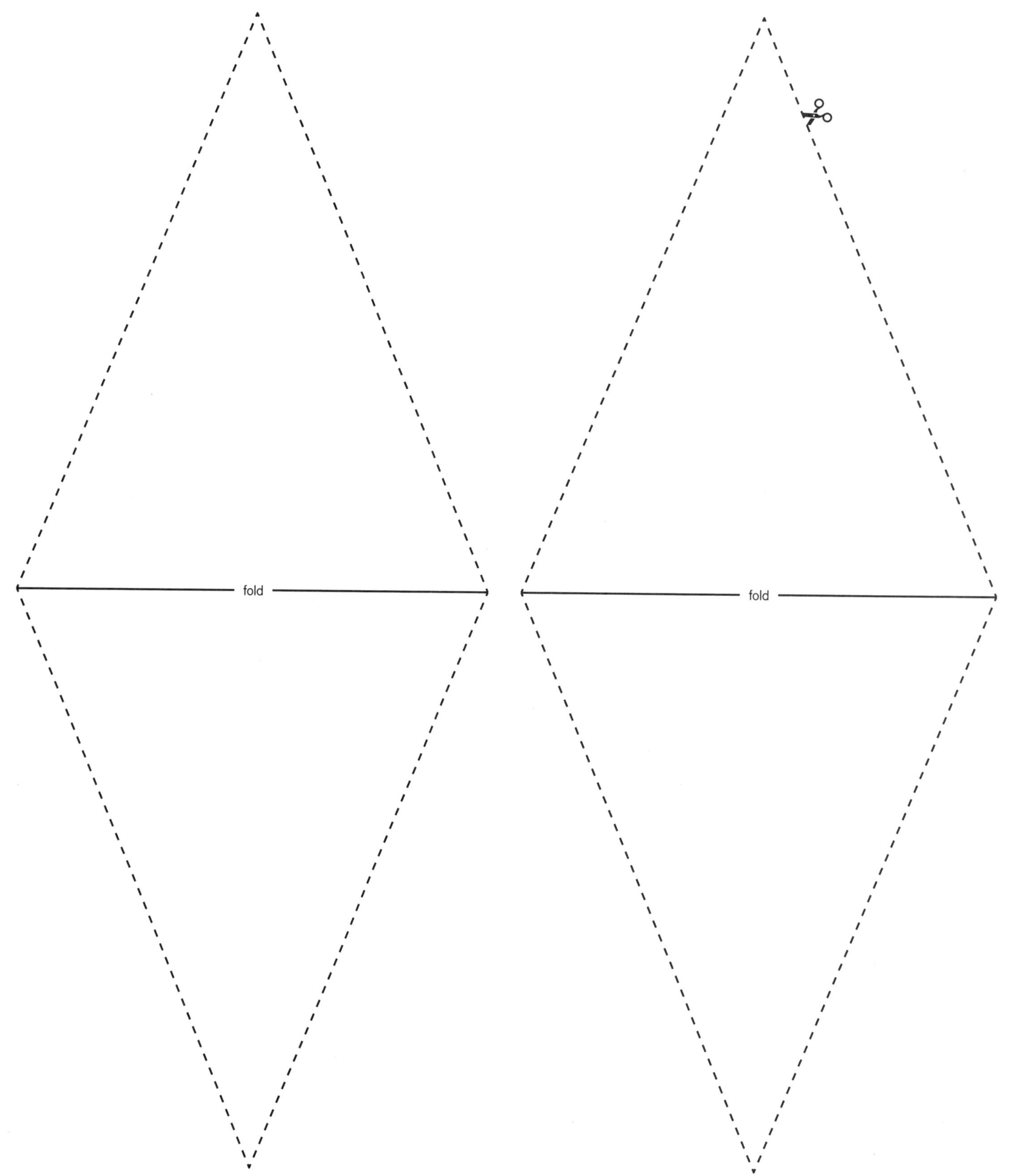

Spelling Games and Activities • EMC 8276 • © Evan-Moor Corporation

HEROES

Practice spelling and using these words about qualities of a hero.

- ☐ protector
- ☐ rescuer
- ☐ voluntary
- ☐ fortitude
- ☐ dedication
- ☐ strength

- ☐ purpose
- ☐ cooperation
- ☐ teamwork
- ☐ support
- ☐ achievement
- ☐ determined

- ☐ inspiring
- ☐ daring
- ☐ admirable
- ☐ humanitarian
- ☐ empathetic
- ☐ trustworthy

SPELLING TIPS

⭐ Long words can be hard to spell. Try dividing the word into syllables and then spell each syllable. Example: **thought | ful**

⭐ An **r**-controlled vowel is any vowel followed by an **r**. The **r** changes the sound of the vowel. **R**-controlled vowels sound different from long and short vowels.

⭐ Consonant digraphs are two consonants that have one sound, such as **th** and **ch**. Examples: **thanks**, **champion**

Classroom Heroes

Mr. Huang put together a bulletin board called "Our Classroom Heroes." He wrote a caption about the student next to each picture. Write the spelling words to complete each caption.

achievement	cooperation	daring	dedication	empathetic	humanitarian
inspiring	purpose	strength	supports	trustworthy	voluntary

Our Classroom Heroes

Aisha is a big fan of ________________________.

She respects others' ideas and always works well

with her classmates.

Blake cares about animals. Last week, he helped with

a ________________________ rescue of a bird trapped

in the sports-equipment shed.

Leo is ________________________ and shows great emotional

________________________. He listens well and can help resolve

arguments between people.

Cora Mae is a ________________________ who cares about the rights of students.

She gives ________________________ speeches about what she believes in.

Spelling Games and Activities • EMC 8276 • © Evan-Moor Corporation

Classroom Heroes, *continued*

> achievement   cooperation   daring   dedication   empathetic   humanitarian
>
> inspiring   purpose   strength   supports   trustworthy   voluntary

Shirin shows great _________________ to her community. She is a _________________ helper at our local food bank.

Milo aims for high _________________ in his studies. He also _________________ his classmates, helping them study for tests.

Pedro is a _________________ friend. His friends can count on him to keep his promises.

Kylie always has a _________________ when she writes. She lets her city government know about issues that kids care about.

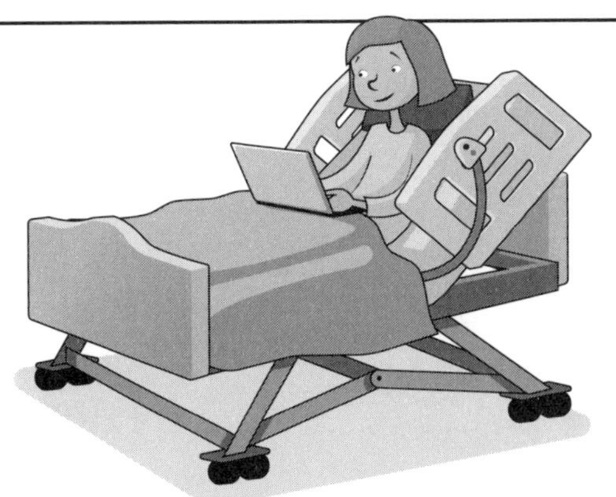

Name _______________

Admirable Anagrams

You can change the silly phrases below to spell heroic spelling words.
After you unscramble each phrase, write the spelling word on the line.

| admirable | cooperation | determined | fortitude |
| inspiring | protector | purpose | teamwork |

1. minted deer 

2. crop otter 

3. tired tofu 

4. pin rising 

5. rose pup 

6. acorn pie too 

7. braid meal

8. two maker

Spelling Games and Activities • EMC 8276 • © Evan-Moor Corporation

Name ___________________________

Honoring Heroes

In an acrostic poem, each line describes the subject of the poem. A letter in each line spells out a word when you read it vertically.

Jing wrote an acrostic poem for her local fire department. Some of the vowels are missing. Finish the acrostic poem using the vowels in the box.

A	A	A	A	E	E	E	E
I	I	I	I	O	O	O	U

**For the Volunteers at the
Pleasant Acres Fire Department**

___MP___T**H**___T___C

D**E**D___C___T_____N

___DM_____**R**___BL___

S_____PP**O**RT

PR___T**E**CT___R

STR_____NGTH

Name ___________________________

Multisyllable Teamwork

Which syllables in the "helping hands" belong together? Match the correct syllables to make words from the box. Write the complete words on the lines.

> achievement   admirable   daring   dedication   determined
>
> fortitude   protector   rescuer   trustworthy   voluntary

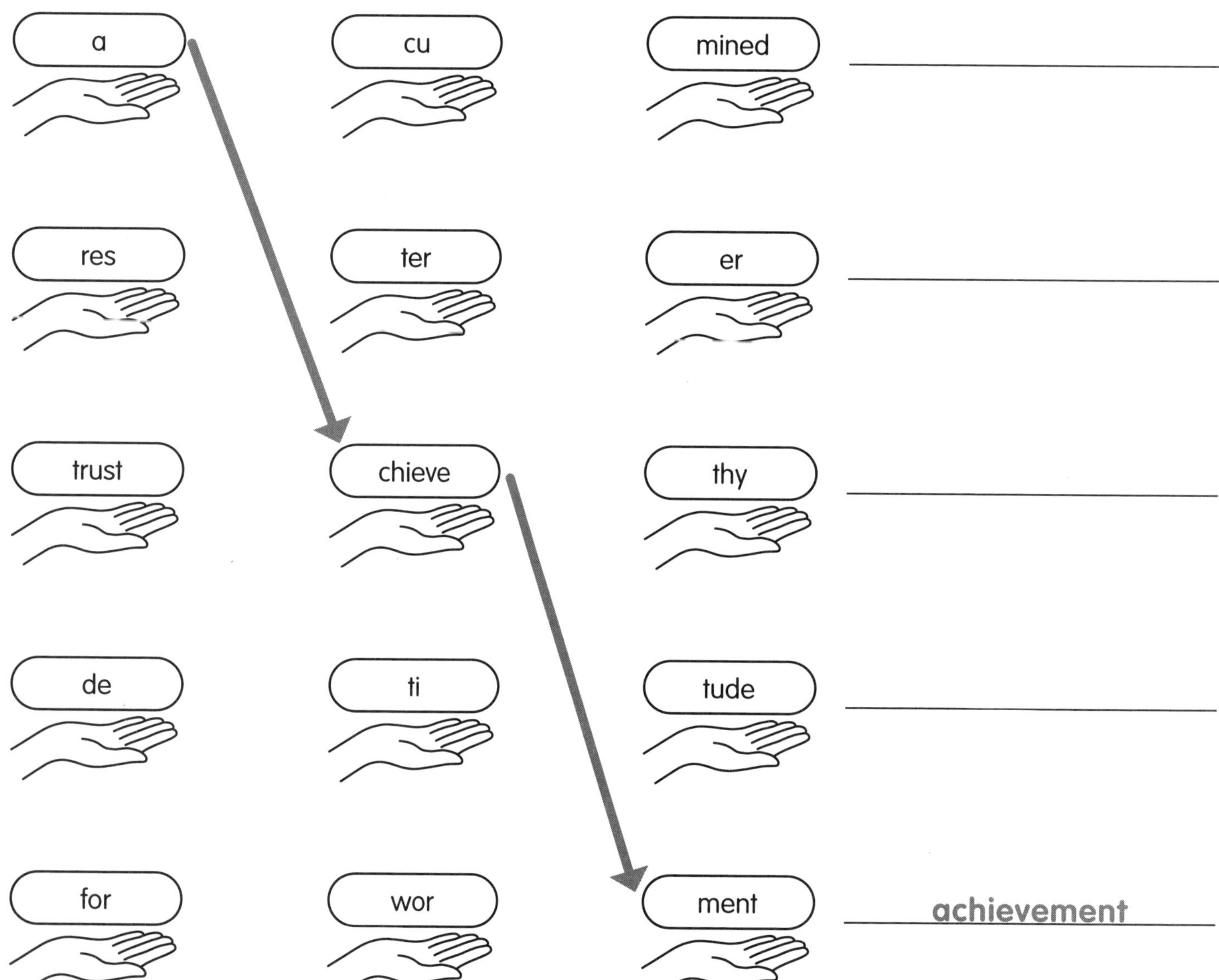

Spelling Games and Activities • EMC 8276 • © Evan-Moor Corporation

Ordinary Heroes

Alisha made a poster to celebrate National Heroes Day on July 20. Read the poster. Circle any misspelled words. Write them correctly below.

Ordinary Heroes in Our Community

Our **mayor** says her perpose is to serve her community. She also showed great fortytude, during the flood evacuations.

Our **delivery person** is trustwerthy. She works hard to deliver our packages on time.

Our local **baker** believes in teamwerk. He suports local businesses by buying his ingredients from them.

Our inspireing city **judge** is a humanatarien who cares about human rights.

Our local **firefighters** are voluntery helpers. They are rescuors who are ready to lend a hand.

Our **librarian** is deturmind to help readers find books they will love to read.

_______________ _______________ _______________

_______________ _______________ _______________

Name _______________________

High-Five a Hero!

Students use their spelling words to thank a local hero with a written "high-five."

What You Need

- Spelling Words, Tips, and Sentence Starters on page 29
- Hero High-Five on page 30
- pencil
- colored pencils or crayons to draw a picture (optional)

What You Do

1. Put students in pairs. Distribute a Spelling Words, Tips, and Sentence Starters to each student and a Hero High-Five to each pair of students. Make sure each student has a pencil; make colored pencils or crayons available, if desired.

2. Explain to students that they will get to use their spelling words to thank a hero with a "high-five." Help students brainstorm different types of "ordinary heroes" in your school or community. Write their ideas on the board for students to refer to.

3. Have pairs choose a local hero to thank for his or her heroic activities.

4. Have students look at the spelling words and the sentence starters. Have them talk with their partner about which spelling words they want to use in their "Hero High-Five."

5. Have students write a "Hero High-Five" using at least five spelling words. If they have time, they can draw a small picture of their hero doing heroic activities.

6. Have students practice saying their "high-five" letter out loud and decide who will say which part of the letter.

7. Have students read their "high-five" letter to the class. Then have them deliver their letters to their local heroes.

Spelling Games and Activities • EMC 8276 • © Evan-Moor Corporation

Name ________________________

Spelling Words, Tips, and Sentence Starters

Include at least five of these spelling words in your "high-five":

protector	strength	achievement	humanitarian
rescuer	purpose	determined	empathetic
voluntary	cooperation	inspiring	trustworthy
fortitude	teamwork	daring	
dedication	support	admirable	

Tips for writing a "high-five" letter:
- Introduce who you are and express your thanks.
- Tell your hero why you admire him or her. Describe some of the person's heroic activities and how he or she helps the school or community.
- Tell why or how the school or community is better because of the hero.

Possible sentence starters:

Hi there! Our names are ______________ and ______________. Thank you for your

hard work doing ______________. We think you are a hero because ______________.

You help our school or community in so many different ways.

For example, you ______________. We want to thank you for your service.

You're our hero! Here's why. First, we think ______________.

Hero High-Five

Name ______________________

Name ______________________

Spelling Games and Activities • EMC 8276 • © Evan-Moor Corporation

LET'S GET IN SHAPE!

Practice spelling and using these words about fun ways to keep your body healthy.

- ☐ exercise
- ☐ impact
- ☐ muscle
- ☐ stretch
- ☐ lunge
- ☐ squat
- ☐ trampoline
- ☐ gymnastics
- ☐ yoga
- ☐ treadmill
- ☐ climbing
- ☐ abdominal
- ☐ cardiovascular
- ☐ condition
- ☐ flexible
- ☐ coordination
- ☐ strengthen
- ☐ repetition

SPELLING TIPS

★ Consonant blends are two or three consonants that say two or three sounds together, such as **tr**, **st**, **cl**, **sc**, **fl**, **ct**, **str**, and **squ**. Examples: **tr**ack, di**st**ance, **cl**imb, **sc**ale, **fl**ip, prote**ct**, **str**ong, **squ**eeze

★ Consonant digraphs are two consonants that spell one sound, such as **ch** and **th**. Examples: **ch**ain, grow**th**

★ Some words have a silent letter. In words ending in **mb**, the letter **b** is silent. Example: **limb**

Marathon Training

Name ______________________

Nessa is getting in shape to run in the Boston Marathon. Look at the words in the maze. Find the words that contain a consonant blend. They will make a path for Nessa to run 26.2 miles for her practice run.

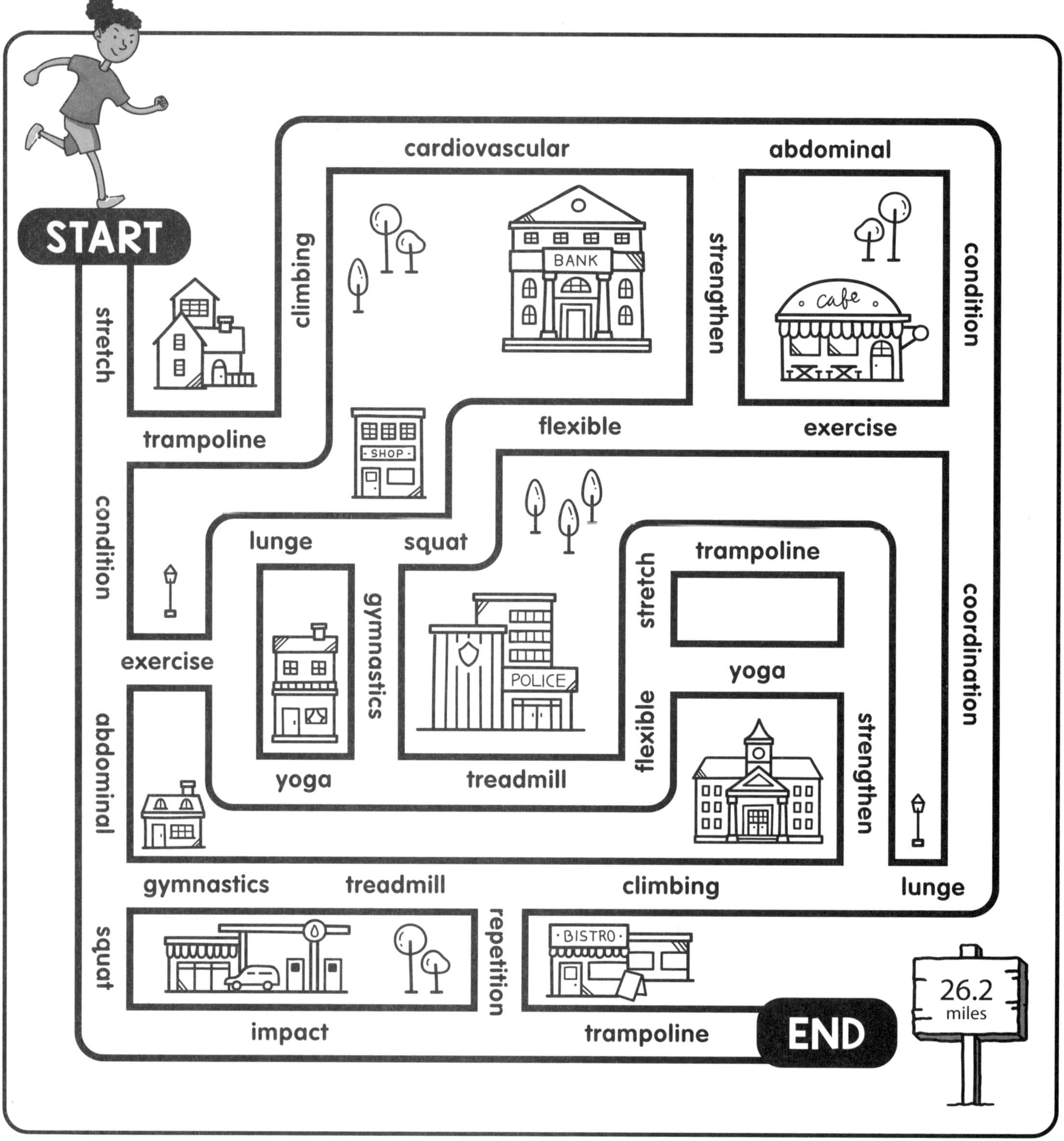

Spelling Games and Activities • EMC 8276 • © Evan-Moor Corporation

Name ________________________

Guess the Workout Word

Read the clue. Write a workout word to solve the riddle.

> abdominal   climbing   condition   coordination   flexible
>
> muscle   repetition   squat   treadmill   yoga

 I rhyme with **position**.

____

 You are me if you are plenty bendy.

____

 Three letters in my name repeat.

____

 I start with a 3-letter blend.

____

 I make everything happen in sync.

____

 You can pair me with **rock**, **ice**, or **mountain**.

____

 I'm full of stretching and posing.

____

 I'm a compound word.

____

 You will be strong when you build more of me.

____

 I start with the same vowel sound you hear in **balance**.

____

© Evan-Moor Corporation • EMC 8276 • Spelling Games and Activities

Riddle Me Right

Name ________________________

Unscramble each word. Then write the numbered letters in the matching spaces of the riddle to answer it.

What is a pirate's least favorite move in yoga?

___ ___ ___   ___ ___ ___ ___ k   ___ ___ ___ ___
1   2   3   4   5   6   7   8   9   10 11

1. pmciat

___ ___ ___ ___ ___ ___
        4

2. cetshrt

___ ___ ___ ___ ___ ___ ___
            11   2

3. eugln

___ ___ ___ ___ ___
        7

4. tpnaeilmor

___ ___ ___ ___ ___ ___ ___ ___ ___ ___
            8   3

5. gtssymcnai

___ ___ ___ ___ ___ ___ ___ ___ ___
        6   10

6. idablmano

___ ___ ___ ___ ___ ___ ___ ___ ___
                            5

7. vcalsdouricara

___ ___ ___ ___ ___ ___ ___ ___ ___ ___ ___ ___ ___ ___
                9

8. gtheennstr

___ ___ ___ ___ ___ ___ ___ ___ ___
1

abdominal
cardiovascular
gymnastics
impact
lunge
strengthen
stretch
trampoline

Spelling Games and Activities • EMC 8276 • © Evan-Moor Corporation

Name ______________________

Get in Shape at Home

Batoul needs help proofreading this poster she made.
Circle any misspelled words. Write them correctly below.

Get in Shape
in the Comfort of Your Home!

Home workouts can have a big impakt on your health!

Try lifting weights while watching an online video.
Make sure to do several repitions to build musle!

Excercize helps us stay healthy. Find ways to move that feel fun to you—and you'll move for a lifetime!

Get in a kardeovaskuler workout! Hop on a tredmill or take a walk. If you have space in your backyard, you can bounce on a trampuleen!

______________ ______________ ______________

______________ ______________

© Evan-Moor Corporation • EMC 8276 • Spelling Games and Activities

Gym Pals

Name _______________________

Lizbeth and Azusa are texting each other about working out.
Write the spelling words to complete the text messages.

> climbing   exercise   flexible   muscles
>
> squats   strengthen   stretch   yoga

Hey, are you coming to _______________ class today?

I feel like I need to _______________ my whole body.

I don't think I'm _______________ enough for

that class. I can never do that "downward dog" pose.

Are you going _______________ on the rock wall? Or

are you going to _______________ at the gym instead?

I'm going to the gym. Coach Li says if I do 10 more

_______________ every day, I'll build up

my leg _______________ .

Okay, go _______________ those legs and make them

strong! Have fun!

Spelling Games and Activities • EMC 8276 • © Evan-Moor Corporation

Name ______________________

Flexible Words

You can take letters in a word and "bend" them into new words. Look at the letters in each spelling word. Use them to make other words. Write them on the floor mat.

Spelling Sprints

Students compete with their classmates to spell words and complete
short exercise sprints.

What You Need

- Spelling Sprints on page 39
- Sprint Scorecard on page 40
- die
- timer

How to Play

The object of the game is to spell as many words
as you can in 3 minutes and do an exercise.

1. Put students in pairs. Distribute a Spelling Sprints sheet and a die
    to each pair. Distribute a Sprint Scorecard to each student.

2. Explain to students that they will roll a die and spell a word. After 3 minutes,
    they will do an exercise sprint.

3. The teacher starts a 3-minute timer and says "Go." Player 1 in each pair rolls the die.
    His or her partner reads the spelling word next to the number rolled. Player 1 writes the
    spelling word in the correct spot on the Sprint Scorecard. Player 2 checks the spelling.

    - If the spelling is correct, Player 1 circles the word.

    - If the spelling is incorrect, Player 1 crosses out the word.

    Player 1 repeats until time is called.

4. After 3 minutes, the teacher calls "Stop, it's time to move!" Have Player 1 in each pair
    follow the exercise directions next to the last number rolled. When completed, Player 1
    checks the corresponding box on the scorecard. If any students have limited mobility,
    have modifications or alternative exercises available for them.

5. Have partners switch roles and repeat steps 3 and 4.

6. Do one or two more rounds for each pair of students, as time allows.

7. At the end of the game, have players count the points for all circled words and checked
    exercises. Then add the scores together. The pair of players with the highest total score wins!

   Spelling Games and Activities • EMC 8276 • © Evan-Moor Corporation

Spelling Sprints

Rolled Number	Roll 1	Roll 2	Roll 3	Time to Move!
⚀ (1)	exercise	trampoline	cardiovascular	Do 10 side bends.
⚁ (2)	impact	gymnastics	condition	Do 10 squats.
⚂ (3)	muscle	yoga	flexible	Do 10 twists, side to side.
⚃ (4)	stretch	treadmill	coordination	Do 10 helicopter arm circles.
⚄ (5)	lunge	climbing	strengthen	Do 10 stretches above your head.
⚅ (6)	squat	abdominal	repetition	Do 10 jumping jacks.

Name _______________________

Sprint Scorecard

Number	1st Spelling Word (3 points)	2nd Spelling Word (4 points)	3rd Spelling Word (5 points)	Time to Move! (2 points)	Total Score for Number
⚀					
⚁					
⚂					
⚃					
⚄					
⚅					

Total Score:

Spelling Games and Activities • EMC 8276 • © Evan-Moor Corporation

FAMILY ROOTS

Practice spelling and using these family words about how family members are related through the past, present, and future.

- ☐ generation
- ☐ genealogy
- ☐ lineage
- ☐ ancestor
- ☐ descendant
- ☐ offspring
- ☐ immigrate
- ☐ surname
- ☐ legacy
- ☐ heritage
- ☐ heredity
- ☐ heir
- ☐ relative
- ☐ relationship
- ☐ marriage
- ☐ maternal
- ☐ paternal
- ☐ sibling

SPELLING TIPS

⭐ Long words can be hard to spell. Try dividing long words into syllables and then spell each syllable. Example: **mul|ti|gen|er|a|tion|al**

⭐ If a **c** comes before an **e**, **i**, or **y**, it is soft and sounds like **s**: **cycle**.
If a **g** comes before an **e**, **i**, or **y**, it usually is soft and sounds like **j**: **age**.

⭐ An **r**-controlled vowel is any vowel followed by an **r**. The **r** changes the sound of the vowel. They sound different from long and short vowels. Examples: p**ar**ent, h**er**, b**or**n, cult**ur**e

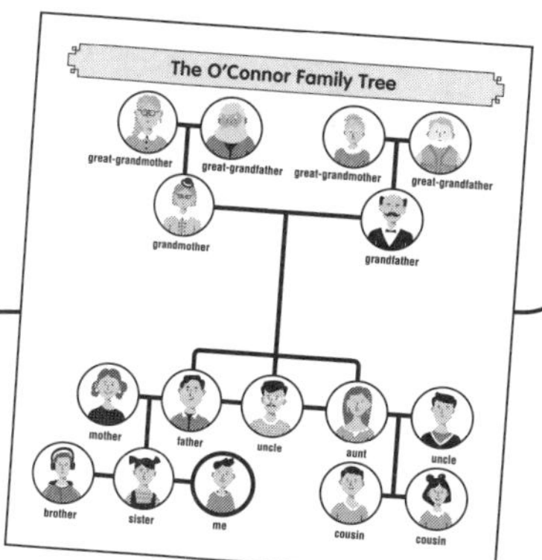

Name ___________________

Exploring Family History

Gina Cengia and her family are driving around the small town where her grandparents grew up. They visit every landmark with a **soft g** or **soft c** in its name. Draw a line from Gina to each stop that she and her family will make.

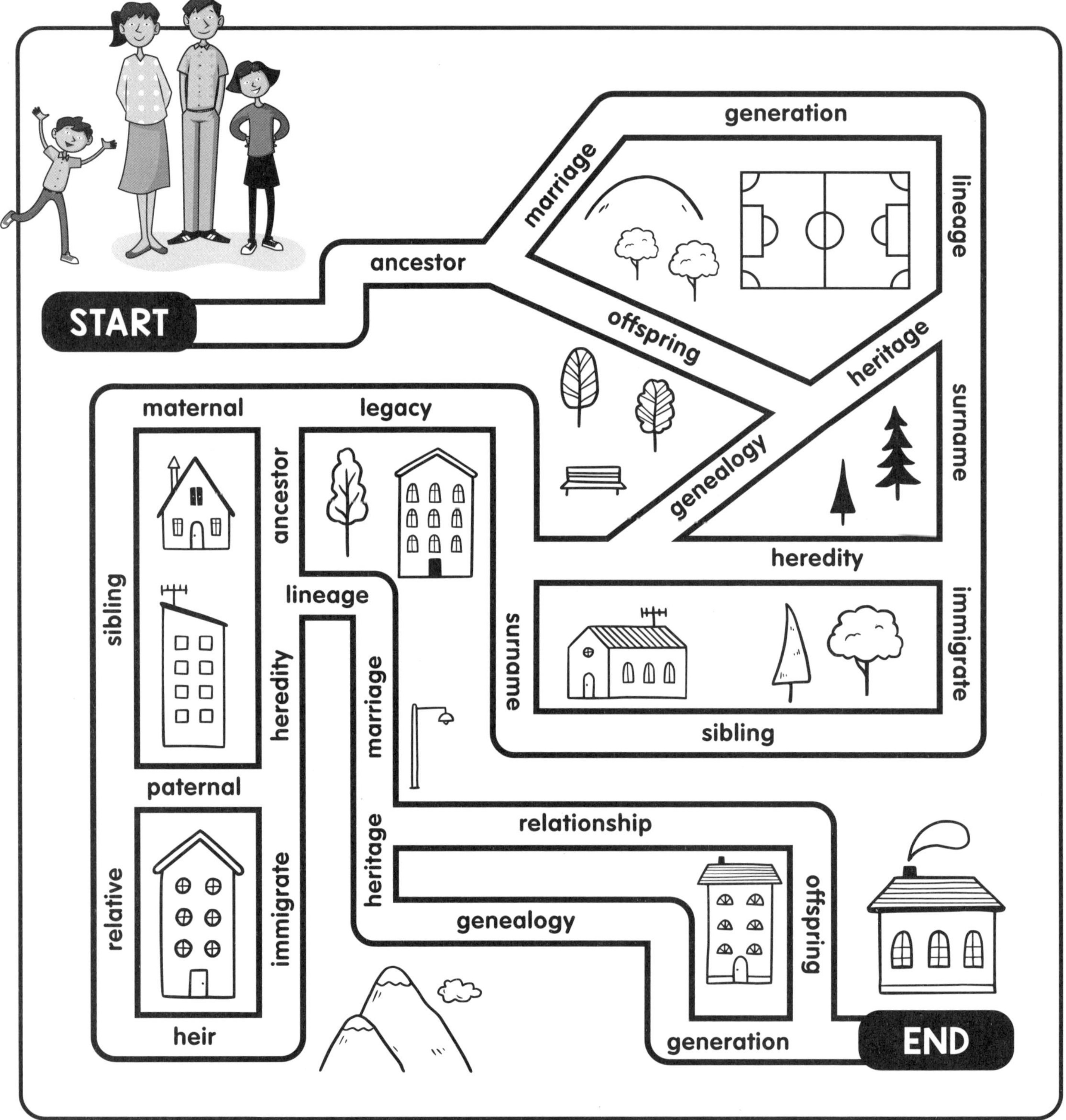

Spelling Games and Activities • EMC 8276 • © Evan-Moor Corporation

My Family Tree

Matthew made a poster about his family tree. Write the spelling words to complete the poster.

Name ___________________________

generations	immigrate	offspring
paternal	relatives	siblings
surname		

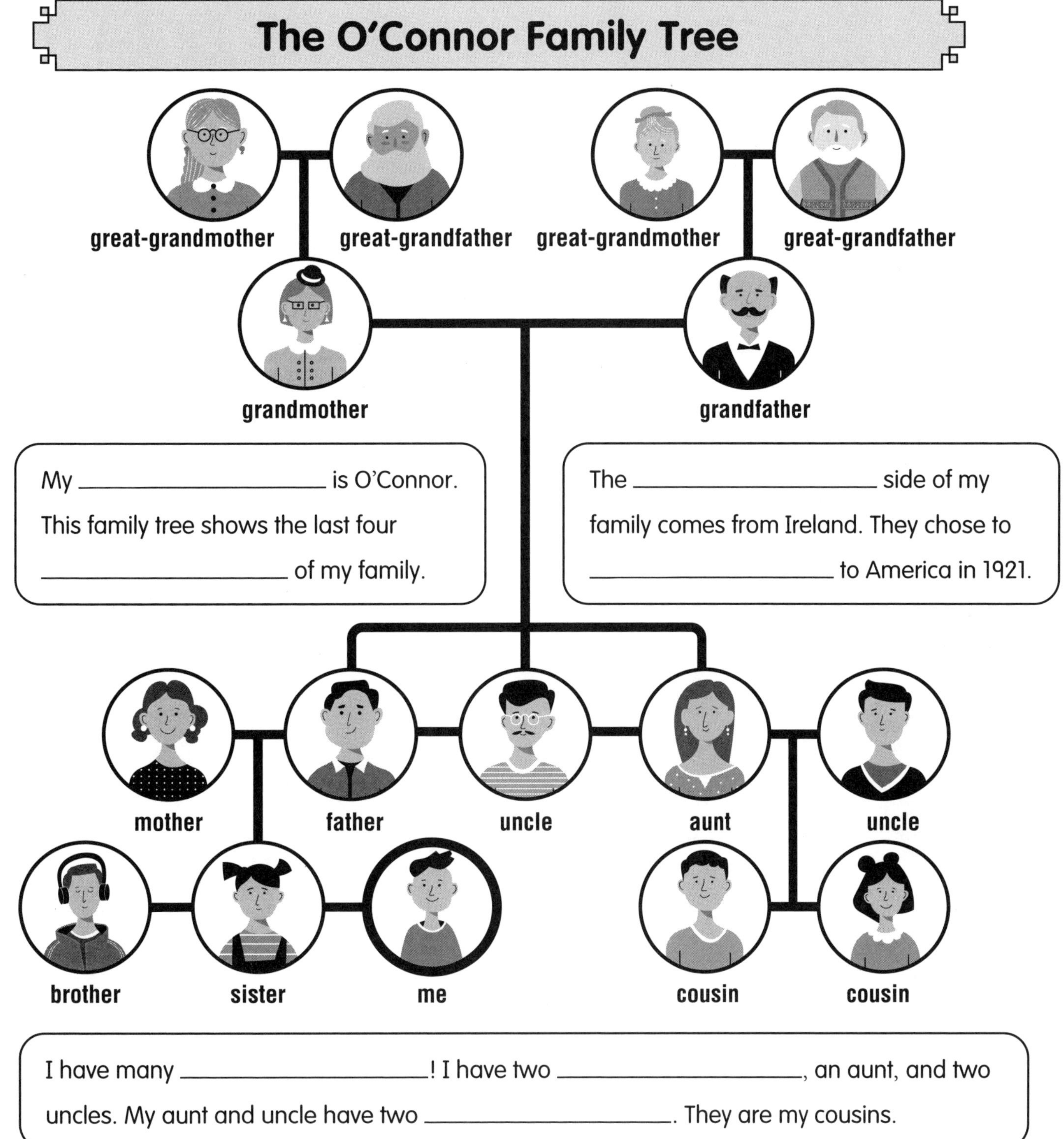

Name ________________________

Our Family Roots

Hiroki and his classmates are discussing their family roots. Read each statement.
Circle any misspelled words. Write them correctly below.

Hiroki

_________________________   _________________________

Olivia

_____________ _____________ _____________

Kiara

_________________________   _________________________

   Spelling Games and Activities • EMC 8276 • © Evan-Moor Corporation

Learning Curve

Elena wrote to her aunt in Mexico City to learn more about her family roots. Read her e-mail. Some letters are missing. Finish the words using the letters in the box. Cross off each letter after you use it.

| a a a c e e e e e g g i l r r |

New Message

To   Tía Sofía

Subject   Questions for you

How have you been? It feels like forever since I last saw you.

I have a school assignment, and Papá told me I should ask you. I'm studying my

lin______ ______ ______e and want to learn more about my an______ ______stors on my

patern______ ______ side of the family.

One of my classmates asked me why I don't look just like my mom or dad. I asked Papá about

it. He said that because of my h______ ______edity, I have his dark hair and Mom's blue eyes.

I'm proud to be multiracial. I know a lot about my Scottish herit______ ______ ______, but I

want to learn more about my Mexican side. I do know a lot about traditional Mexican foods.

(I'll be the h______ ______ ______ to your famous pozole recipe one day!) But I'd love to chat with

you more about other parts of Mexican culture. Please let me know when you have time for

a video call.

Hugs, Elena

Send        

It's All Related

One word in each group is spelled incorrectly. Find the word and spell it correctly in the spaces below the group. Then write the numbered letters in the matching spaces of the riddle to answer it.

> **I am your father's nephew's aunt. Who am I?**
>
> ___ ___ ___ ___   ___ ___ ___ ___ ___ ___
> 1   2   3   4   5   6   7   8   9 10

1. marridge, maternal, relative

   ___ ___ ___ ___ ___ ___ ___ ___
            4

2. paternal, sibling, ansester

   ___ ___ ___ ___ ___ ___ ___ ___
                            6

3. immigrate, descandent, geneulogy

   ___ ___ ___ ___ ___ ___ ___ ___ ___ ___ ___
    9

4. offspring, sirname, lineage

   ___ ___ ___ ___ ___ ___ ___
        3

5. descendant, relationship, genieology

   ___ ___ ___ ___ ___ ___ ___ ___ ___ ___
                            2   1

6. immigreat, generation, paternal

   ___ ___ ___ ___ ___ ___ ___ ___ ___
        5   10

7. lineage, legacy, heretaj

   ___ ___ ___ ___ ___ ___ ___
    8   7

Name ______________________

Ancestral Anagrams

You can change the silly phrases below to spell ancestral words.
After you unscramble each phrase, write the spelling word on the line.

> ancestor   descendant   generation   heredity
>
> immigrate   relationship   relative   surname

1. trim image   ______________________

2. nose cart   ______________________

3. tea liver   ______________________

4. neat ignore   ______________________

5. dented cans   ______________________

6. aspirin hotel   ______________________

7. near sum   ______________________

8. hey tired   ______________________

Name ___________________________

The Generations Game

Students race each other through family-tree generations.

What You Need

- Word Cards on page 49, cut out
- Game Board on page 50
- game pieces
- die

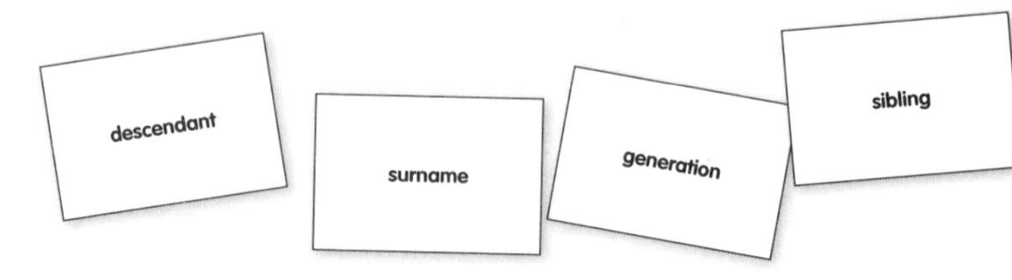

How to Play

The object of the game is to spell words and be the first player
to get through a family tree and back again.

1. Put students in groups of four. Distribute one set of words cards and a game board to each group, along with a die. Distribute a game piece to each player. Have students place the word cards facedown in a stack.

2. Have each group choose one person to be the Card Reader. The other three players in the group place their game piece on START on the game board.

3. Explain to students that players will take turns. On each turn, the Card Reader takes a card from the stack and reads the word aloud. The player must spell the word.

   - If it is correct, the player rolls the die and moves the same number of spaces. If the player lands on a space with more movement directions, he or she completes them.

   - If the spelling is incorrect, the player does not move on the board.

4. Players follow the arrows through the family tree. After they reach Nikita's square, they start moving back through the generations on the family tree.

5. Whoever reaches FINISH first wins. That player switches places with the Card Reader to play the game again.

Spelling Games and Activities • EMC 8276 • © Evan-Moor Corporation

Word Cards

generation	immigrate	relative
genealogy	surname	relationship
lineage	legacy	marriage
ancestor	heritage	maternal
descendant	heredity	paternal
offspring	heir	sibling

Game Board

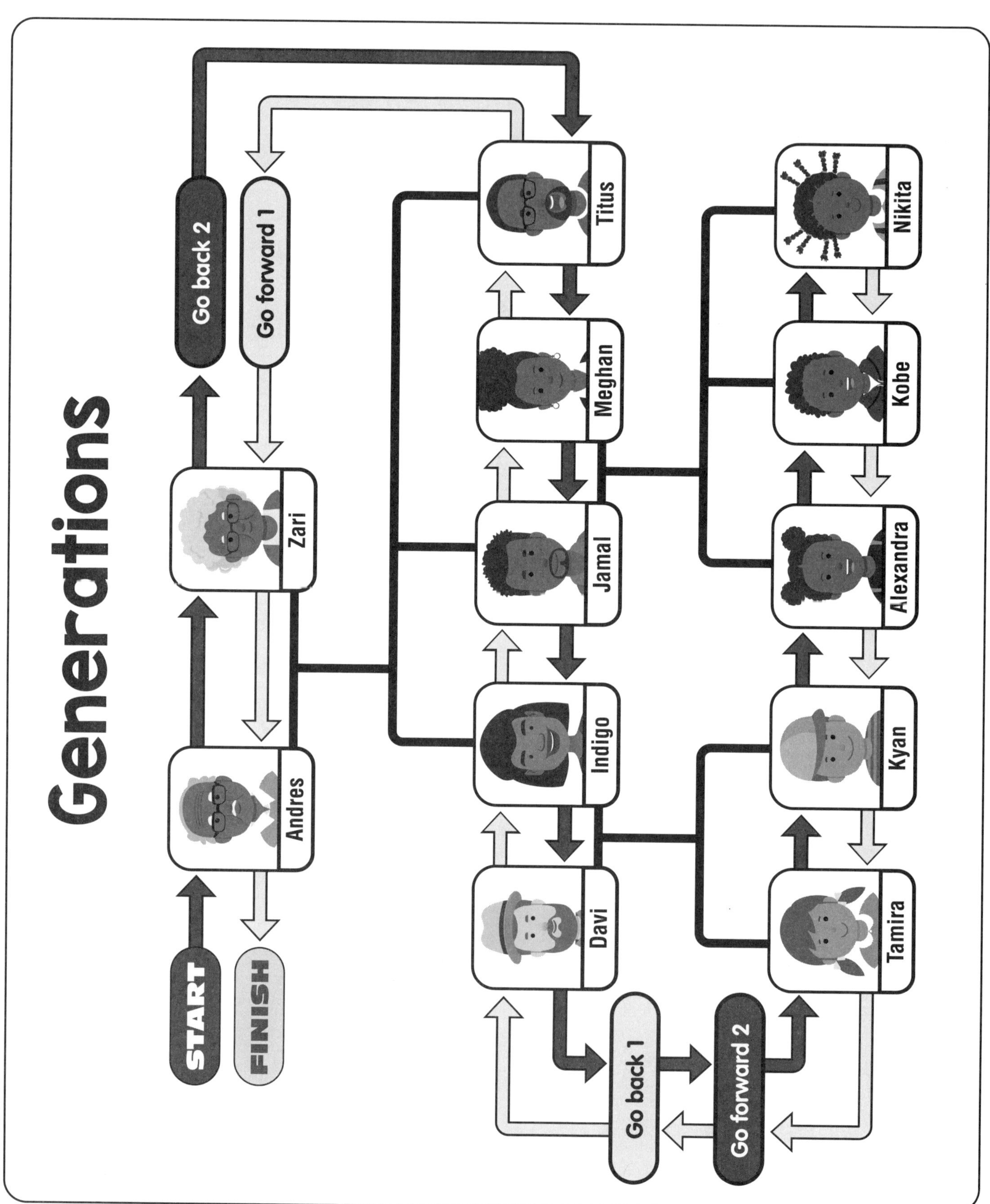

Spelling Games and Activities • EMC 8276 • © Evan-Moor Corporation

EXPLORATION

Practice spelling and using these words about discovering space, Earth, and our world's past and present.

☐ ancient   ☐ inhabit   ☐ subterranean

☐ survey   ☐ navigation   ☐ scientific

☐ expedition   ☐ latitude   ☐ phenomenon

☐ satellite   ☐ longitude   ☐ curiosity

☐ terrain   ☐ coordinates   ☐ inquire

☐ territory   ☐ oceanographer   ☐ investigate

SPELLING TIPS

☆ If a **c** comes before an **e**, **i**, or **y**, it is soft and sounds like **s**: **space**.

Sometimes **ci** followed by other vowels sounds like **sh**: **spacious**.

If a **c** comes before a different letter or at the end, it is hard and sounds like **k**: **discover**.

☆ Vowel digraphs are two vowels that have one sound, such as **ey**, **ai**, and **ea**. Examples: journ**ey**, s**ai**l, s**ea**

☆ When a vowel pair makes two separate long or short sounds, one vowel is at the end of one syllable and the second vowel is at the beginning of the next syllable. Examples: **co|operate**, **are|a**, **soci|ety**, **pi|oneer**

☆ Most multisyllable words have a **schwa** sound. The schwa sound is found in unaccented syllables. There is no rule for which vowel to use to spell it.

Image Inquiry

Name _______________

What picture is hidden in the image below? Read the word in each space.
Color each space following these rules:

- Use **purple** for words that have vowel pairs with two sounds.
- Use **blue** for words that start with **in**.
- Use **yellow** for words with the **ey** or **ai** vowel digraph.
- Use **gray** for words with the **-tion** or **-tude** suffix.
- Use **orange** for words with **c** that sounds like **sh**.

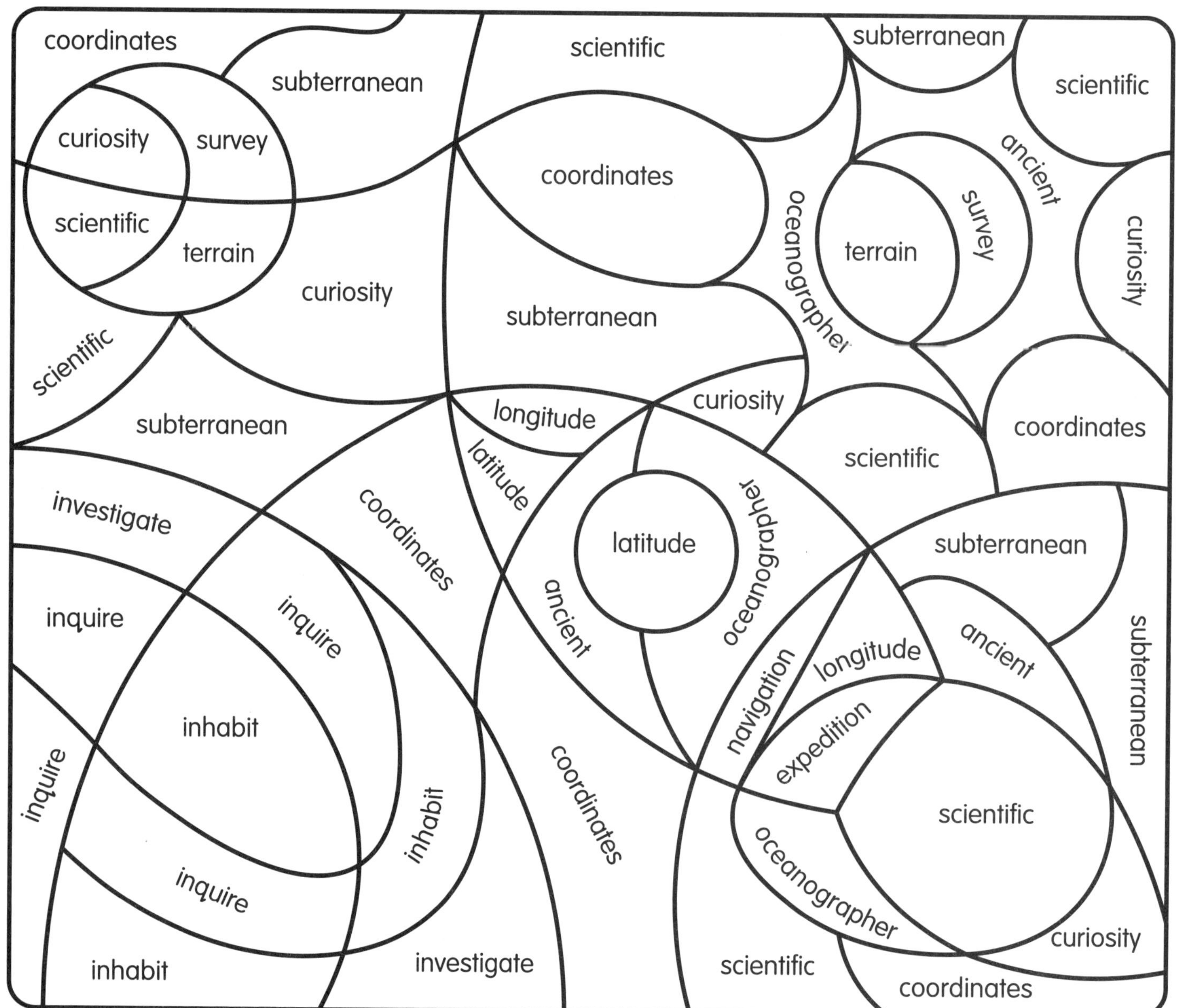

Spelling Games and Activities • EMC 8276 • © Evan-Moor Corporation

Name ______________________

Riddle Me Right

One word in each group is spelled incorrectly. Find the word and spell it correctly in the spaces below the group. Then write the numbered letters in the matching spaces of the riddle to answer it.

> **You can find me in Mercury, Earth, Mars, and Jupiter.**
> **But you won't find me in Venus or Neptune. What am I?**
>
> ___ ___ ___ ___ ___ ___ ___ ___ ___ ___
> 1   2   3   4   5   6   7   8   9   10

1. ancient, inhabit, servey

    ___ ___ ___ ___ ___ ___
                  5

2. subteranian, oceanographer, investigate

    ___ ___ ___ ___ ___ ___ ___ ___ ___ ___ ___
                        9   8

3. expidishin, curiosity, navigation

    ___ ___ ___ ___ ___ ___ ___ ___ ___
                        7

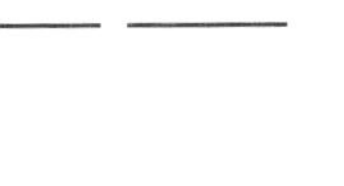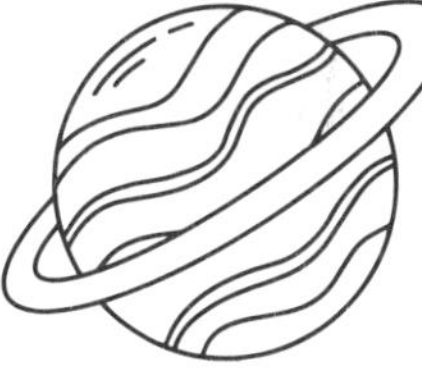

4. coordinates, scientific, tearitory

    ___ ___ ___ ___ ___ ___ ___ ___ ___
     1   10

5. latitude, fenomenon, satellite

    ___ ___ ___ ___ ___ ___ ___ ___ ___
         2

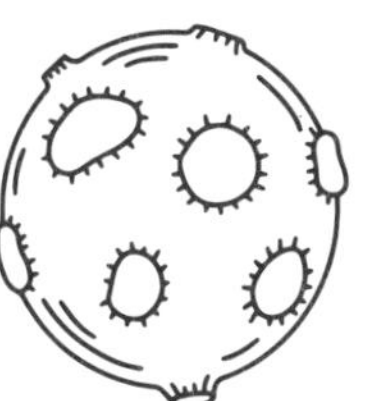

6. terrain, inquire, lonjitude

    ___ ___ ___ ___ ___ ___ ___ ___ ___
     4   6

7. satellite, navigation, cyantifick

    ___ ___ ___ ___ ___ ___ ___ ___ ___ ___
             3

© Evan-Moor Corporation • EMC 8276 • Spelling Games and Activities

Survey the Word

Name ________________

When you use a powerful telescope to look at the sky, you might find hidden surprises! Look at the letters in each spelling word. Use them to make other words. Write them on the sun.

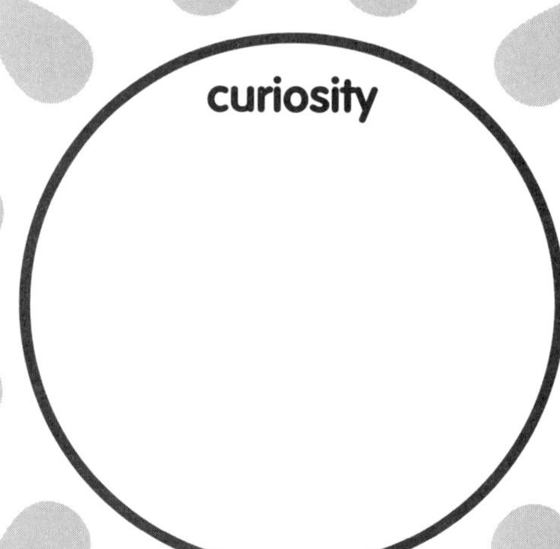

Spelling Games and Activities   EMC 8276 • Evan-Moor Corporation

Name _______________________________

A Sea of Vowels

The words below are missing their vowels! Luckily, there's a whole sea of vowels nearby.
Finish the words using vowels in the sea. Cross off each vowel after you use it.

a a a a a a a a e e e e e e e e e e e
e e i i i i i i o o o o o o o o u y

1. ____xp____d____t________n

2. s____t____ll____t____

3. t____rr____t____r____

4. s____bt____rr____n________n

5. ph____n____m____n____n

6. ____nv____st____g____t____

7. c________rd____n____t____s

8. ____c________n____gr____ph____r

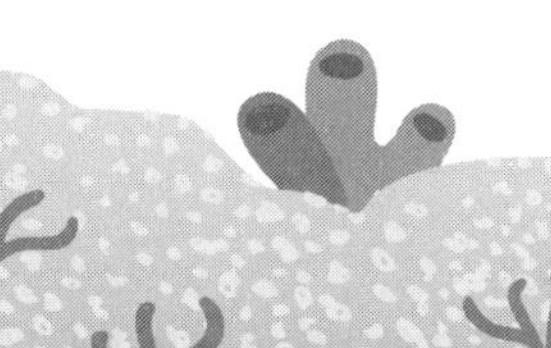
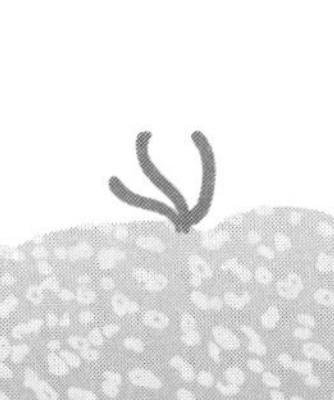

Name ___________________

Spelling Investigation

Look closely at the starting, ending, and vowel sounds of the clue words in the example. They describe an exploration word in the box. The exploration word will have the same sounds, but the spelling may be different from the clue words.

> coordinates   curiosity   inhabit
>
> inquire   latitude   longitude

Example

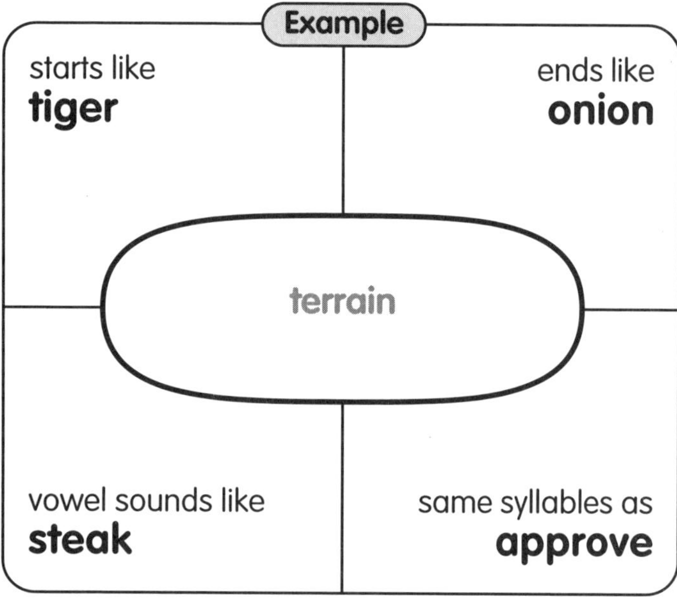

starts like **tiger** · ends like **onion**

terrain

vowel sounds like **steak** · same syllables as **approve**

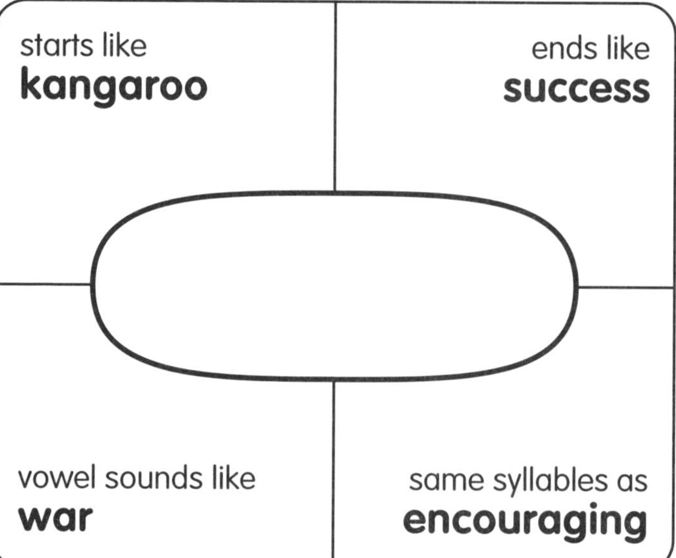

starts like **kangaroo** · ends like **success**

vowel sounds like **war** · same syllables as **encouraging**

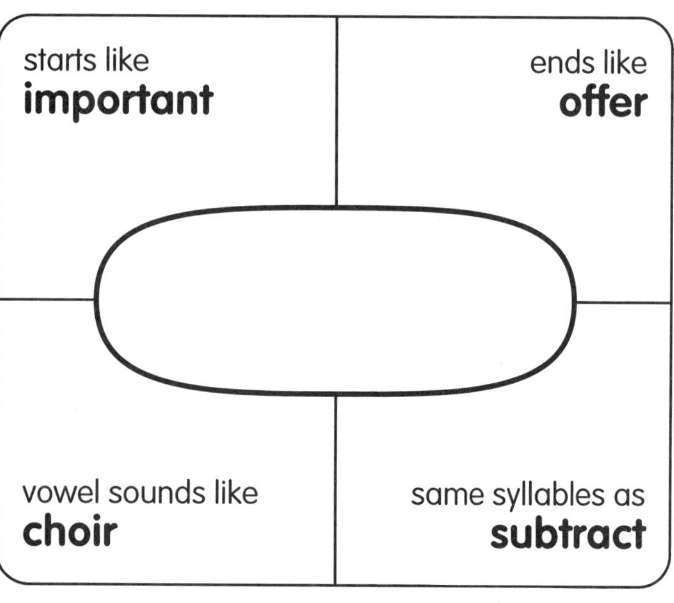

starts like **important** · ends like **offer**

vowel sounds like **choir** · same syllables as **subtract**

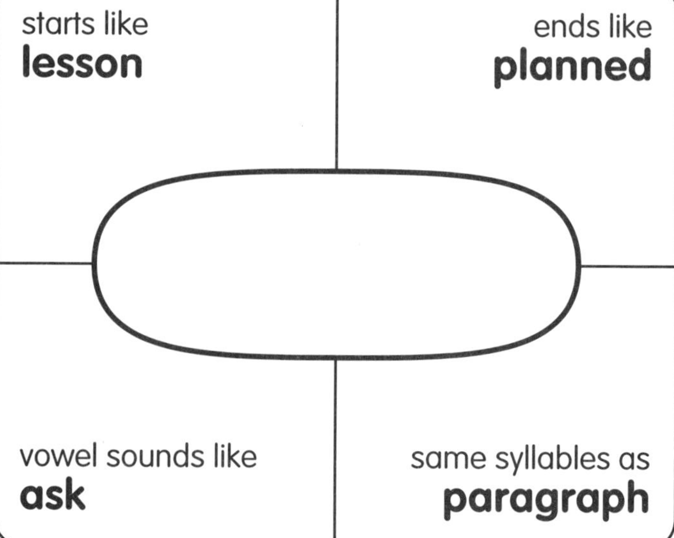

starts like **lesson** · ends like **planned**

vowel sounds like **ask** · same syllables as **paragraph**

Spelling Games and Activities • EMC 8276 • © Evan-Moor Corporation

Future Explorer

After Career Day, Keisha's class wrote about their possible careers. Read Keisha's assignment. Circle any misspelled words and write them correctly below.

Olga Popova / Shutterstock.com

I want to be a deep-ocean explorer someday. I have had a lot of sientific curiocity ever since I read about Jacques Cousteau. He wasn't a trained scientist, but his research inspired many to study science. He was a diver who loved to investagate the plants and animals that inhabut this terretory. He even turned a navy ship into a research ship. He and his crew used it for hundreds of expaditions. Unlike ainchent explorers, Cousteau used navagation to learn about the hidden surface and life under the sea. His crew made survays of the undersea terane in many places. They studied the fenominon of "blue holes" and many other land formations. They even worked with NASA to confirm that a satellight could accurately measure shallow distances underwater!

These days, an ocianogrepher might study certain animals or plants. Or they might do research on how their habitats are changing. They are

learning more about places that are deeper or at a colder lattitude that few people have visited. I'm sure there will still be new things to discover when I become one!

___________ ___________ ___________ ___________ ___________

___________ ___________ ___________ ___________ ___________

___________ ___________ ___________ ___________

Name ______________________

Exploration Bingo

Students give each other clues to spell words on their bingo sheet.

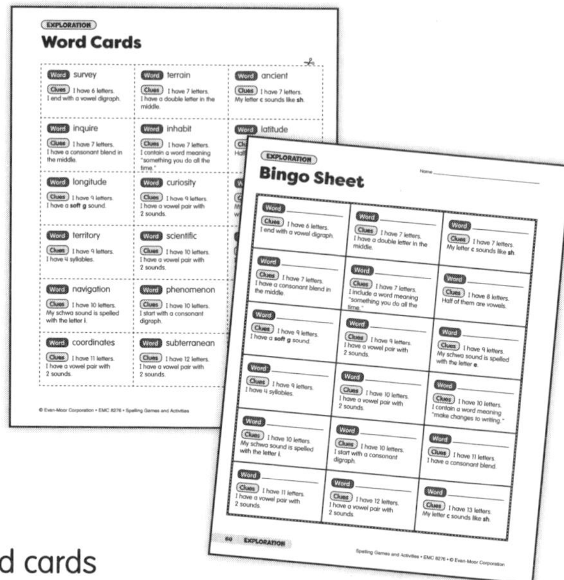

What You Need

- Word Cards on page 59, cut out (enough to give each student 9 cards)
- Bingo Sheet on page 60
- pencil

How to Play

The object of the game is to correctly write as many words as possible next to their descriptions.

1. Put students in pairs. Distribute a bingo sheet and 9 word cards to each student.

2. Explain to students that they will work with their partner using clues to write exploration words on their bingo sheets. Have students read the clues on their bingo sheets before they start the game to become familiar with the types of clues given. They will use these clues to decide where to write the words they hear.

3. Player 1 chooses one of his or her word cards and reads aloud the spelling word and first clue (the length of the word). Player 2 finds a space with the same number of letters and a clue that fits the word. He or she writes the spelling word in that space on his or her own bingo sheet.

4. Players switch roles for the next turn.

5. The two players alternate until they use all of their word cards. They trade bingo sheets and use the word cards to check that each word is spelled correctly and that the words are in the correct spaces.

6. If time allows, have players get their bingo sheet back and exchange word cards to play another round.

Spelling Games and Activities • EMC 8276 • © Evan-Moor Corporation

Word Cards

Word survey

Clues I have 6 letters. I end with a vowel digraph.

Word terrain

Clues I have 7 letters. I have a double letter in the middle.

Word ancient

Clues I have 7 letters. My letter **c** sounds like **sh**.

Word inquire

Clues I have 7 letters. I have a consonant blend in the middle.

Word inhabit

Clues I have 7 letters. I contain a word meaning "something you do all the time."

Word latitude

Clues I have 8 letters. Half of them are vowels.

Word longitude

Clues I have 9 letters. I have a **soft g** sound.

Word curiosity

Clues I have 9 letters. I have a vowel pair with 2 sounds.

Word satellite

Clues I have 9 letters. My schwa sound is spelled with the letter **e**.

Word territory

Clues I have 9 letters. I have 4 syllables.

Word scientific

Clues I have 10 letters. I have a vowel pair with 2 sounds.

Word expedition

Clues I have 10 letters. I contain a word meaning "make changes to writing."

Word navigation

Clues I have 10 letters. My schwa sound is spelled with the letter **i**.

Word phenomenon

Clues I have 10 letters. I start with a consonant digraph.

Word investigate

Clues I have 11 letters. I have a consonant blend.

Word coordinates

Clues I have 11 letters. I have a vowel pair with 2 sounds.

Word subterranean

Clues I have 12 letters. I have a vowel pair with 2 sounds.

Word oceanographer

Clues I have 13 letters. My letter **c** sounds like **sh**.

Name ___________________

Bingo Sheet

Word ___________________
Clues I have 6 letters. I end with a vowel digraph.

Word ___________________
Clues I have 7 letters. I have a double letter in the middle.

Word ___________________
Clues I have 7 letters. My letter **c** sounds like **sh**.

Word ___________________
Clues I have 7 letters. I have a consonant blend in the middle.

Word ___________________
Clues I have 7 letters. I include a word meaning "something you do all the time."

Word ___________________
Clues I have 8 letters. Half of them are vowels.

Word ___________________
Clues I have 9 letters. I have a **soft g** sound.

Word ___________________
Clues I have 9 letters. I have a vowel pair with 2 sounds.

Word ___________________
Clues I have 9 letters. My schwa sound is spelled with the letter **e**.

Word ___________________
Clues I have 9 letters. I have 4 syllables.

Word ___________________
Clues I have 10 letters. I have a vowel pair with 2 sounds.

Word ___________________
Clues I have 10 letters. I contain a word meaning "make changes to writing."

Word ___________________
Clues I have 10 letters. My schwa sound is spelled with the letter **i**.

Word ___________________
Clues I have 10 letters. I start with a consonant digraph.

Word ___________________
Clues I have 11 letters. I have a consonant blend.

Word ___________________
Clues I have 11 letters. I have a vowel pair with 2 sounds.

Word ___________________
Clues I have 12 letters. I have a vowel pair with 2 sounds.

Word ___________________
Clues I have 13 letters. My letter **c** sounds like **sh**.

Spelling Games and Activities • EMC 8276 • © Evan-Moor Corporation

A WORLD OF FOOD

Practice spelling and using these food words from all around the globe.

- ☐ carnitas
- ☐ barbeque
- ☐ tikka masala
- ☐ fajitas
- ☐ spaghetti
- ☐ couscous
- ☐ guacamole
- ☐ crepe
- ☐ schnitzel
- ☐ quesadilla
- ☐ quiche
- ☐ challah
- ☐ sushi
- ☐ fondue
- ☐ goulash
- ☐ tempura
- ☐ yogurt
- ☐ chow mein

SPELLING TIPS

Many food words have roots from different countries and cultures (Latin American, Japanese, French, Indian, Arabic, German, Hebrew, Hungarian, Chinese). Some of these words can be sounded out using English rules. But certain letters from some countries will sound different.

⭐ In words with a Latin American root, **j** sounds like **h**: **fajitas** is pronounced "fuh HEE tuhz."

⭐ In words with Spanish and French roots, **qu** sounds like **k**: **quesadilla** is pronounced "KAY suh DEE yuh"; **quiche** is pronounced "KEESH."

⭐ In words with a German root, **sch** sounds like **sh**: **schnitzel** is pronounced "SHNIT suhl."

⭐ If a word has a Hebrew root, **ch** sounds like a rough **h**: **challah** is pronounced "HAH luh."

Name __________________

Guess the Food Word

Read the clue. Write the food word to solve the riddle.

> barbeque   challah   crepe   fajitas   goulash
>
> guacamole   quiche   schnitzel   tikka masala

I'm cooked on an open fire and have a letter in my name.

____

I'm grilled meat with peppers that put "heat" in my name.

____

I'm an egg, milk, and cheese pie that starts with a **k** sound.

____

I'm a braided bread with a double letter in my name.

____

I'm a Hungarian stew, which rhymes with my first syllable.

____

I'm a slice of meat whose name starts with a lot of consonants.

____

I'm chicken in a spicy sauce, and my name sounds like it looks.

____

I'm a thin filled pancake with a **long a** sound in my name.

____

I'm mashed avocado, and my name contains an animal that lives underground.

____

Spelling Games and Activities • EMC 8276 • © Evan-Moor Corporation

Name ___________________________

Scrambled Servings

The International Food Fair showcases dishes from across the world. The dish names on the signs are scrambled words. Write them correctly below.

> couscous   fondue   schnitzel
> spaghetti   sushi

ucusosco:
a North African dish

____

hiuss:
a Japanese dish

____

ounedf:
a Swiss dish

____

tielhzscn:
a German dish

____

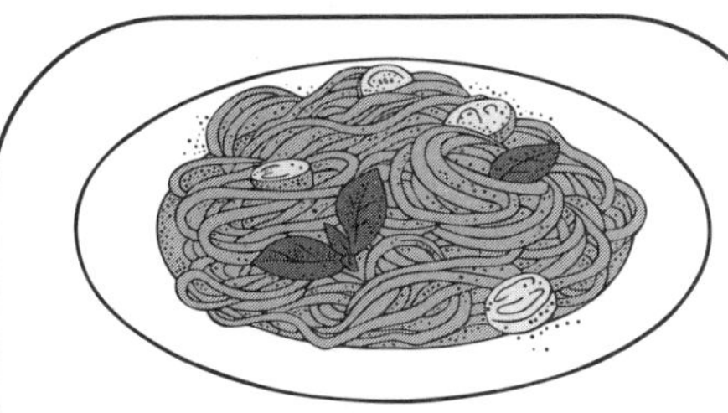

iestaphgt:
an Italian dish

____

Name _______________________

What to Eat?

Daniel and Riya are texting each other using rhymes. Write a spelling word that rhymes with the underlined word or words to complete each text message.

carnitas	crepes	guacamole
sushi	tempura	

Mom will take us to that new Japanese restaurant. You knew she would want to eat _______________________.

Oh no! Dad said they will meet us at the food truck for _______________________.

I hope we have lots of time. I eat chips with _______________________ very slowly.

Maybe Mom's plan is best. I know that you're a big fan of _______________________.

Okay! Next week we'll try the new French café. Some cooks fold _______________________ into fan shapes!

We'll add it to our foodie bucket list!

Spelling Games and Activities • EMC 8276 • © Evan-Moor Corporation

Name ___________________

Rave Restaurant Reviews

Visitors often leave reviews for restaurants they love. Read each review.
Circle any misspelled words. Write them correctly below.

Nate ★★★★★ 2 months ago

The Cardamon Bistro is my favorite restaurant. Its food is a fusion
of Indian and North African dishes. Last time, I ordered the chicken
ticca massala with a side of Moroccan kooskoos. Amazing!

______________________   ______________________

Meghan ★★★★★ 3 weeks ago

If you're a fan of cheese, you'll definitely want to check out
Casual Cow. My mom and I shared the classic cheese phondoo
and split spinach and feta cheese krapes.

______________________   ______________________

Eun ★★★★★ 5 days ago

Cantina La Vida is a hidden gem. We go there every Friday and
always have great service. I recommend ordering any of the
fahitas or a kesodiya. You can't go wrong with either one!

______________________   ______________________

© Evan-Moor Corporation • EMC 8276 • Spelling Games and Activities

Name ______________________

Foodie Favorites

Elijah sometimes writes for his older sister's food blog. Some of the letters are missing. Finish the words using the letters in the box. Cross off each letter after you use it.

c	c	e	e	e	g	h	h
h	i	q	q	u	u	u	w

Elijah's Foodie Recommendations

My sister helped me braid my first loaf of _____ _____ alla _____ for Shabbat. It's my favorite bread— and isn't it pretty to look at, too?

My dad makes a homemade barb_____ _____ _____ _____ _____ sauce for our beef brisket. It's so good that we dip other foods into it as well!

My mom's cheesy zucchini _____ _____ i _____ _____ e is too good to be missed. Her recipe is a family secret!

If you only try one dessert *ever*, it should definitely be the yo_____ _____ rt parfait from Murphy's Café.

My family usually orders takeout on Fridays. If I'm lucky, we order the chicken cho_____ m_____ _____ n from the Golden Rice House. It's delicious!

     Spelling Games and Activities • EMC 8276 • © Evan-Moor Corporation

Name _______________________

Appetizing Anagrams

You can change the silly phrases below to spell appetizing words.
After you unscramble each phrase, write the spelling word on the line.

carnitas	chow mein
goulash	quesadilla
spaghetti	tempura
yogurt	

1. true map _______________________

2. quail deals _______________________

3. also hug _______________________

4. toy rug _______________________

5. hi cow men _______________________

6. rain cats _______________________

7. tight peas _______________________

© Evan-Moor Corporation • EMC 8276 • Spelling Games and Activities

Name ______________________________

Would You Rather...

Students talk and write in pairs as they answer "Would You Rather" questions and write spelling words.

What You Need

- Would You Rather on page 69
- Our Spelling Words on page 70
- 2 dice

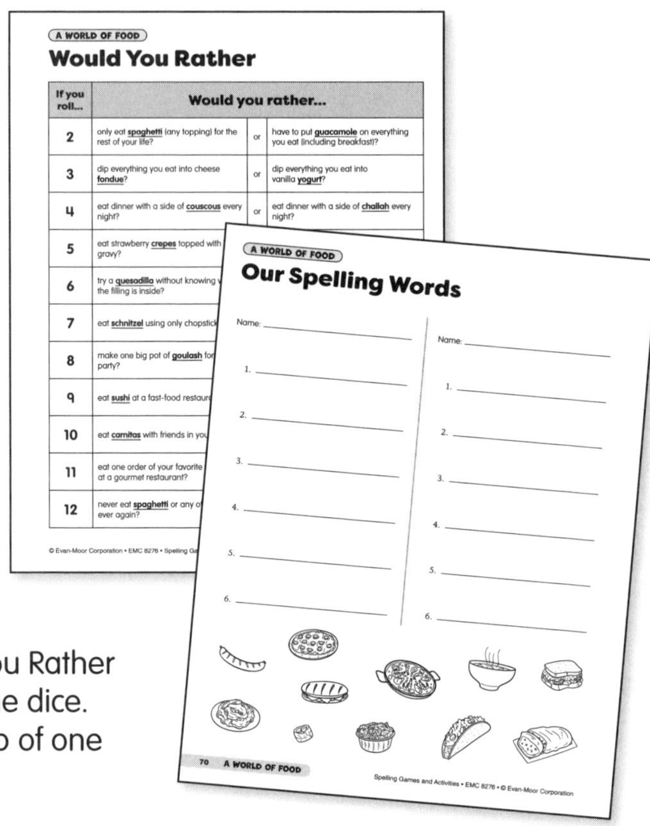

What You Do

1. Put students in pairs. Distribute a copy of Would You Rather and Our Spelling Words to each pair, along with the dice. Have each student write his or her name at the top of one column on Our Spelling Words.

2. Explain to students that they will take turns choosing between two options.

3. To start, Player 1 rolls the pair of dice and adds the total number rolled.

   - Player 2 finds that number on the Would You Rather sheet and reads the two options on that row to Player 1. Player 1 chooses an option. Player 2 then tells Player 1 the underlined spelling word in the chosen option.

   - Player 1 writes the spelling word on his or her column on Our Spelling Words. Player 2 checks the spelling.

     - If it is correct, it is now Player 2's turn.

     - If the spelling is incorrect, Player 2 can offer tips on how to spell the word.

4. Continue until each player has 6 words spelled correctly on the sheet.

Spelling Games and Activities • EMC 8276 • © Evan-Moor Corporation

Would You Rather

If you roll...	Would you rather...		
2	eat only **spaghetti** with the same sauce for the rest of your life?	or	have to put **guacamole** on everything you eat (including breakfast)?
3	dip everything you eat into cheese **fondue**?	or	dip everything you eat into vanilla **yogurt**?
4	eat dinner with a side of **couscous** every night?	or	eat dinner with a side of **challah** every night?
5	eat banana strawberry **crepes** topped with gravy?	or	eat **quiche** filled with brussels sprouts and chocolate?
6	try a **quesadilla** without knowing what the filling is inside?	or	eat a whole tray of **sushi** with your eyes closed?
7	eat **schnitzel** using only chopsticks?	or	eat **chow mein** using only a spoon?
8	make one big pot of **goulash** for a party?	or	make twenty individual **fajitas** for a party?
9	eat **sushi** at a fast-food restaurant?	or	eat a **barbeque** dish at a gourmet restaurant?
10	eat **carnitas** with friends in your home?	or	eat **tikka masala** alone in a cafeteria?
11	eat one order of your favorite **tempura** at a gourmet restaurant?	or	eat whatever you want at an all-you-can-eat **fondue** restaurant?
12	never eat **spaghetti** or any other pasta ever again?	or	never eat **yogurt** or ice cream ever again?

© Evan-Moor Corporation • EMC 8276 • Spelling Games and Activities

Our Spelling Words

Name: _______________________

1. _______________________

2. _______________________

3. _______________________

4. _______________________

5. _______________________

6. _______________________

Name: _______________________

1. _______________________

2. _______________________

3. _______________________

4. _______________________

5. _______________________

6. _______________________

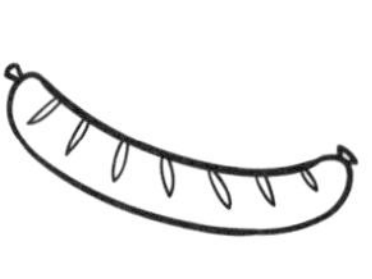

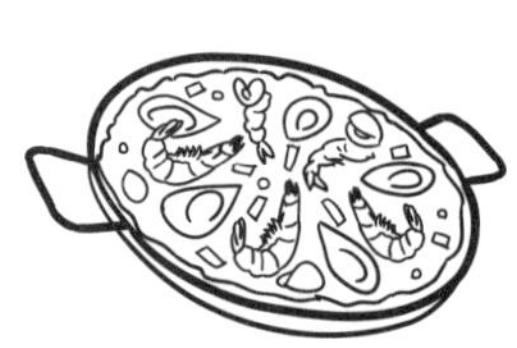

Spelling Games and Activities • EMC 8276 • © Evan-Moor Corporation

SOLVING MYSTERIES

Practice spelling and using these words about solving mysteries.

☐ detective	☐ decipher	☐ suspicion
☐ investigator	☐ cryptic	☐ explanation
☐ sleuth	☐ puzzling	☐ disappearance
☐ evidence	☐ fascinating	☐ alibi
☐ deduce	☐ intriguing	☐ logical
☐ motive	☐ peculiar	☐ theory

⭐ An **r**-controlled vowel is any vowel or vowel pair followed by an **r**. The **r** changes the sound of the vowel. They sound different from long and short vowels. Examples: overh**ear**, th**eor**y, m**ar**k, fing**er**print, inf**or**mation

⭐ Consonant digraphs are two consonants that spell one sound, such as **th**, **ph**, and **sc**. Examples: **th**ink, **ph**oto, **sc**ene

⭐ If a **c** comes before an **e**, **i**, or **y**, it is soft and sounds like **s**: **decide**.

Sometimes **ci** followed by other vowels sounds like **sh**: **official**.

If a **c** comes before a different letter or at the end, it is hard and sounds like **k**: **tragic**.

⭐ Most multisyllable words have a **schwa** sound. The schwa sound is found in unaccented syllables. There is no rule for which vowel to use to spell it.

Name _______________________

Mystery Maze

Look at the words in the maze. Find the words that contain an **r-controlled vowel**, a **hard c**, or both. They will make a path for Detective Simmons to find an important clue for his investigation.

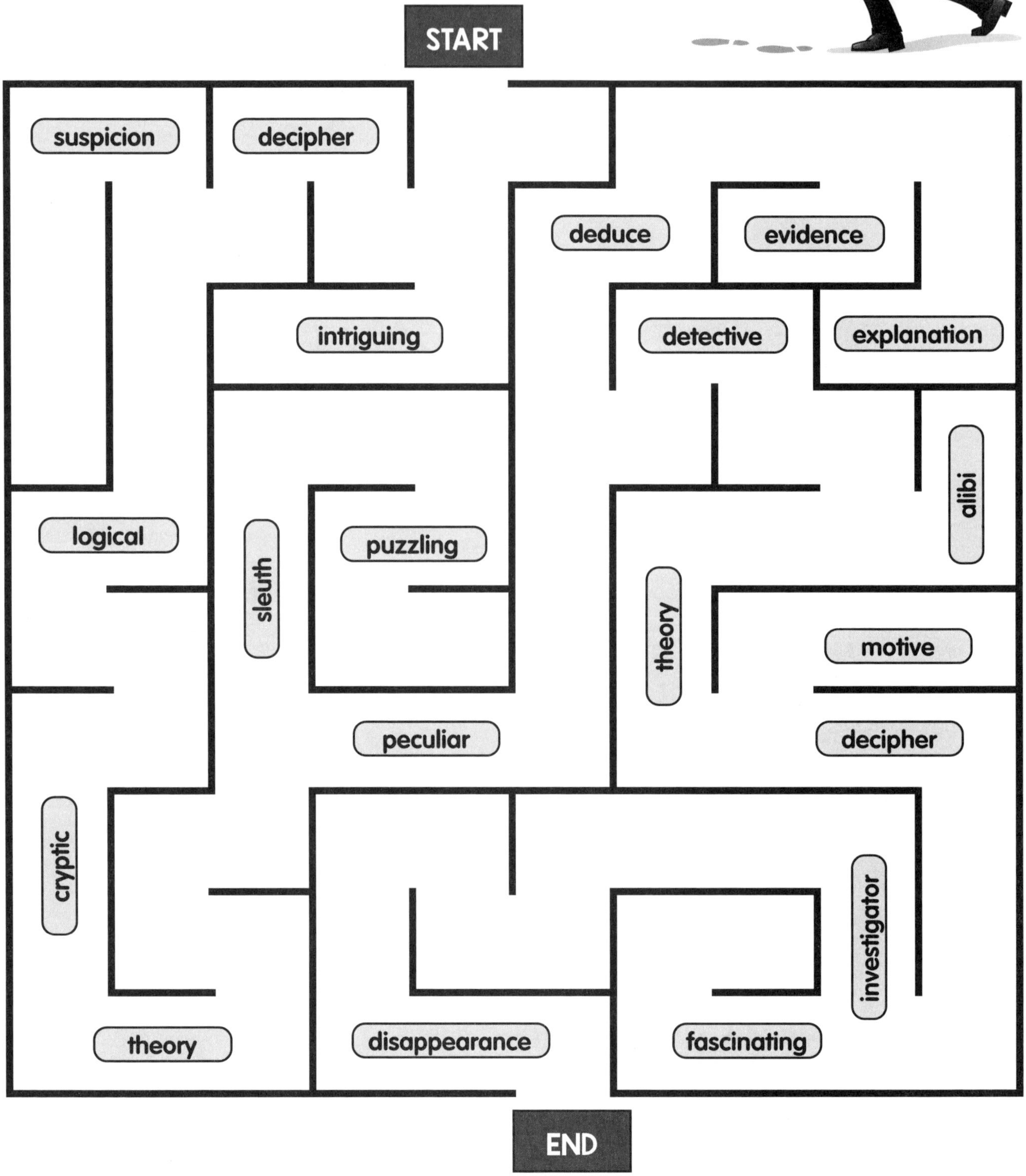

START

suspicion

decipher

deduce

evidence

intriguing

detective

explanation

alibi

logical

sleuth

puzzling

theory

cryptic

peculiar

motive

decipher

investigator

theory

disappearance

fascinating

END

Spelling Games and Activities • EMC 8276 • © Evan-Moor Corporation

Let's Investigate

Name _______________________

Investigate the letters in each spelling word.
Use them to make other words. Write them
on each magnifying glass.

decipher

cryptic

city   cry   crypt
icy   it   pit   pity
pricy   pry
rip   tip   trip
try   yip

puzzling

theory

peculiar

© Evan-Moor Corporation • EMC 8276 • Spelling Games and Activities

Name _______________________

Use Your Clues

Look closely at the starting, ending, and vowel sounds of the clue words in the example. They describe a mystery word in the box. The mystery word will have the same sounds, but the spelling may be different from the clue words.

> detective   disappearance   evidence   explanation
> intriguing   investigator   sleuth   suspicion

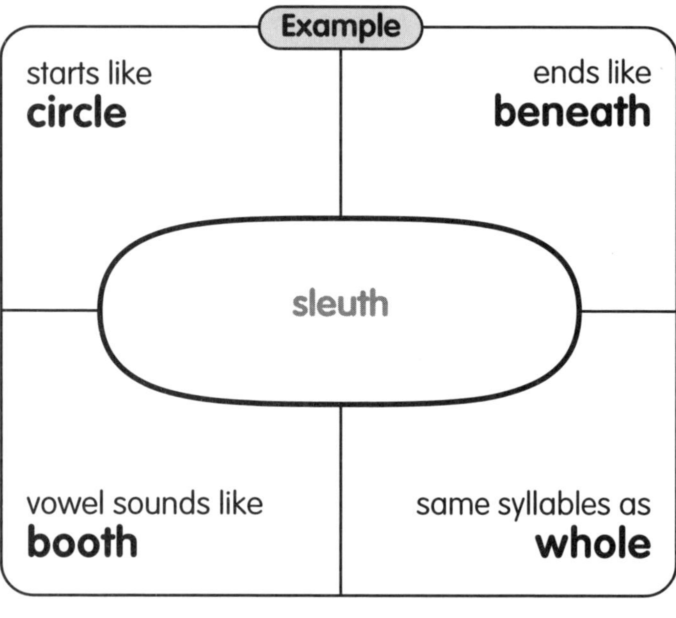

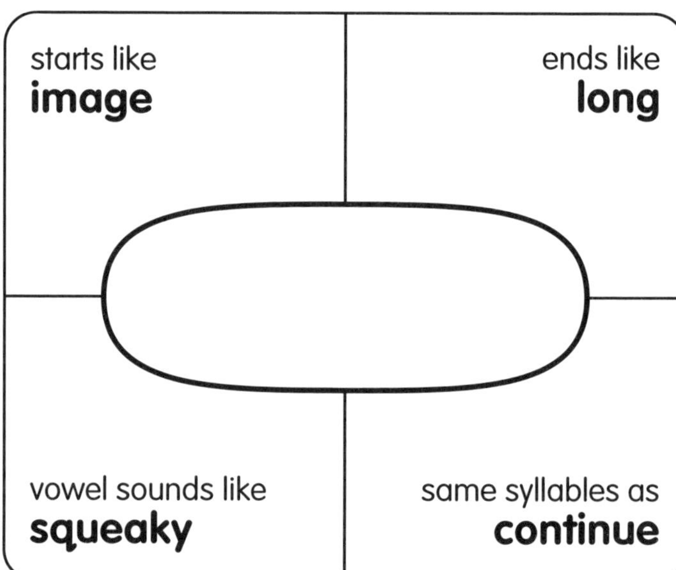

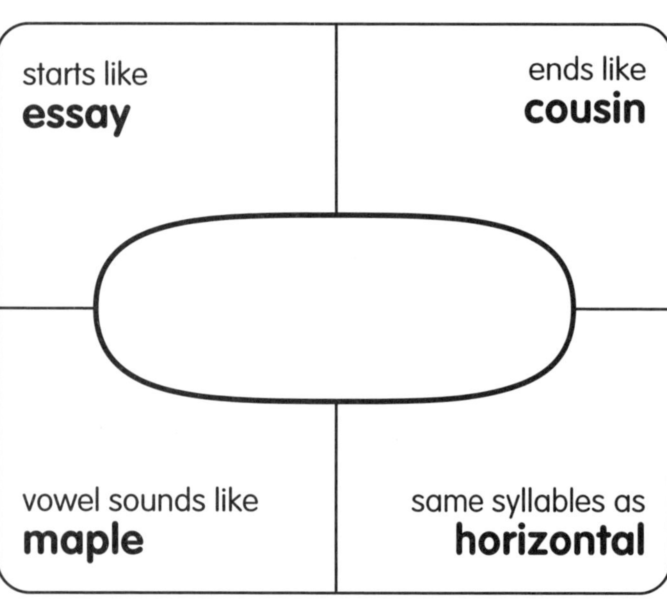

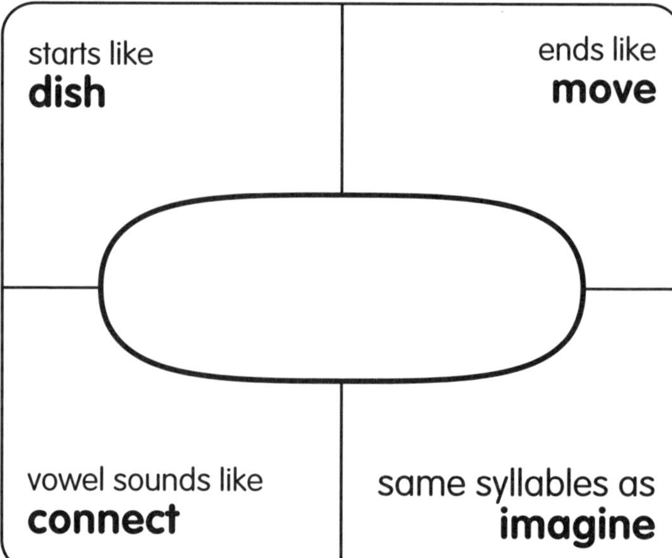

    Spelling Games and Activities • EMC 8276 • © Evan-Moor Corporation

Word Suspects

Read the clue. Write a spelling word
to solve the riddle.

Name ________________________

cryptic   decipher

deduce   fascinating

intriguing   motive

sleuth

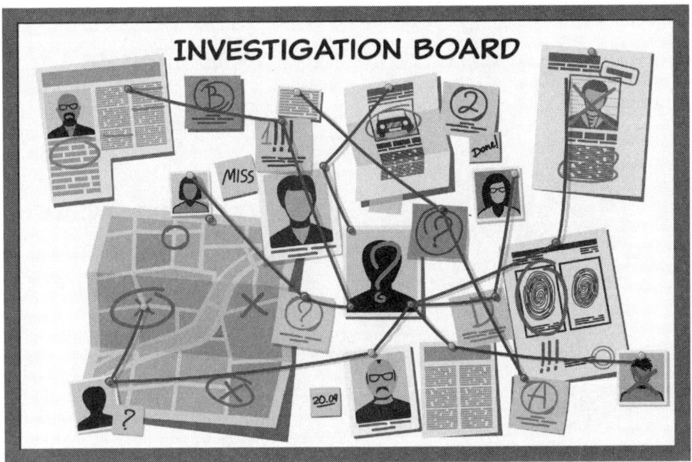

1. I have a vowel digraph, and I solve crimes.   ________________________

2. I have a consonant digraph and will amaze you!   ________________________

3. Ooh, my **hard g** sound is from the letter added after it!   ________________________

4. I have a **long o**, and I know your reason why.   ________________________

5. Use hard work and a **soft c** to do this.   ________________________

6. Hidden clue: my 2 **short i** sounds aren't spelled the same!   ________________________

7. My consonant digraph is "code" for a different letter.   ________________________

Name ___________________

Alibi Typos

Someone ate the last snickerdoodle from Mr. Yun's cookie jar! Read the alibis of his students. Circle any misspelled words. Write them correctly below.

Dak-Ho

_______________________   _______________________

____

Lindsay

_______________________   _______________________

_______________________   _______________________

Imani

_______________________   _______________________

_______________________   _______________________

____

Spelling Games and Activities • EMC 8276 • © Evan-Moor Corporation

Name ______________________

Schwa Sleuth

Put on your sleuthing cap and find the quiet schwa vowels hiding in the spelling words. Read each word in the box and decide which vowels are making each schwa sound. Circle the vowels. Then write the word in its Schwa Zone. If a word has more than one schwa, write the word in each zone. Use a different color for each zone.

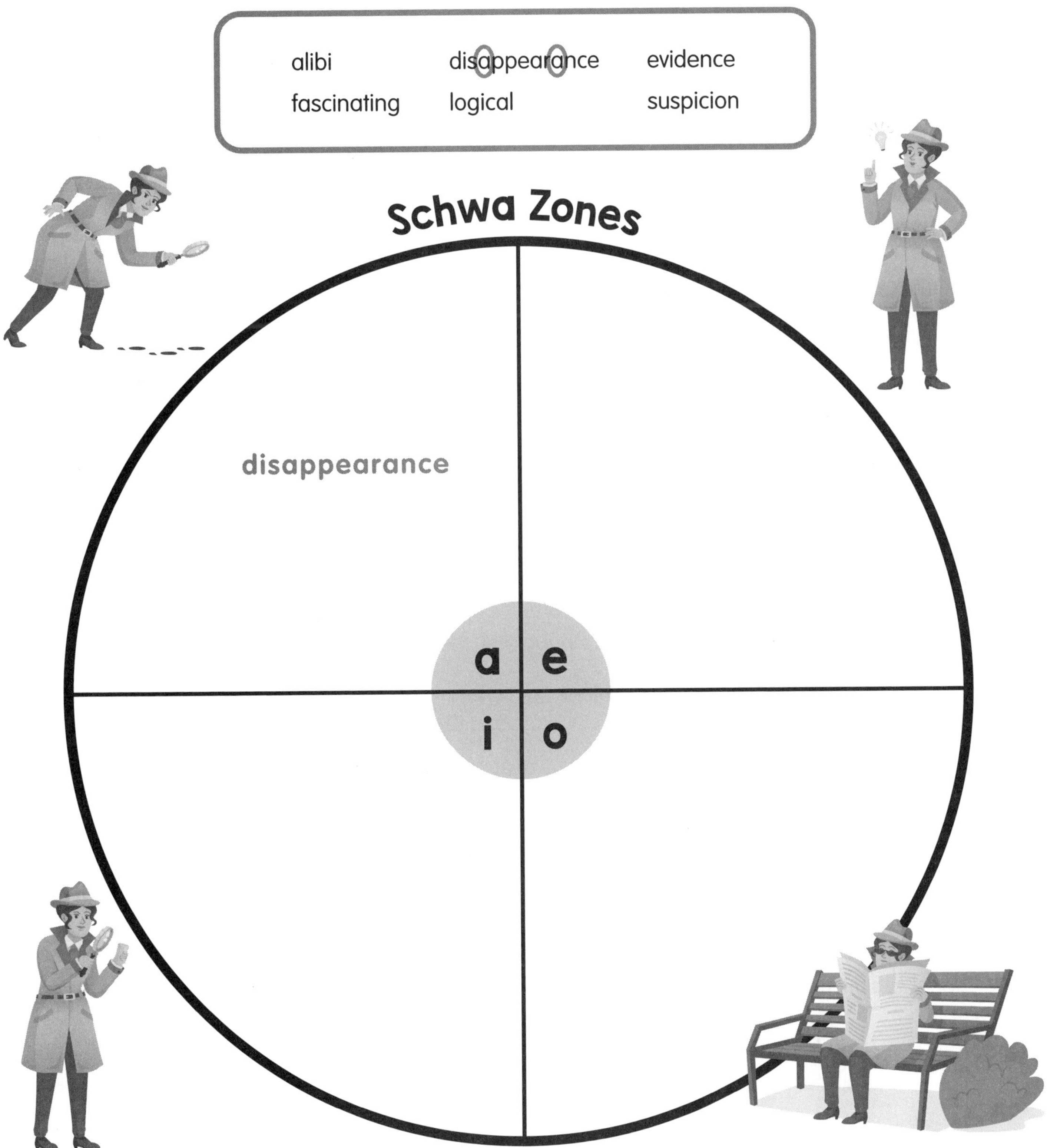

Write a Mystery

Name ___________________

Students work in pairs to write a mystery story using their spelling words.

What You Need

- Dice Options on page 79
- Write a Mystery on page 80
- die
- pencil

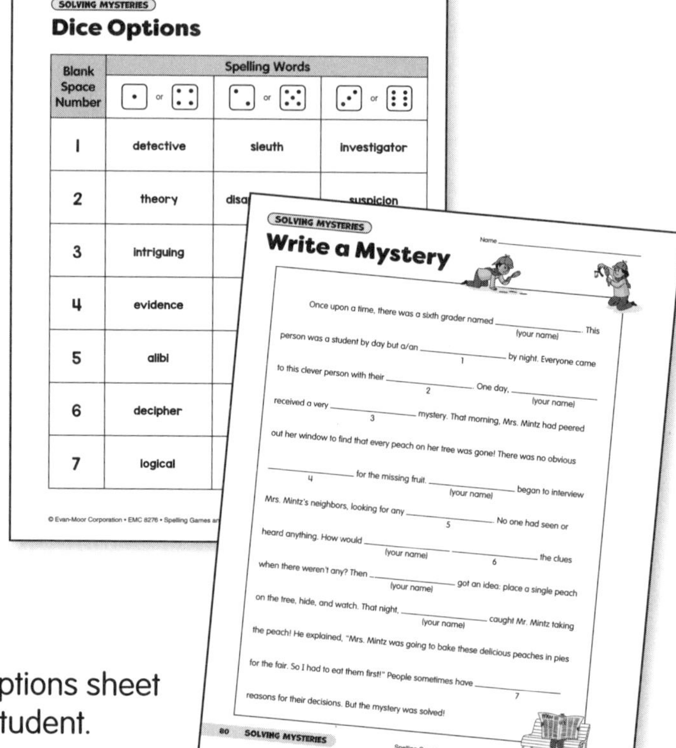

What You Do

1. Put students in pairs. Distribute a die and a Dice Options sheet to each pair and a Write a Mystery sheet to each student.

2. Have students write their first name in all the blank spaces above "your name" on their Write a Mystery sheet.

3. Explain to students that they will be filling in blanks in a mystery story by rolling a die.

4. Student 1 in each pair has the die and a pencil. Student 2 has the Dice Options sheet.

   - Student 1 finds the first numbered blank space on his or her Write a Mystery Sheet, rolls the die, and calls out the number rolled.

   - Student 2 finds the column for the number rolled on the Dice Options sheet, looks down to the row for blank space 1, and tells Student 1 the word.

   - Student 1 writes the word in the blank space 1 on the Write a Mystery sheet.

5. Students repeat for all the numbered blank spaces in the story. Then Student 1 reads his or her story aloud.

6. Students switch rolls and repeat.

7. If there is time, invite students to share their mystery stories with the class.

Spelling Games and Activities • EMC 8276 • © Evan-Moor Corporation

Dice Options

Blank Space Number	Spelling Words		
	⚀ or ⚃	⚁ or ⚄	⚂ or ⚅
1	detective	sleuth	investigator
2	theory	disappearance	suspicion
3	intriguing	cryptic	fascinating
4	evidence	theory	motive
5	alibi	motive	explanation
6	decipher	deduce	decipher
7	logical	peculiar	puzzling

Write a Mystery

Name _______________________

Once upon a time, there was a sixth grader named _______________________. This
(your name)

person was a student by day but a/an _______________________ by night. Everyone came
1

to this clever person with their _______________________. One day, _______________________
2   (your name)

received a very _______________________ mystery. That morning, Mrs. Mintz had peered
3

out her window to find that every peach on her tree was gone! There was no obvious

_______________________ for the missing fruit. _______________________ began to interview
4   (your name)

Mrs. Mintz's neighbors, looking for any _______________________. No one had seen or
5

heard anything. How would _______________________ _______________________ the clues
(your name)   6

when there weren't any? Then _______________________ got an idea: place a single peach
(your name)

on the tree, hide, and watch. That night, _______________________ caught Mr. Mintz taking
(your name)

the peach! He explained, "Mrs. Mintz was going to bake these delicious peaches in pies

for the fair. So I had to eat them first!" People sometimes have _______________________
7

reasons for their decisions. But the mystery was solved!

Spelling Games and Activities • EMC 8276 • © Evan-Moor Corporation

IT CAME FROM OUTER SPACE!

Practice spelling and using these science words about things that are in space or that come from space words.

☐ astronaut	☐ stellar	☐ gravity
☐ astronomy	☐ constellation	☐ gravitational
☐ astronomic	☐ solar	☐ gravitate
☐ astronomer	☐ solarium	☐ meteor
☐ asteroid	☐ solstice	☐ eclipse
☐ asterisk	☐ parasol	☐ galaxy

SPELLING TIPS

⭐ Some spelling words have Greek or Latin roots. Learning about these roots can tell you more about a word. **Ast** comes from the Greek word for **star**. **Stell** comes from the Latin word for **star**. **Sol** comes from the Latin word for **sun**. **Grav** comes from the Latin word for **weight** or **heavy**.

⭐ Consonant blends are two or more consonants that say their sounds together, such as **str**, **st**, **gr**, and **cl**. Examples: **str**ipe, sy**st**em, **gr**ound, **cl**oud

⭐ An **r**-controlled vowel is any vowel followed by an **r**. The **r** changes the sound of the vowel. They sound different from long and short vowels. Examples: st**ar**, univ**er**se, **or**bit

Name ______________________

Wonder Jars

Some of the words in the box have a Greek or Latin root that means **star** (**ast** or **stell**). Some of the words have a Latin root that means **sun** (**sol**). Some of the words have a Latin root that means **weight** or **heavy** (**grav**). Sort the words into the correct wonder jar.

solar	astronaut
stellar	gravitate
gravity	astronomy
solstice	astronomic
parasol	gravitational
solarium	constellation

Spelling Games and Activities • EMC 8276 • © Evan-Moor Corporation

Name ________________________

Space Party Riddle

One word in each group is spelled incorrectly. Find the word and spell it correctly in the spaces below the group. Then write the numbered letters in the matching spaces of the riddle to answer it.

How do you organize a space party?

___ ___ ___   ___ ___ ___ ___ ___ ___ !
1   2   3   4   5   6   7   8   9

1. stellar, eklips, galaxy

___ ___ ___ ___ ___ ___ ___
        5   4

2. metier, solstice, parasol

___ ___ ___ ___ ___ ___ ___
            8

3. asterisk, galaxy, gravetie

___ ___ ___ ___ ___ ___ ___ ___
                        1

4. gravatate, constellation, astronomy

___ ___ ___ ___ ___ ___ ___ ___
                9

5. astronomic, asturoide, gravitational

___ ___ ___ ___ ___ ___ ___ ___
6   2

6. astronaut, asterisk, astronimur

___ ___ ___ ___ ___ ___ ___ ___
                7

7. soularum, stellar, solstice

___ ___ ___ ___ ___ ___ ___ ___
                3

© Evan-Moor Corporation • EMC 8276 • Spelling Games and Activities

Name _______________

Guess the Galaxy Word

Read the clue. Write the spelling word to solve the riddle.

asterisk	asteroid	astronomer	eclipse	galaxy
meteor	parasol	solar	stellar	

I keep the sun off your face, so carry me just in case.  _______________

If you shine like a star, with a double letter, you'll go far.  _______________

Like a star, I have a consonant blend,
but I also have a diphthong near my end. 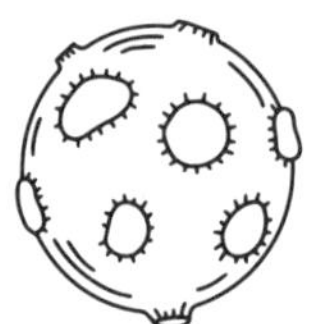 _______________

I help mark a spot from afar, and I look like a small star.  _______________

With planets and stars all around,
I end with a **long e** sound. 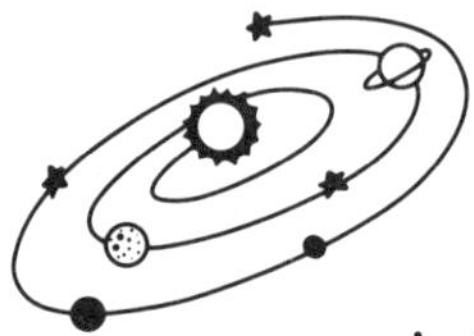 _______________

I'm a sight to see, and I have a **hard c**.  _______________

I study planets like Mars, along with millions of stars.  _______________

I'm a falling rock that burns bright. I'll light up a dark night.  _______________

I am the sun's power.
I rhyme with **polar** and start like **sour**.  _______________

Spelling Games and Activities • EMC 8276 • © Evan-Moor Corporation

Name _______________________

Constellation Vowels

The words below are missing their vowels! Luckily, there are some orbiting Neptune on its moons. Finish the words using the vowels. Cross off each vowel after you use it.

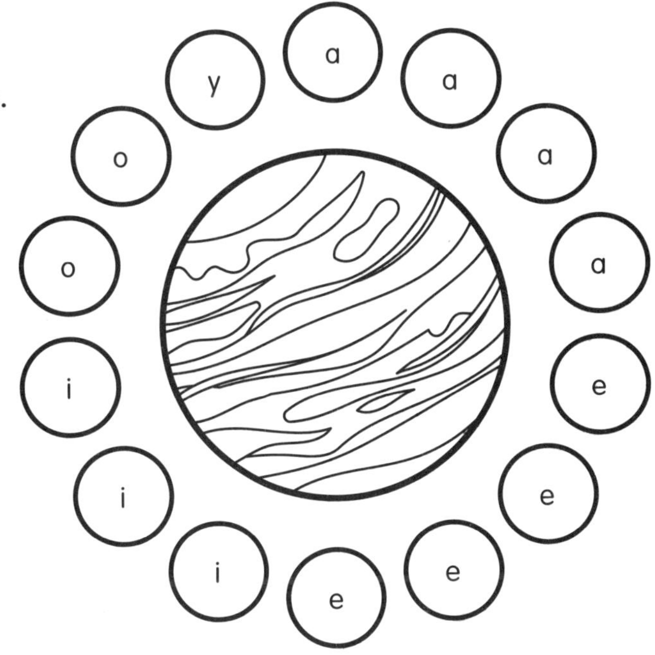

1. ast _____ r _____ _____ d

2. const _____ llation

3. sol _____ r

4. solst _____ c _____

5. stell _____ r

6. gal _____ x _____

7. met _____ _____ r

8. grav _____ tation _____ l

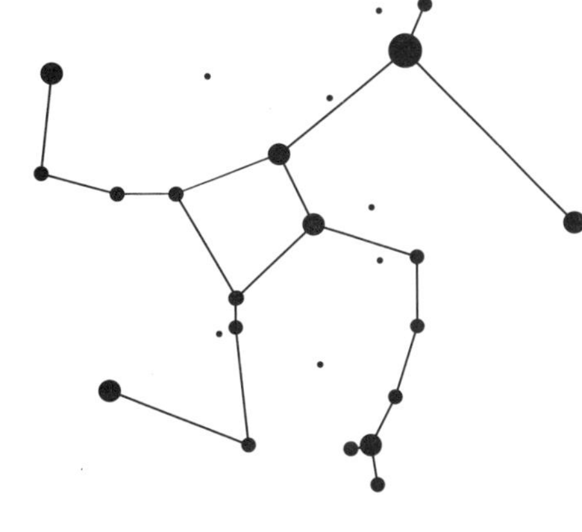

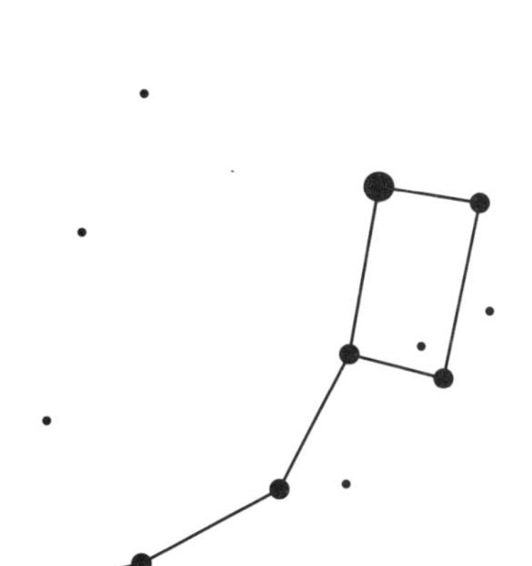

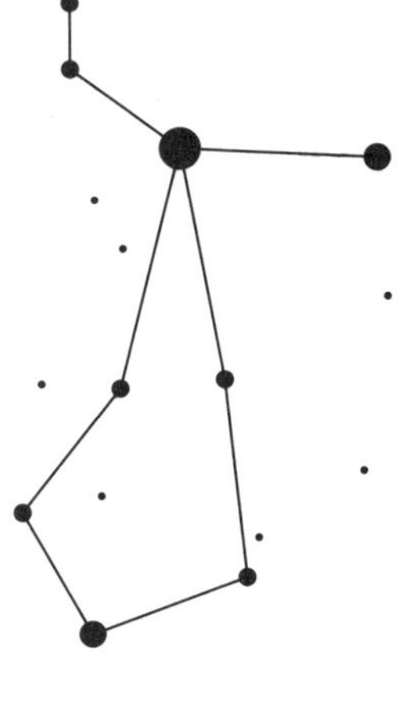

Stay in Touch

Name ___________________________

Jessie works on the International Space Station and writes to her father every day. Read her e-mail. The underlined words are scrambled. Write the words correctly below.

astronaut	astronomer	constellations
galaxy	gravity	meteor
stellar		

New Message

To Dad

Subject Your daily note from space!

Hey Dad,

Space greetings from your favorite <u>sarouattn</u>! You asked me yesterday how I can eat at a table without much <u>ryvigat</u>. I strap my meal trays to my lap or to the wall. When I make a meal, I tape my ingredients to the table!

My crewmate has a daughter in 6th grade. I started thinking about when I was that age. Remember how I wrote "future <u>oesoramrnt</u>" on my 6th-grade vision board? I thought studying the stars and planets would be a "<u>rasltel</u>" job way back then!

I remember looking up at all the <u>stinaslnleooct</u> in the night sky. I felt so small. I'm still in awe of our <u>axglya</u>. It is so vast and full of mystery. I'm grateful that I get to live out my 6th-grade dream from space! Also, I'm so glad that you got to see a <u>terome</u> shower last night. Please send pictures!

Love, Jessie

Send

___________________ ___________________ ___________________

___________________ ___________________

  Spelling Games and Activities • EMC 8276 • © Evan-Moor Corporation

Name _______________________

Astronomic Anagrams

You can change the silly phrases below to spell words from outer space.
After you unscramble each phrase, write the spelling word on the line.

asterisk	astronaut	astronomic	astronomy
constellation	gravitational	parasol	solstice

1. moon trays _______________________

2. soar pal _______________________

3. tuna roast _______________________

4. isle cost _______________________

5. sea skirt _______________________

6. colonial tents _______________________

7. tail navigator _______________________

8. moist acorn _______________________

Name _______________________

Space Odyssey

Playing in pairs, students will spell words together on a space odyssey.

What You Need

- Spelling List and Space Die on page 89
- Odyssey Game Board on page 90
- game pieces
- scissors
- glue or tape
- sheet of paper
- pencil

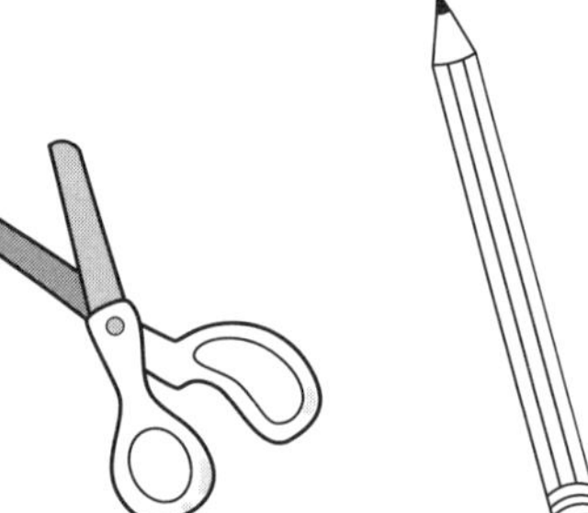

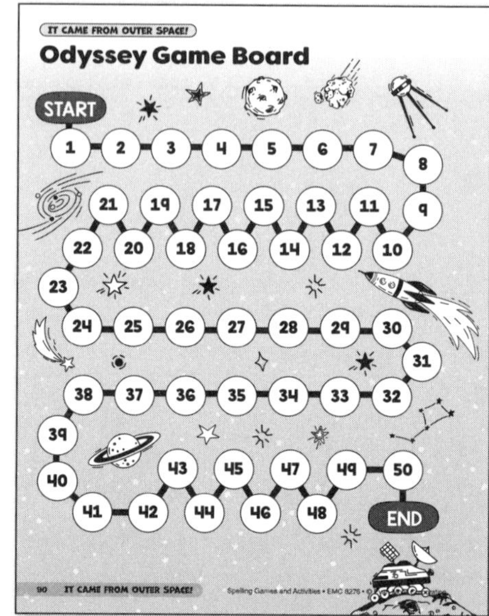

How to Play

The object of the game is to move through the odyssey voyage as quickly as possible.

1. Put students in pairs. Distribute a Spelling List and Space Die sheet and an Odyssey Game Board to each pair. Make sure they have scissors, glue or tape, a blank sheet of paper, and a pencil. Each student should have a game piece.

2. Have students cut out the spelling list and the die. Have them make the die by folding on the lines to make a cube and gluing or taping the tabs. Then have them place their game pieces on START on the game board.

3. Explain to students that Player 1 rolls the space die and reads the top side aloud. Player 2 then finds a word on the spelling list that fits the description and reads it for Player 1 to write on the sheet of paper. Player 2 checks the spelling.
   - If the spelling is correct, Player 1 moves his or her game piece as shown on the die.
   - If the spelling is incorrect, Player 2 can give tips on how to spell the word. Player 1 gets one more try to spell the word.

4. Players switch roles each turn until both reach END on the game board.

5. Players say "Odyssey complete!" The teacher then checks the spelling words.

Spelling List and Space Die

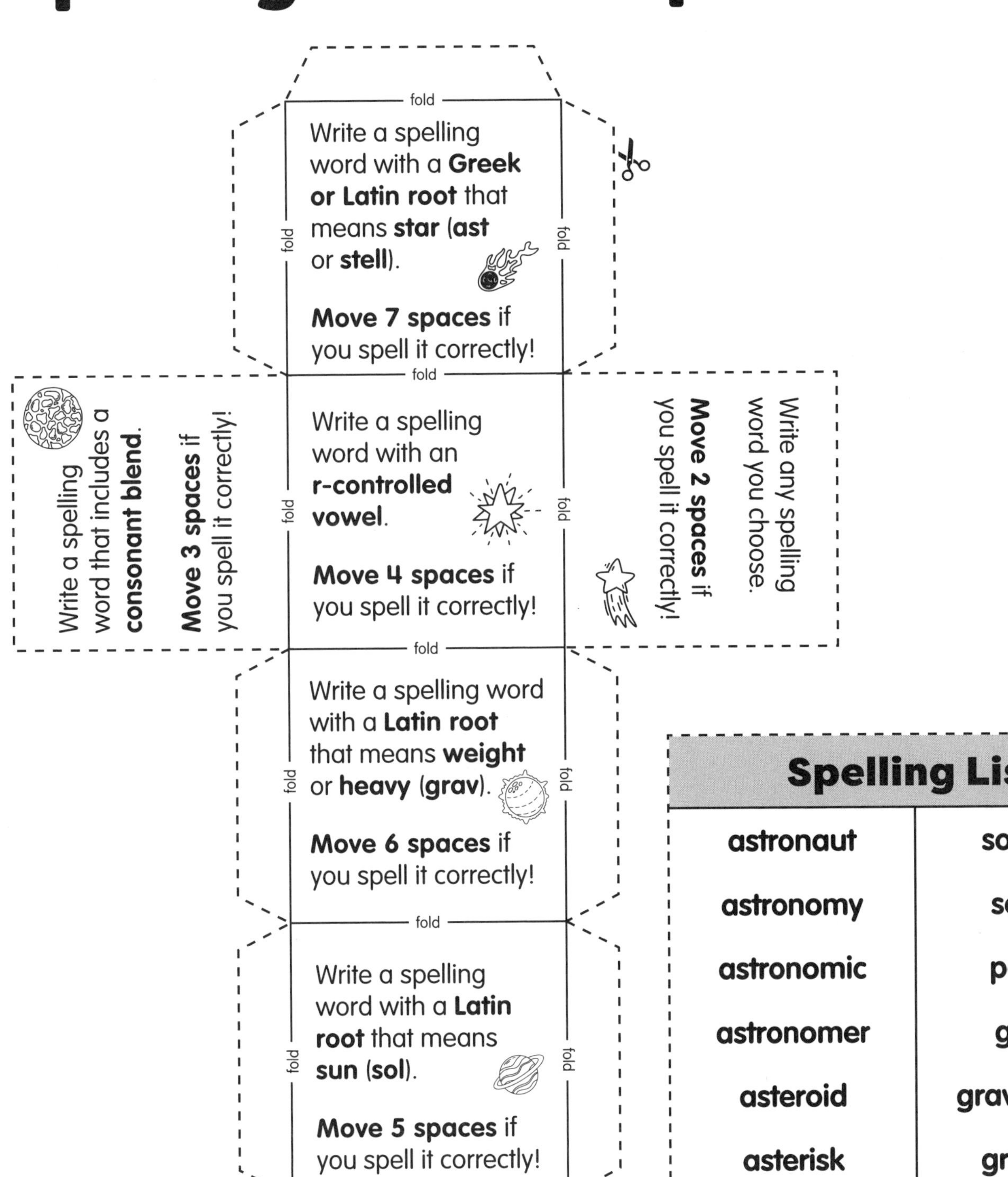

Spelling List

astronaut	solarium
astronomy	solstice
astronomic	parasol
astronomer	gravity
asteroid	gravitational
asterisk	gravitate
stellar	meteor
constellation	eclipse
solar	galaxy

Odyssey Game Board

START

1 2 3 4 5 6 7 8

21 19 17 15 13 11 9

22 20 18 16 14 12 10

23

24 25 26 27 28 29 30

31

38 37 36 35 34 33 32

39

40 43 45 47 49 50

41 42 44 46 48

END

Spelling Games and Activities • EMC 8276 • © Evan-Moor Corporation

Extra Practice Worksheets

This section provides an additional 534 words to give students even more practice with spelling patterns and word study! The activity pages can be used independently or to enhance *Building Spelling Skills* weekly lessons.

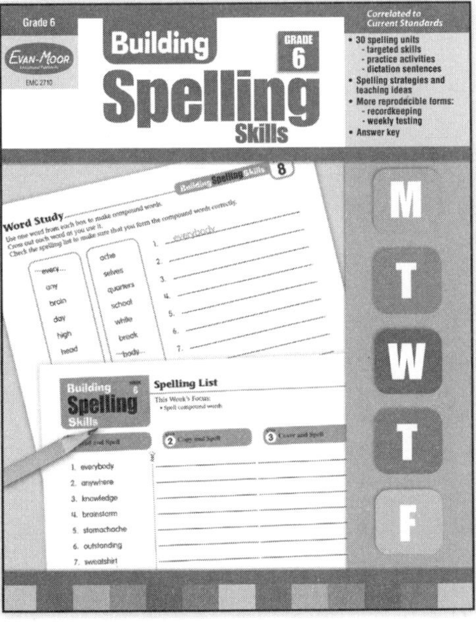

Better Together!

The worksheets in this section correspond to each week in *Building Spelling Skills*, grade 6.

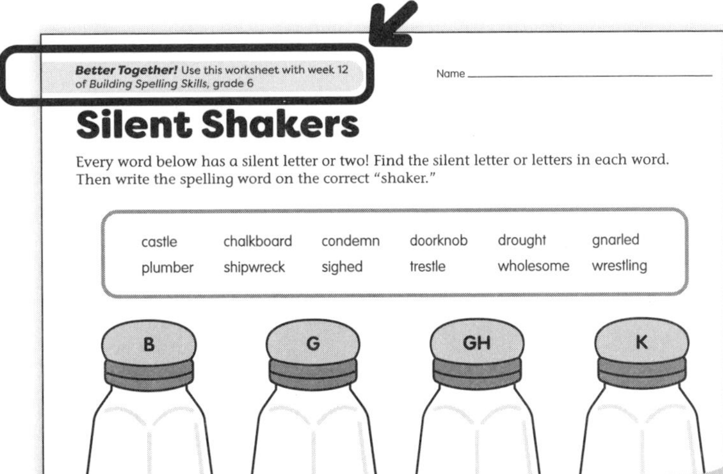

Riddle by the Numbers

Write the answer to each clue using the words in the box.
Then use the letters to answer the riddle below.

agent	anticipate	famous	fragile
mayor	persuade	restrain	survey

1. the **second letter** in the leader of a city ______

2. the **sixth letter** in the opposite of **sturdy** ______

3. the **fourth letter** in a word with a **soft c** ______

4. the **last letter** in a word with a **short e** ______

5. the **fifth letter** in a word with 4 syllables ______

6. the **second letter** in a word that means **well known** ______

7. the **last letter** in a word that contains a type of weather ______

8. the **seventh letter** in a word with a vowel that sounds like a **w** ______

9. the **sixth letter** in a word with a **soft g** and a **silent e** ______

10. the **fifth letter** in a word with a **long a** sound spelled without an **a** ______

What grows smaller with time?

____

Name ___________________________

Vegetable Vowels

The words below are missing their vowels! Luckily, there are vowels growing
on vegetables nearby. Finish the words using the vowels on the vegetables.
Cross off each vowel after you use it.

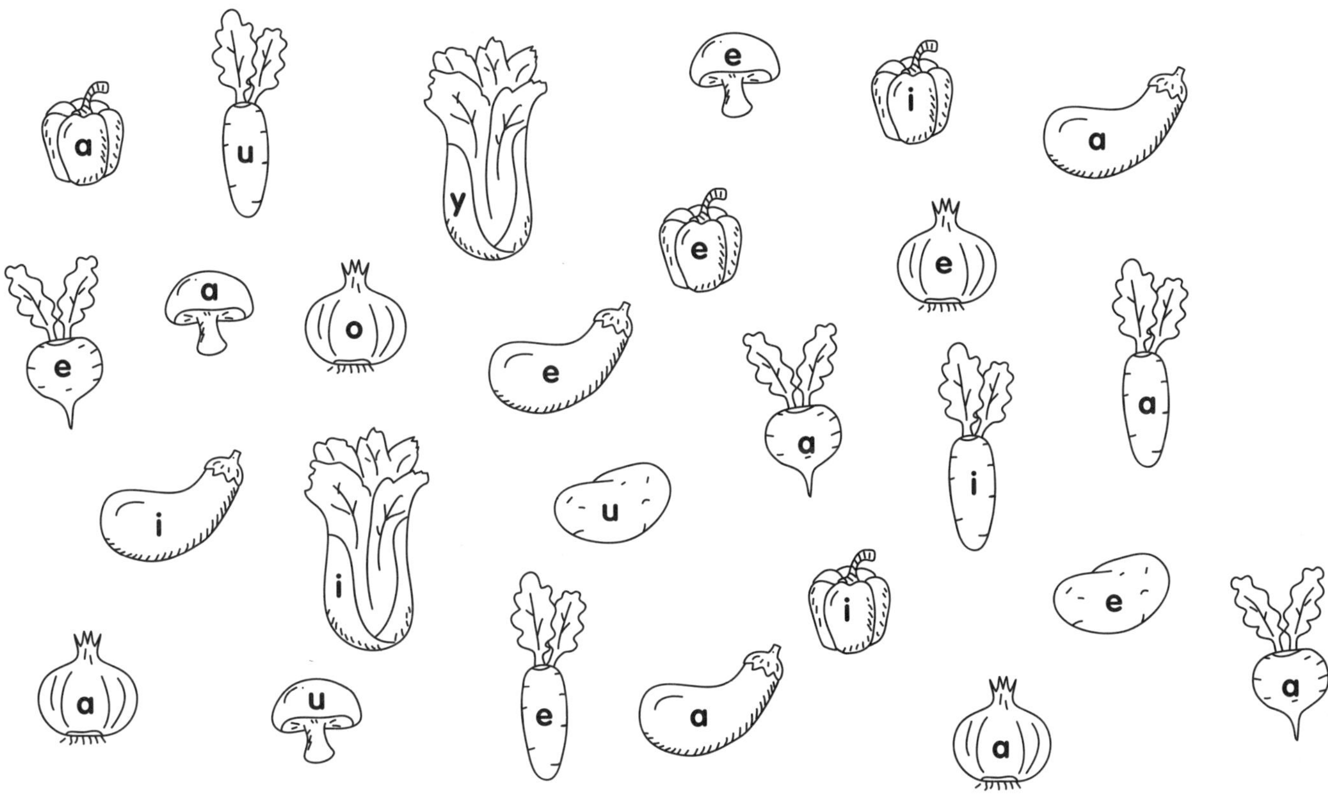

1. _____ cr _____

2. _____ xl _____

3. _________ nt

4. _____ b _________

5. pl _____ g _______

6. str ________ _____ ght

7. w __________ st

8. c _____ mp _____ _____ gn

9. _____ pt _____ t _____ d _____

10. fr __________ ght _____ r

Name _______________________

Word Sort

Read each word in the box. Figure out
which letters are making the **long e** sound.
Write each word on the word wheel in the
parts that match. Use a different color for
each part.

abbreviate	eagerly	easel
electricity	equality	frequent
illegal	neither	received
tedious		

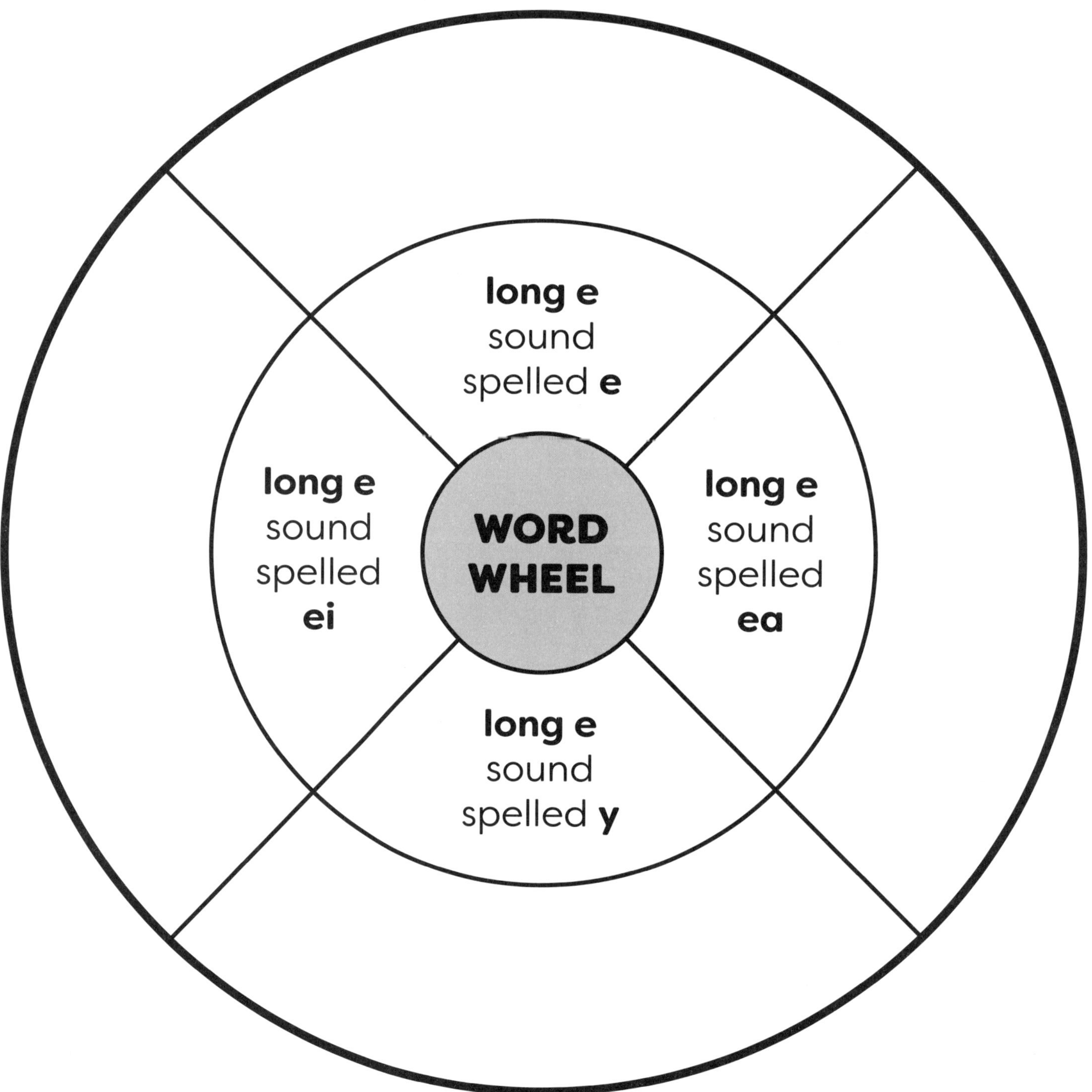

Dear Mei

Daniela e-mails her friend who moved to another state. Read her e-mail.
Some words are misspelled. Circle them. Then write the words correctly below.

New Message   — ↗ ✕

To   Mei

Subject   A weekly update on Daniela's mega-interesting life

Hey friend!

How was your week? Mine was a mix of highs and lows.

On the low side, my ice hockie team lost the final game of the championship.
I can't blame it on the reffurey; we just didn't play our best. My dad reminded
me that it was a great acheivment to make it all the way to the finals.

On the high side, I had a plessent surprise. I'm a final nominy to win that
short-story contest I entered! People can now vote for my story if they like it.
Remember when you encouraged me to submit my entery? The contest did picke
my interest, but without you, I might not have entered! It means a lot that you
always belleve in me. Keep your fingers crossed for me! And please vote!

What's new on your side of the continent? As always, I'm egarly waiting for
your reply!

Hugs, Daniela

Send   A   🔗 🙂   🗑

________________   ________________   ________________

________________   ________________   ________________

________________   ________________   ________________

© Evan-Moor Corporation • EMC 8276 • Spelling Games and Activities

Name ___________________

Puzzling Anagrams

You can change the silly phrases below to spell the words in the box.
After you unscramble each phrase, write the spelling word on the line.

although	antelope	ceremony	envelope
goalie	molecule	obstacle	trolley

1. peel oven   _______________________

2. oil age   _______________________

3. emu cello   _______________________

4. hot laugh   _______________________

5. one mercy   _______________________

6. yet roll   _______________________

7. able cost   _______________________

8. neat pole   _______________________

Spelling Games and Activities • EMC 8276 • © Evan-Moor Corporation

Baffling Riddle

One word in each group is spelled incorrectly. Find the word and spell it correctly in the spaces below the group. Then write the numbered letters in the matching spaces of the riddle to answer it.

I'm constantly running, but I never get tired or hot. What am I?

___ ___ ___ ___ ___ ___ ___ ___ ___ ___ ___ ___ ___
1   2   3   4   5   6   7   8   9   10   11   12   13

---

1. aproche, ceremony, obstacle

   ___ ___ ___ ___ ___ ___ ___
   1   2

2. although, goalie, poatrey

   ___ ___ ___ ___
   3   5

3. trolley, poem, offin

   ___ ___ ___ ___
   4

4. proverb, oxigin, goalie

   ___ ___ ___ ___ ___
   7   8

5. momint, antelope, officer

   ___ ___ ___ ___ ___ ___
   11

6. ceremony, stoaway, although

   ___ ___ ___ ___ ___ ___ ___
   12   10

7. trolley, envelope, provurb

   ___ ___ ___ ___ ___ ___
   9   13

8. envelope, antelope, obstinant

   ___ ___ ___ ___ ___ ___ ___
   6

Name _______________________

Subway Travel

Kareem is traveling with his mother across town on the subway to see his grandparents.
Look at the map of the subway stops. The route they take goes to every stop name that
is a multisyllable word with a **long i** sound. Circle all stops on their route. Then draw
a line from Kareem and his mother to each stop the subway train will make.

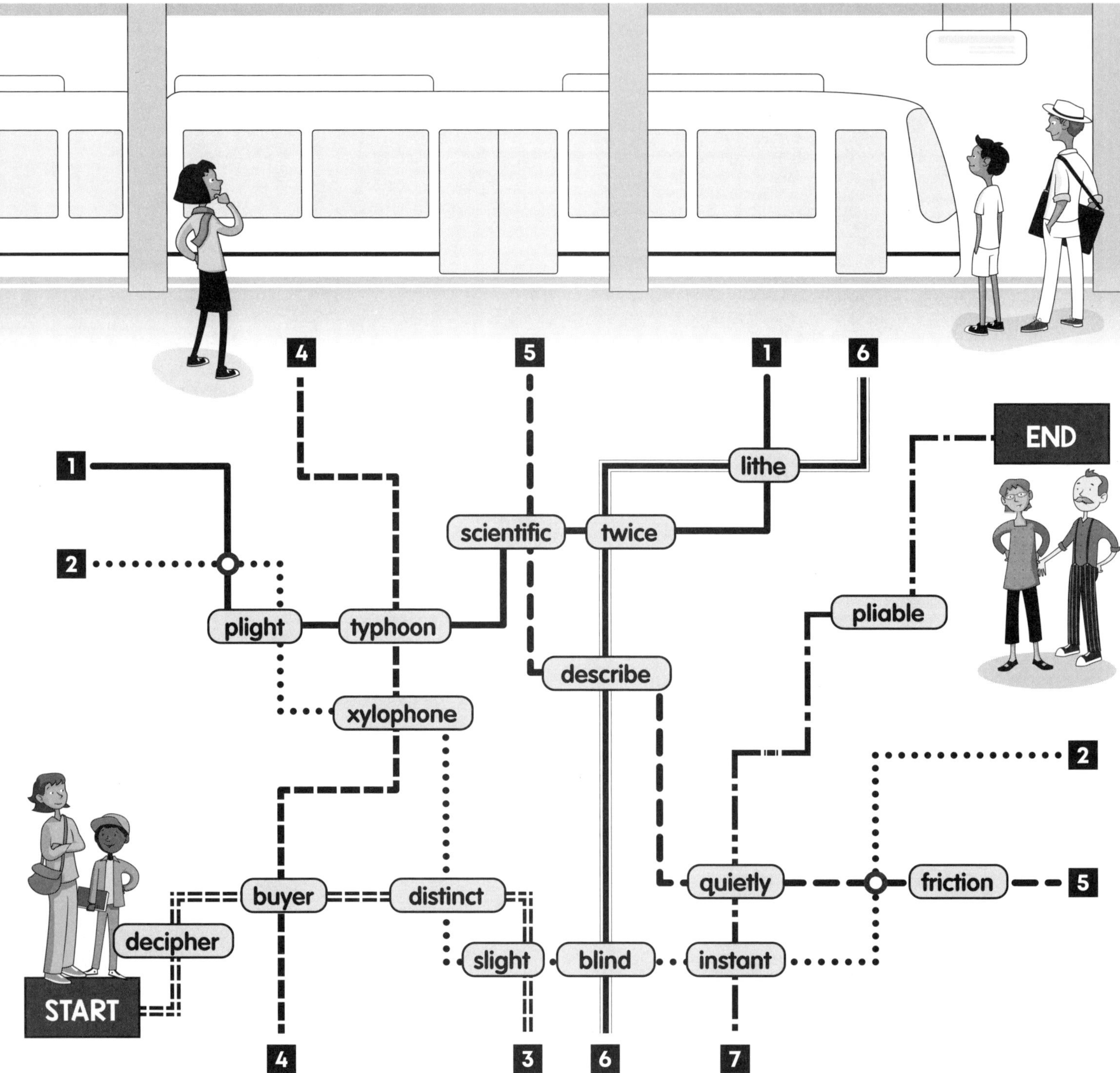

Making Room

Isabella and Jordan are texting each other. Write the spelling words to complete the text messages.

acquire	buyer	glimpse	instant
plight	quietly	twice	xylophone

Hey, I think I have a ______________________ for that ______________________ of yours. A friend is interested in learning how to play a new instrument!

Seriously?! I haven't had anyone look at it ______________________.

No one has even wanted to take a tiny ______________________ at it. Which friend is it?

It's Marissa. She was in our class in fifth grade. She always sat ______________________ at the back. She wants to ______________________ a new skill.

That's fantastic! I'll sell it to her in an ______________________. I'll give her a good deal. Mom says I have to make room if I want a piano.

Haha, what a ______________________ for you! I'll give her your phone number.

Name ______________________________

Postcard Pals

Ezra sent his pal, Nova, a postcard from his vacation in Italy. Write the spelling words to complete the postcard.

beautiful country menu

museums once sculpture

unusual

Hey Nova,

Hello from Italy! It's my first time visiting this ______________, but my mother was here ______________ before. We've had such a fun time. This country is full of ______________ landscapes.

We've seen many ______________ and a ton of art. We saw Michelangelo's famous ______________ of David. It has a lot of lifelike details when you see it up close!

After dinner, we're going to a nearby gelato shop. Their ______________ has many ______________ flavors. My last gelato was cherry ricotta, made out of cheese!

I can't wait to tell you more when I get back!

Your friend,

Ezra

Spelling Games and Activities • EMC 8276 • © Evan-Moor Corporation

Secret Tongue Twister

Find 11 words in the word search that have a **short u** or **long u** sound.
Words may go forward, backward, up, down, or diagonally.

Word list:
- customary
- does
- fugitive
- luxury
- suffocate
- sulfur
- thumbprint
- unit
- universe
- utilize
- valuable

S	L	K	I	L	L	E	D	E	S	T	C
E	T	U	E	L	L	A	L	S	E	N	U
E	T	L	X	L	S	B	S	S	Q	I	S
T	U	A	A	U	A	R	R	E	S	R	T
C	I	U	C	U	R	E	L	F	E	P	O
P	T	N	L	O	V	Y	U	U	Z	B	M
R	E	A	U	I	F	G	S	J	I	M	A
B	V	Y	N	L	I	F	N	H	L	U	R
L	A	U	S	T	W	H	U	U	I	H	Y
W	Q	E	I	S	K	E	T	S	T	T	M
E	O	V	S	U	L	F	U	R	U	R	C
D	E	I	R	X	F	E	I	R	H	B	E

Now write the unused letters in the blank spaces below,
starting in the top left corner. You will find a secret tongue twister!

______________________________   ______________________________

______________________________   ______________________________

______________________________ .

© Evan-Moor Corporation • EMC 8276 • Spelling Games and Activities

Name _______________________

Red Light, Green Light

Some of the sentences below have misspelled words! Read each sentence. If the sentence is correct, **color the traffic light green**. If there is a misspelled word, **color the traffic light red**. Then write the correct spelling word in the last column.

1. Read the sentence.	**2.** Is there a **misspelled word** in this sentence?	**3.** Write the correct spelling word.
My birthday is my favorite **ocassion** to celebrate.	● ○ ○	occasion
A butterfly is an example of **symmetry** in nature.	○ ○ ○	
It's a rare **occurrence** when someone can **embarass** me.	○ ○ ○	
The **terane** is uneven in the countryside.	○ ○ ○	
There is an **alliance** between those two teams.	○ ○ ○	
Can you **reccomend** a good restaurant?	○ ○ ○	
An audience will usually **aplod** if they have the **opportunity**.	○ ○ ○	
Watch out for the **barricade** on the **oposite** side of the road.	○ ○ ○	
Horray! Your story was selected for the final competition!	○ ○ ○	
They sometimes **exxagerate** their stories.	○ ○ ○	

Under the Microscope

Look at the letters in each spelling word. Use them to make other words. Write them on each microscope slide.

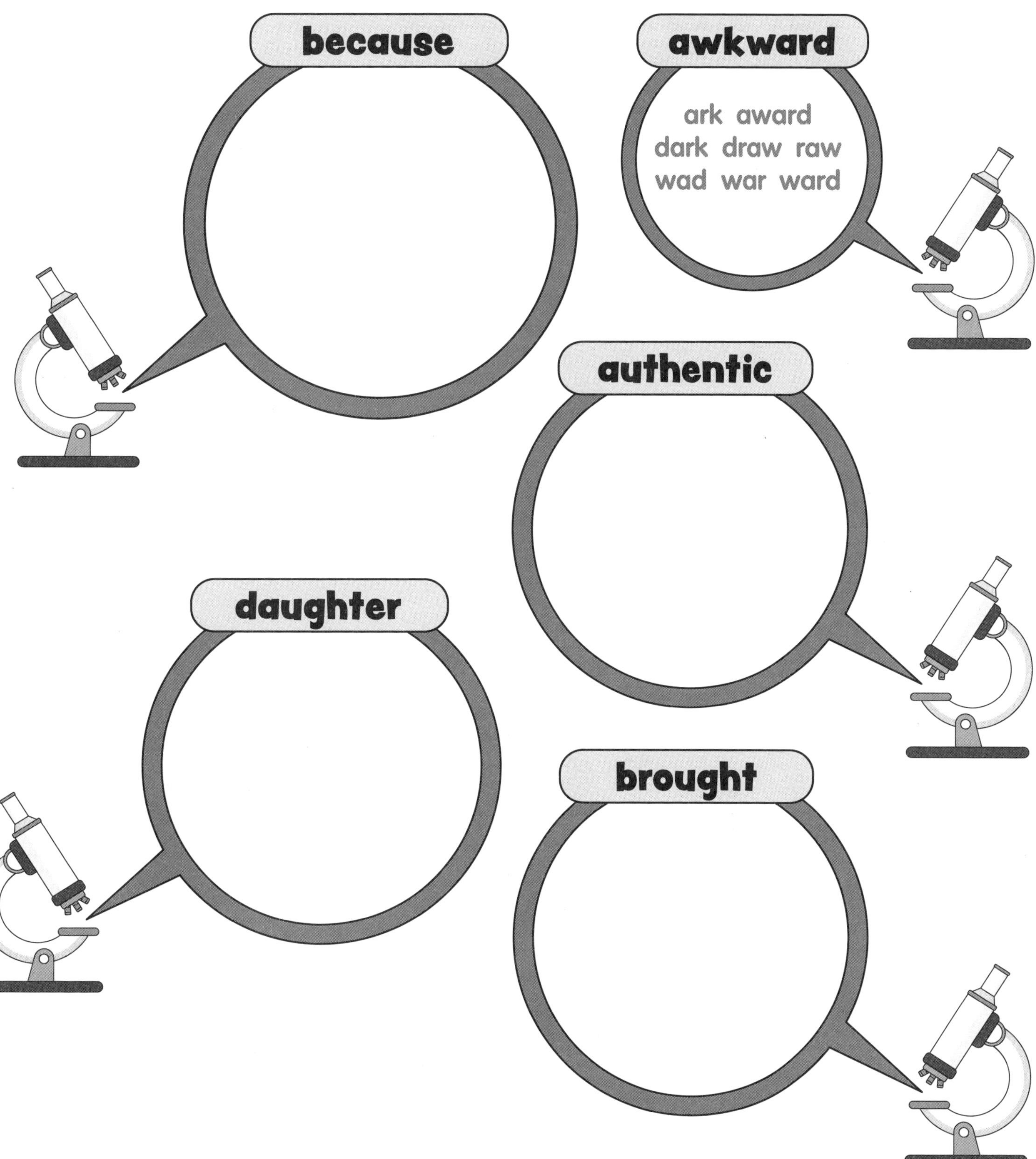

Baffling Riddle

One word in each group is spelled incorrectly. Find the word and spell it correctly in the spaces below the group. Then write the numbered letters in the matching space of the riddle to answer it.

You see me twice every afternoon, once every morning, but never in the night. What am I?

___ ___ ___ ___ ___ ___ ___ ___ ___ ___
 1   2   3   4   5   6   7   8   9   10

1. skiing, angryer, studied

___ ___ ___ ___ ___ ___ ___
        9

2. lonelier, skiing, cleanist

___ ___ ___ ___ ___ ___ ___ ___
    4   7

3. studying, angriest, hesitatid

___ ___ ___ ___ ___ ___ ___ ___ ___
  2   6

4. perscribed, friendliest, gestured

___ ___ ___ ___ ___ ___ ___ ___ ___
        3

5. cleaner, skeed, studied

___ ___ ___ ___ ___
        8

6. studying, geschured, loneliest

___ ___ ___ ___ ___ ___ ___
    5   1

7. angrier, cleaner, lonlier

___ ___ ___ ___ ___ ___ ___
    10

8. frendlyier, prescribing, hesitating

___ ___ ___ ___ ___ ___ ___ ___ ___ ___

    Spelling Games and Activities • EMC 8276 • © Evan-Moor Corporation

Name _______________________

Suffix Soups

Look at the base words. For some words, you can add the ending **-ing**.
You can add the ending **-est** to other words. Add the correct ending to
each word and write it on the matching soup pot.

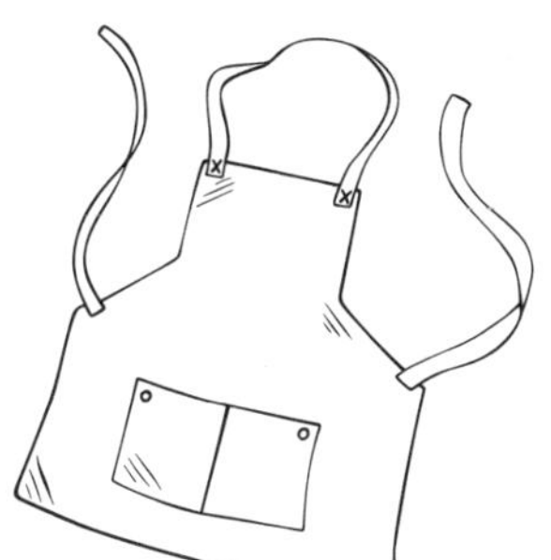

Base Words

angry	friendly	gesture	hesitate
lonely	prescribe	ski	study

**The -ing
Suffix Soup**

**The -est
Suffix Soup**

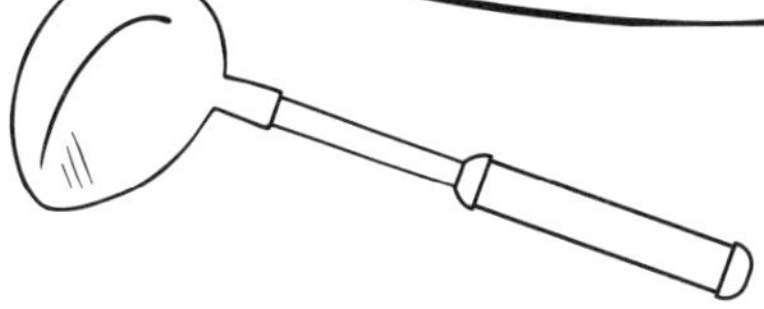

© Evan-Moor Corporation • EMC 8276 • Spelling Games and Activities

Swimmer Pairs

A bunch of words have gone swimming in their own lane.
But some words often swim together as a pair. Use the
words to make as many compound words as you can.
Write them in the box.

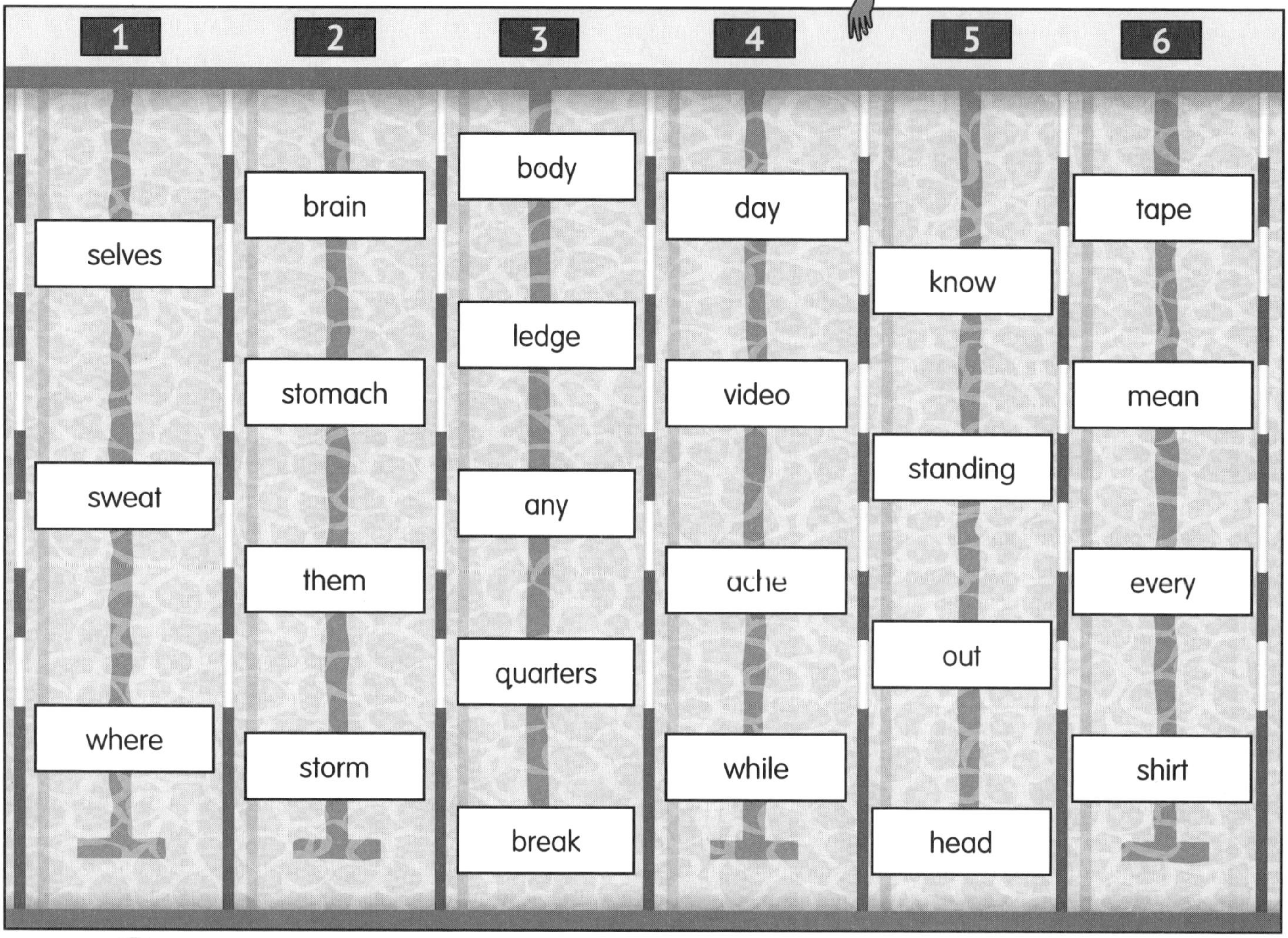

1	2	3	4	5	6
selves	brain	body	day	know	tape
sweat	stomach	ledge	video	standing	mean
where	them	any	ache	out	every
	storm	quarters	while		shirt
		break	head		

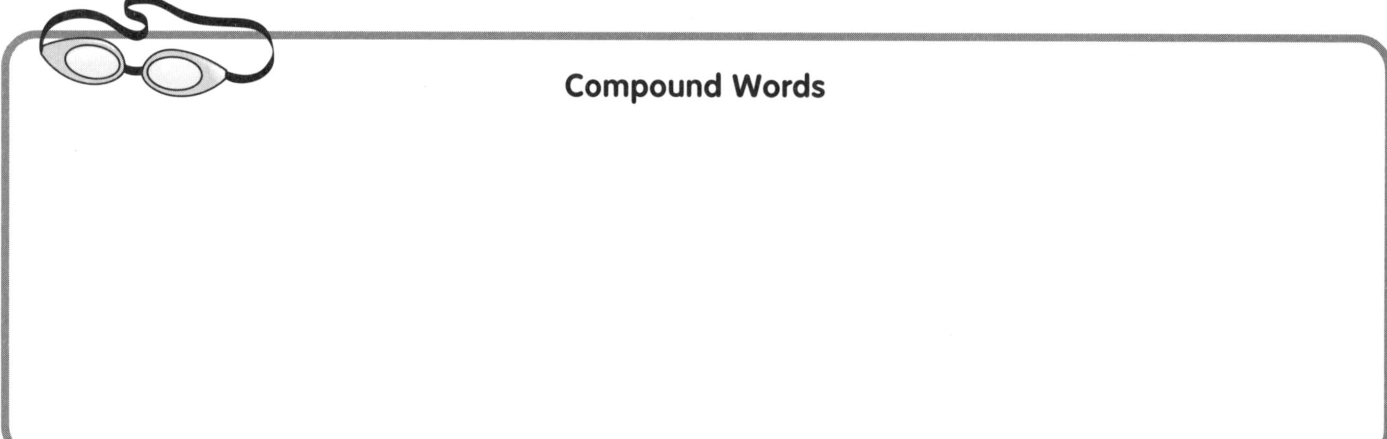

Compound Words

Spelling Games and Activities • EMC 8276 • © Evan-Moor Corporation

Name ______________________

Seasonal Fun

What's the hidden image? Read the word in each space.
Color each space following these rules:

- Use blue for **hyphenated compound words**.
- Use white for **compound words with two words**.
- Use red for **4-syllable words**.
- Use gray for **3-syllable words**.
- Use brown for **2-syllable words**.

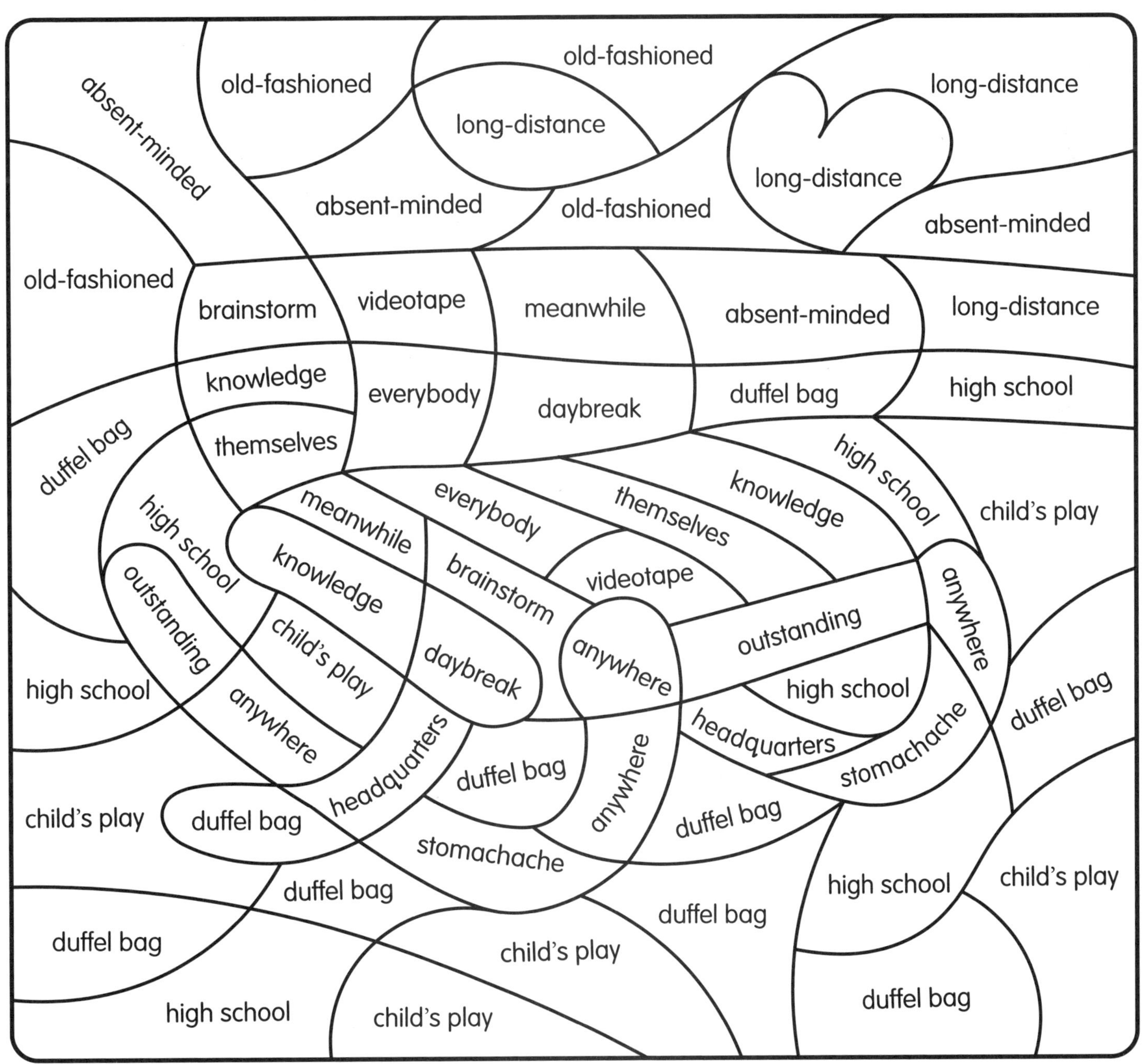

Name ___________________________

Violet Vowels

The words below are missing their vowels! Luckily, there are vowels growing on the violet petals. Finish the words using the vowels on the violets. Cross off each vowel after you use it.

1. w____rth____

2. tr____ ____t____r

3. c____rc____ ____t

4. c____rc____mv____nt

5. r____h____ ____rs____

6. c____ ____r____g____

7. ____n____rg____t____c

8. ____ ____ ____rthw____rm

Words of Encouragement

Hai and his classmates are offering each other words of encouragement.
Read each text message. Circle any misspelled words. Write them correctly below.

Hai

___________________________   ___________________________

____

Brooke

___________________________   ___________________________

___________________________   ___________________________

Maya

___________________________   ___________________________

____

Name _______________________

Bleacher Buddies

Rod is walking through the bleachers at the game to sit with his friends. Look at the words on the seats. Find the words with the **cher** sound. They will make a path for Rod to reach his friends.

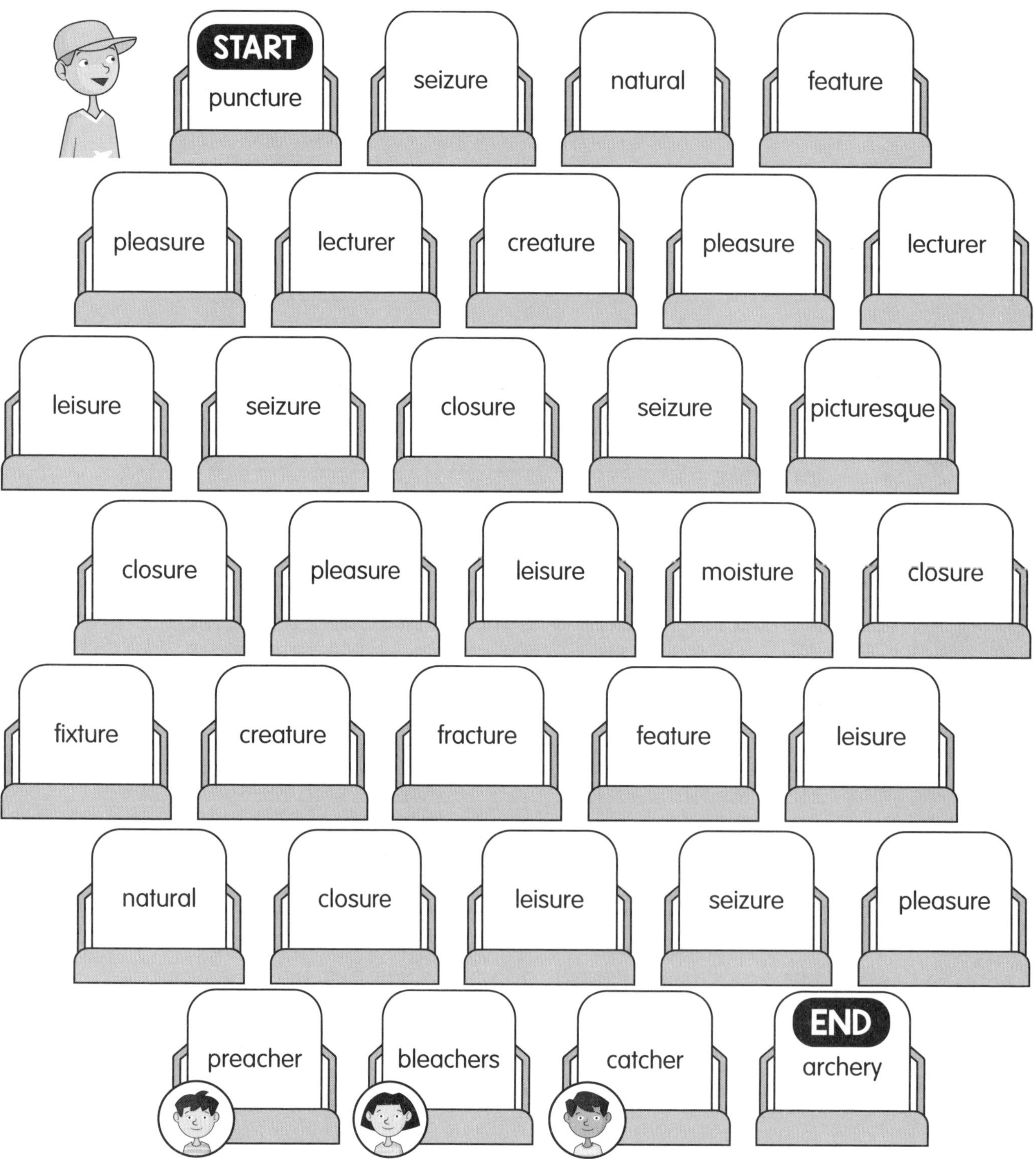

What do the words on Rod's friends' seats have in common?

Name _______________________

Use Your Clues

Look closely at the starting, ending, and vowel sounds of the clue words in the example. They describe a mystery word in the box. The mystery word will have the same sounds, but the spelling may be different from the clue words. Write the mystery word.

bleachers   closure   creature   natural

pitcher   preacher   puncture   seizure

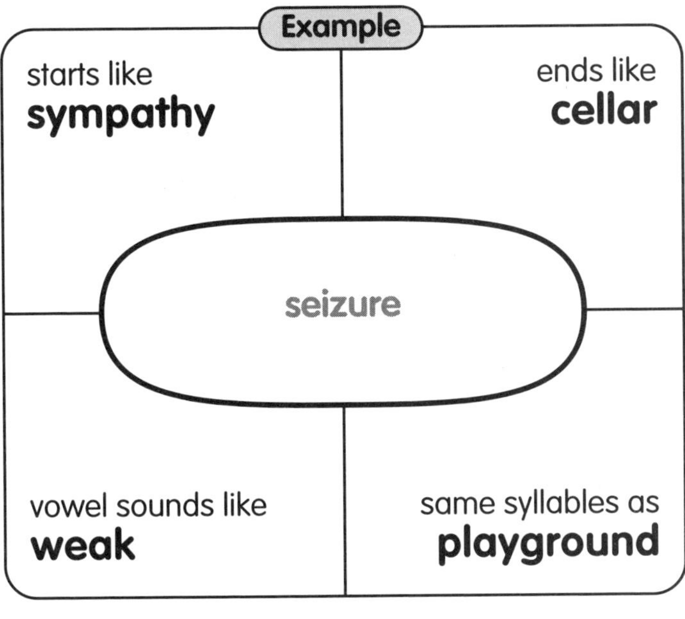

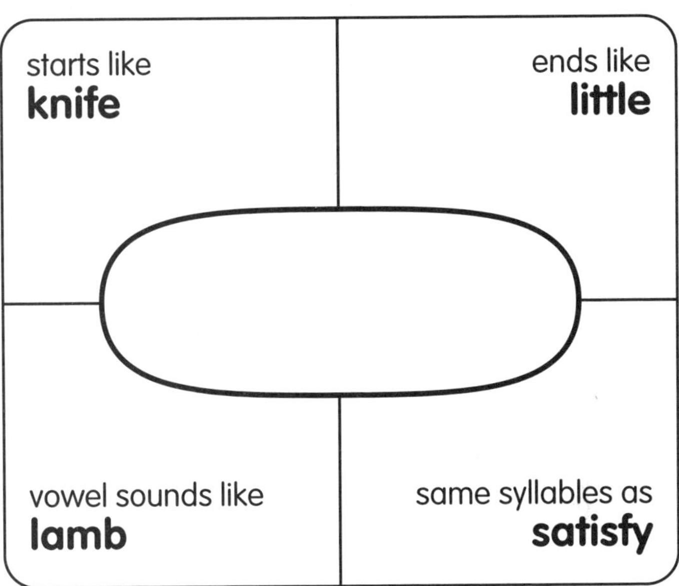

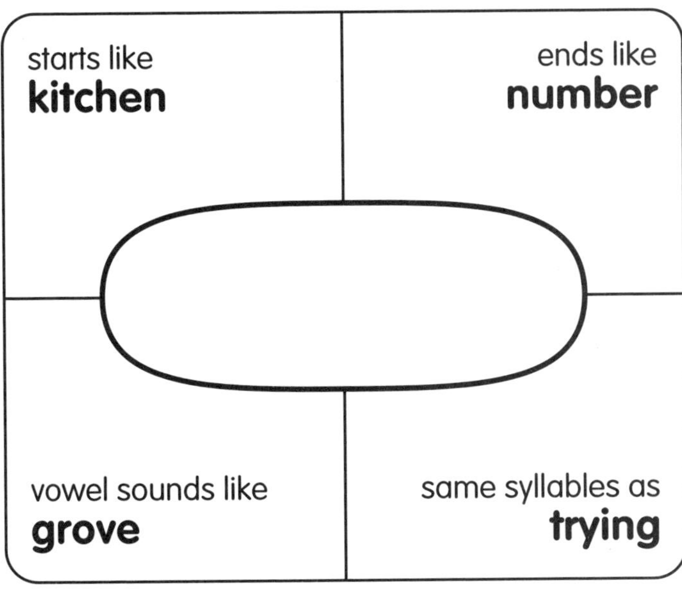

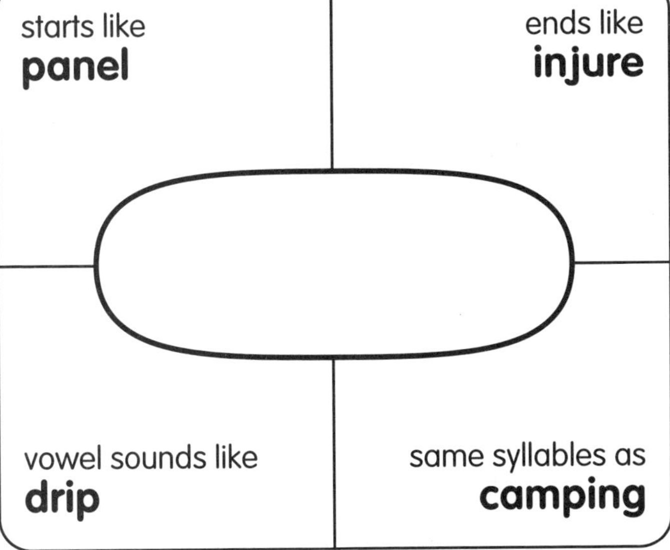

Name _______________________________

Baffling Riddle

One word in each group is spelled incorrectly. Find the word and spell it correctly
in the spaces below the group. Then write the numbered letters in the matching
spaces of the riddle to answer it.

> **What type of tree can you fit in your hand?**
>
> ___ ___ ___ ___ ___ ___ ___ ___ ___
> 1   2   3   4   5   6   7   8   9

1. enough, sinfony, chieftain

   ___ ___ ___ ___ ___ ___ ___ ___
       2

2. termoyl, flexible, loyalty

   ___ ___ ___ ___ ___ ___ ___
                           4

3. lyphoid, ointment, korderoi

   ___ ___ ___ ___ ___ ___ ___ ___
           7

4. boycott, pamflet, coughing

   ___ ___ ___ ___ ___ ___ ___ ___
       1   6

5. breffly, flexible, enough

   ___ ___ ___ ___ ___ ___ ___
           9

6. efishent, loyalty, physical

   ___ ___ ___ ___ ___ ___ ___ ___ ___
                       8

7. ointment, voyager, amfibean

   ___ ___ ___ ___ ___ ___ ___
       5   3

Spelling Games and Activities • EMC 8276 • © Evan-Moor Corporation

Name ___________________

Puzzling Anagrams

You can change the silly phrases below to spell the word in the box.
After you unscramble each phrase, write the spelling word on the line.

> | chieftain | corduroy | enough | loyalty |
> |-----------|----------|--------|---------|
> | ointment | physical | typhoid | voyager |

1. toy ally _______________________

2. mint note _______________________

3. very ago _______________________

4. do our cry _______________________

5. one hug _______________________

6. nice faith _______________________

7. tidy hop _______________________

8. hay clips _______________________

© Evan-Moor Corporation • EMC 8276 • Spelling Games and Activities

Silent Shakers

Every word below has a silent letter or two! Find the silent letter or letters in each word.
Then write the spelling word on the correct "shaker."

castle   chalkboard   condemn   doorknob   drought   gnarled

plumber   shipwreck   sighed   trestle   wholesome   wrestling

Name _______________________

Under the Microscope

Look at the letters in each spelling word. Use them to make other words. Write them on each microscope slide.

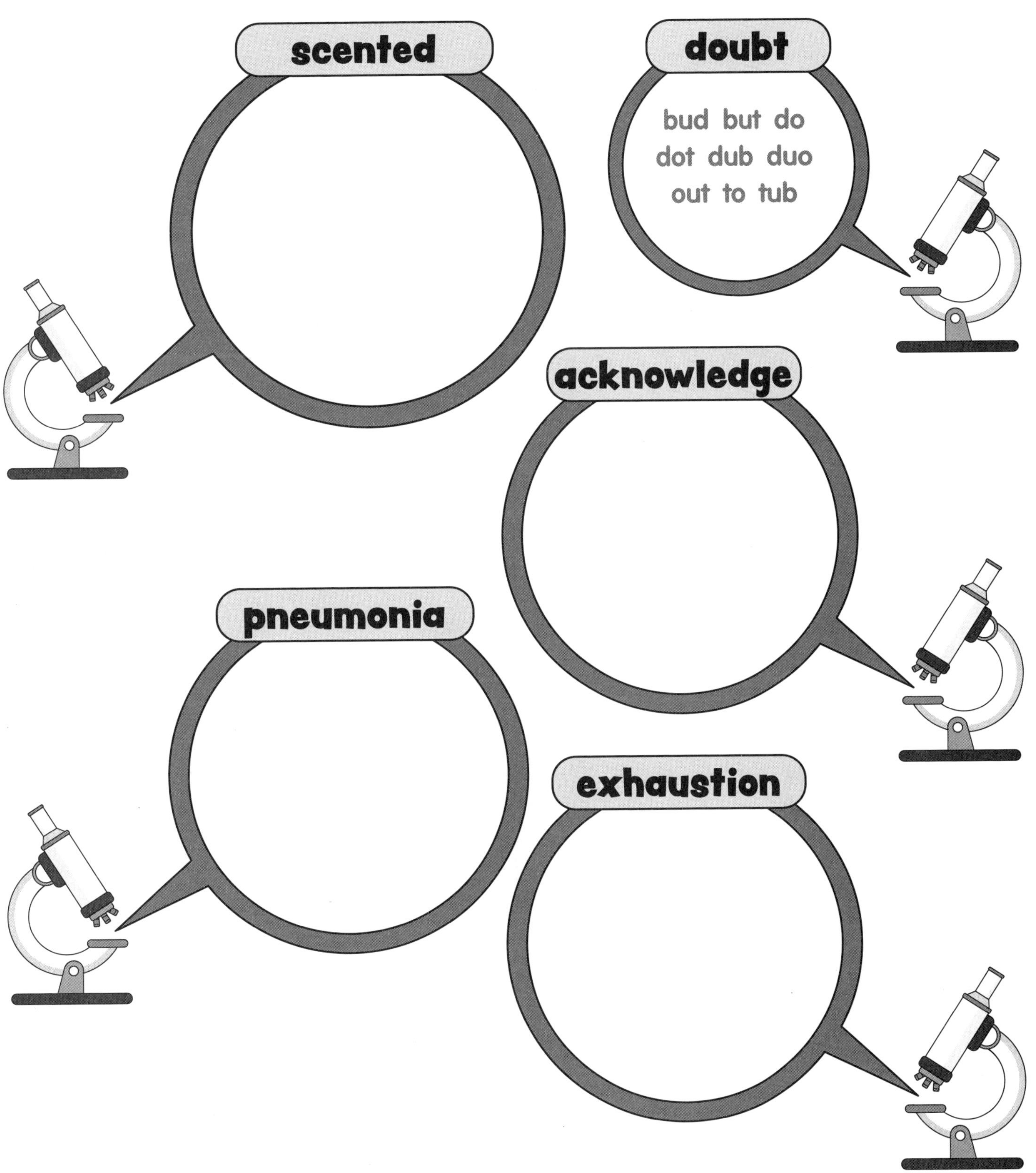

Spot the Schwa

Most words with more than one syllable have a **schwa** sound. Read each word in the box and decide which vowels are making each schwa sound. Circle the vowels. Then write each word in its Schwa Zone. If a word has more than one schwa, write the word in each zone. Use a different color for each zone.

absolutely	algebra	antenna	architect	argument
efficiency	opinion	orchestra	ordinary	participant

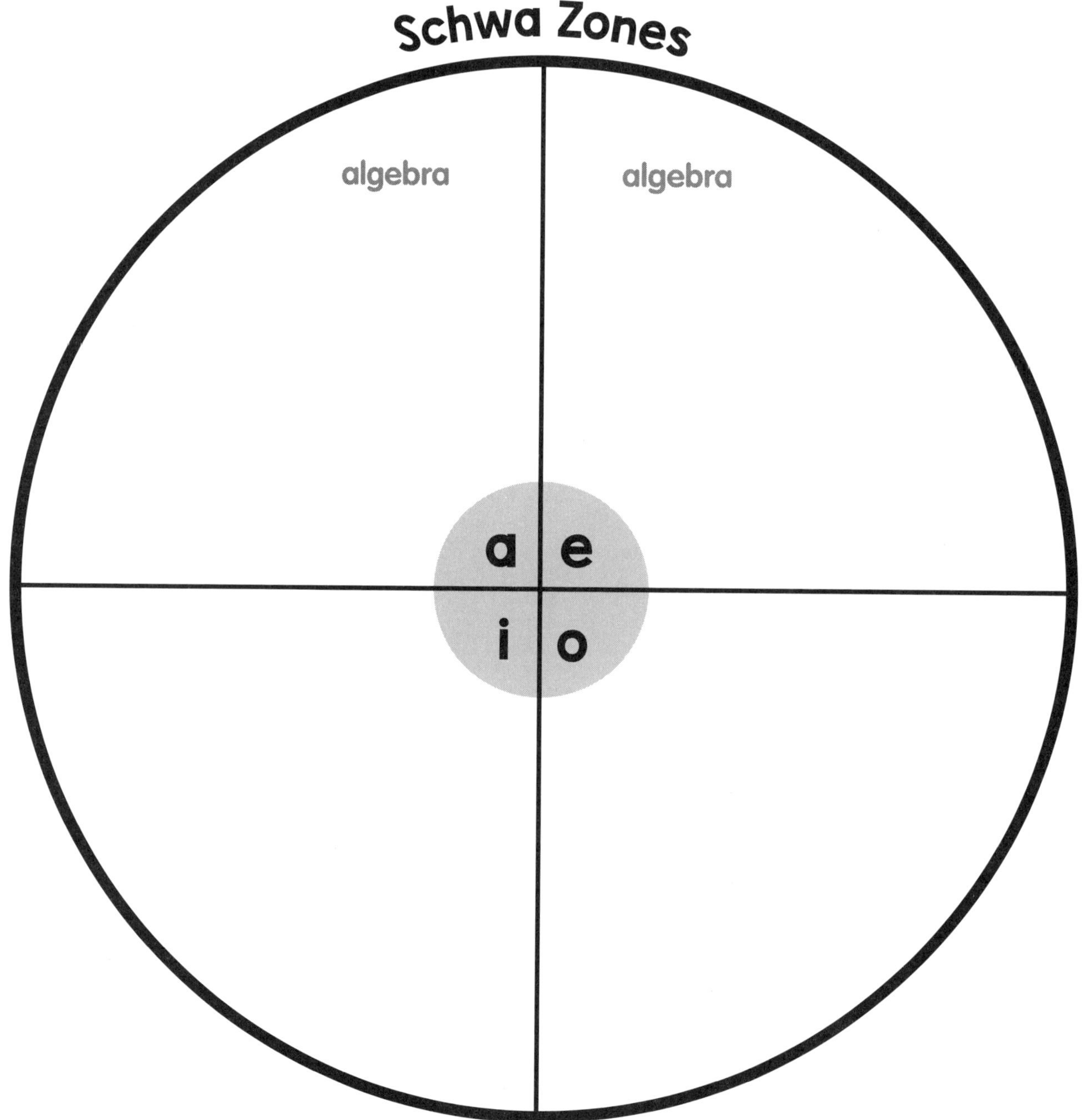

Name ___________________

Secret Tongue Twister

Find 11 words in the word search with a **schwa** sound or an **r-controlled** vowel sound. Words may go forward, backward, up, down, or diagonally.

Y	C	N	E	I	C	I	F	F	E	A	R
A	R	T	I	C	L	E	C	C	H	I	T
G	E	C	T	C	H	U	N	C	Y	K	C
N	N	R	E	E	G	A	T	R	O	H	S
A	A	I	T	E	R	D	A	C	C	E	O
T	R	M	N	A	P	N	L	A	O	N	I
I	C	G	E	R	I	A	T	L	L	I	E
O	D	P	U	D	A	A	R	U	O	Z	C
N	P	H	R	M	E	W	S	M	N	A	D
A	M	O	D	S	E	E	D	R	E	G	R
L	M	C	V	V	B	N	H	O	L	A	S
N	N	S	G	N	Z	C	T	F	F	M	D

appearance

argument

article

colonel

efficiency

formula

magazine

national

ordinary

shortage

warning

Now write the unused letters in the blank spaces below, starting on the top row. You will find a secret tongue twister!

___ ___ ___ ___ ___ ___ ___ ___ ___ ___ ___ ___ ___

___ ___ ___ ___ ___ ___   ___ ___ ___ ___ ___ ___

___ ___ ___ ___ ___ ___ ___ ___ ___ ___ ___

___ ___ ___ ___ ___ ___ ___ .

Red Light, Green Light

Some of the sentences below are using incorrect homophones. Read each sentence. If the sentence is correct, **color the traffic light green**. If you find an incorrect homophone, **color the traffic light red**. Then write the correct homophone in the last column.

1. Read the sentence.	2. Is there an **incorrect homophone** in this sentence?	3. Write the correct homophone.
I had sudden **insight** into solving my problem while taking a walk.		
Prairie dogs like to **borough** underground.		
Glenn wears a leg brace for **assistants** while walking.		
Hurry up! **They're** already at the hockey rink.		
The **censor** on the back of the car helps Dad parallel park.		
We have an emergency kit and are **already** for bad weather.		
She is wearing a sparkly **broach** on her jacket.		
The carriage driver took the **reins** and clip-clopped away.		
The singers in the school's **corral** are selling tickets to their show.		

Spelling Games and Activities • EMC 8276 • © Evan-Moor Corporation

Red Light, Green Light, *continued*

1. Read the sentence.	**2.** Is there an **incorrect homophone** in this sentence?	**3.** Write the correct homophone.
In the fall, the trees start to lose **their** leaves.		
The city of London is made of 32 **burrows**.		
The local farm keeps livestock in a large **chorale**.		
His doctor started to **brooch** a difficult topic.		
I've **already** eaten today, but thanks for asking!		
Ms. Detlef's **assistance** help her set up the lab experiments.		
Her **rein** as the top skateboard champion has come to an end.		
The **sensor** asked to cut a scene out of a movie.		
Huy didn't want to **incite** an argument, so he changed the subject.		

Name ______________________

Suffix Socks

Look at the beginning of each word. Write the complete word in the correct suffix sock.

ac _____ applica _____ colli _____ estima _____ musi _____

predic _____ separa _____ starva _____ succes _____ viola _____

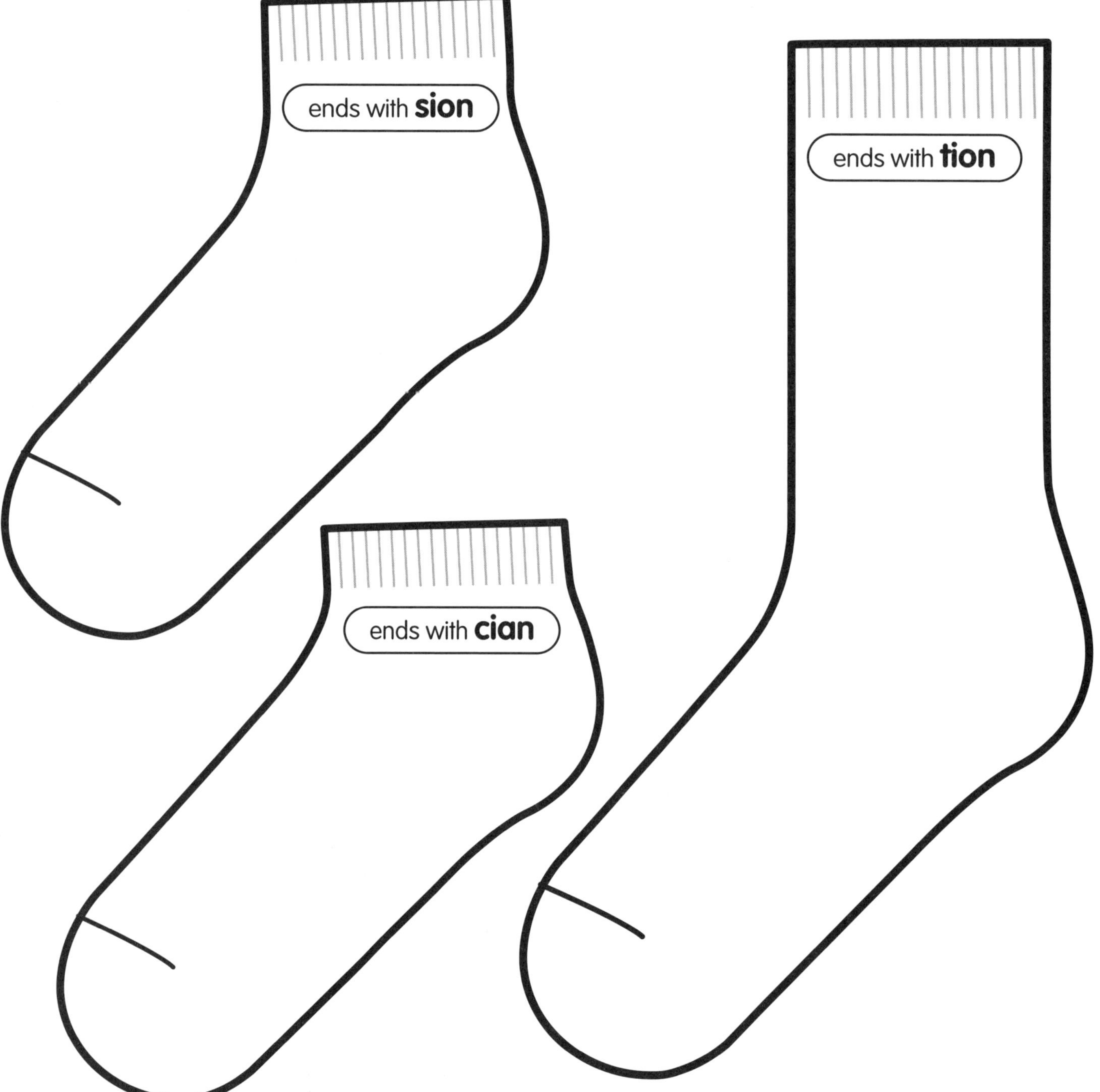

Spelling Games and Activities • EMC 8276 • © Evan-Moor Corporation

Name ______________________

A Form of Flattery

Lola and Anna are texting each other. Circle any misspelled words.
Write them correctly below.

______________________ ______________________ ______________________

______________________ ______________________ ______________________

______________________ ______________________ ______________________

Spelling Seesaw

Read each sentence. Look at the two words on the seesaw. Circle and write the correct
one to complete the sentence.

My jeans are a little _______________
at the waist.

She did a _______________ job raking
the leaves.

The white walls have the _______________
of making the room look bigger.

I don't have the _______________ to
wait in this long line.

Our school _______________ treats the
students and staff fairly.

I love riding my _______________ bike
to stay active.

Spelling Games and Activities • EMC 8276 • © Evan-Moor Corporation

Dear Diary

Ariana is writing in her diary. Read her entry. Some letters are missing. Finish the words using the letters in the box. Cross off each letter after you use it.

| a | a | e | e | e | e | e | e | i | i | l | l |
| l | l | l | n | o | o | r | r | s | s | u | z |

Dear Diary,

The summer holidays are fin ____ ____ ____ y here, and I'm so excited to see my dad. I like living with my mom in Seattle, but in the summer, it's so special to go traveling with my dad!

We might travel by train down the West Coast. He says we might stay at a youth host ____ ____ one night and at a nice hotel another night. We'll collect shells at the beach one day and see fi ____ ____ ____ y painted masterpieces at a museum the next day. He says we must try new things and "s ____ ____ ____ e the day"! That's his favorite saying.

My parents are always there for me. When they divorced, they told me I would never l ____ ____ e them. They said, "We will never c ____ ____ ____ e to be in your life." I've seen how true that is th ____ ____ ____ gh the years. They don't have a host ____ ____ ____ relationship at all. That makes everything easier.

I'm going to take some station ____ ____ y with me and write letters to my mom. I'll miss her, but I'll be back in Seattle soon.

© Evan-Moor Corporation • EMC 8276 • Spelling Games and Activities

Words of Encouragement

Medhi and his classmates are offering each other words of encouragement. Read each speech bubble. The underlined words are scrambled. Write them correctly below.

brilliant	confident	equivalent	immigrant	magnificent
persistent	reluctant	significant	valiant	

_______________   _______________   _______________

_______________   _______________   _______________

_______________   _______________   _______________

Name _______________

Rave Reviews

People often leave reviews for services they use. Read each review.
Circle any misspelled words. Write them correctly below.

Amar ★★★★★ 2 months ago

I can't say enough about Giuliana's Gym! There was an insidant
in which a guy dropped a weight on his foot. A first-aid atendent
came immediately and helped with the acsidant.

_______________   _______________   _______________

Morgan ★★★★★ 3 weeks ago

We were so lucky to attend the puppy class at Debjani's Dog
Training! I was completely iggnorent on how to train my new
Husky puppy. Debjani showed us how to get our puppy
to be obeadiant. It was hard, but we were vijalent.

_______________   _______________   _______________

Xiuying ★★★★★ 5 days ago

I love Mickey's Parlor hair salon! Mickey always takes her time
when coloring my hair. I walk out with a radyent hairstyle every
time. She'll even do flooresent colors! I'm konfedent you'll love
your hair!

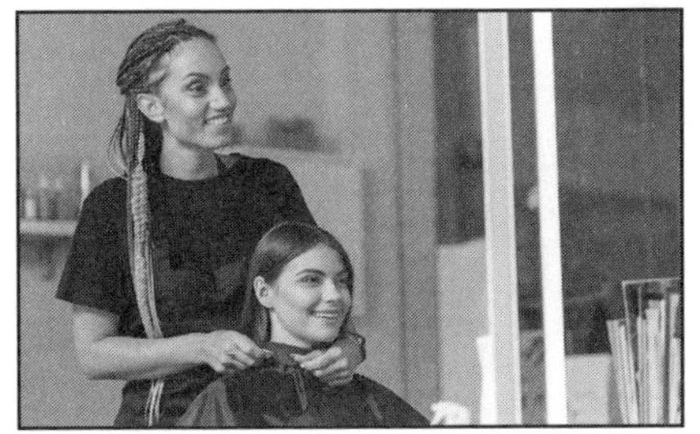

_______________   _______________   _______________

Laces and Letters

The **sh** sound fell out of the words below! Luckily, there are **sh** sounds on the shoe rack. Finish the words using the letter pairs on the shoes. Cross off each letter pair after you use it.

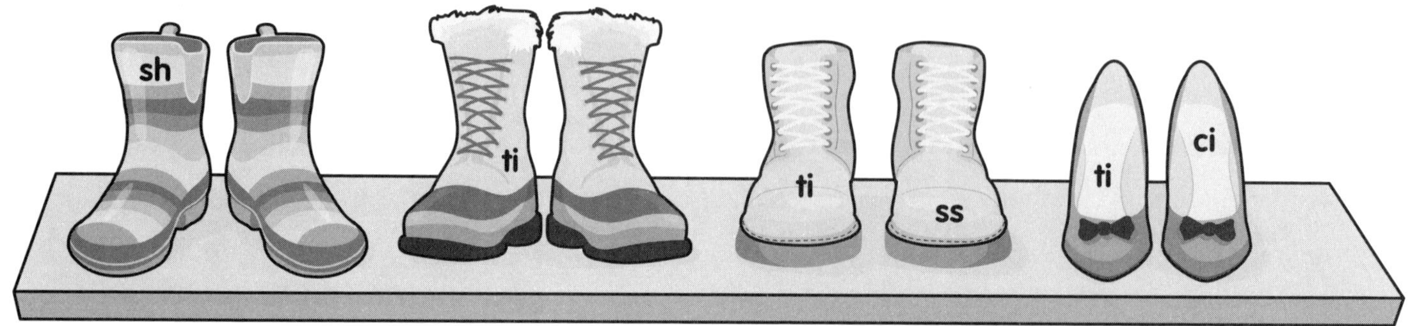

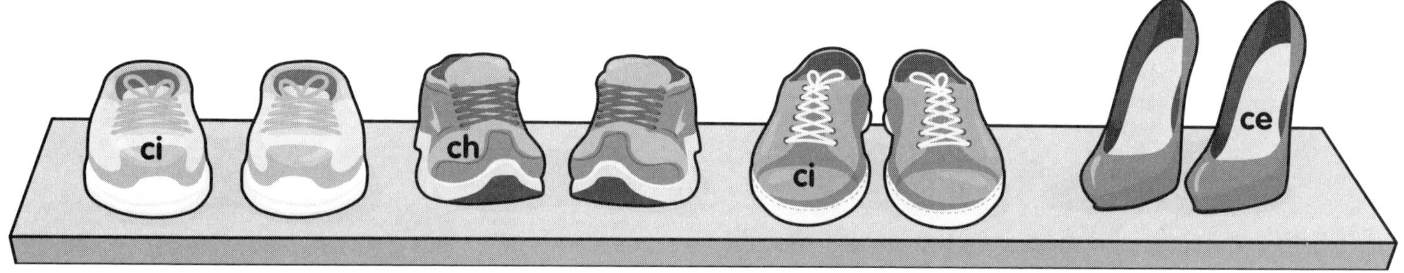

1. conversa______on

2. offi______al

3. permi______ion

4. impa______ent

5. physi______an

6. o______an

7. ambi______ous

8. bro______ure

9. establi______

10. magi______an

Guess the Word

Read the clue. Write the spelling word to solve the riddle.

| ashes | delicious | dictionary | friendship |
| glacier | inertia | sufficient | surely |

 I'm the bond between a pair where there's a lot of care. _______________________

 Yes indeed, I am all that you need. _______________________

 I'm the form of wood where a campfire once stood. _______________________

 I'm food that tastes great on your dinner plate. _______________________

 I'm a river of ice on a list of travel sights. _______________________

 Take a look in this definition book. _______________________

 I rhyme with **securely** and **obscurely**. _______________________

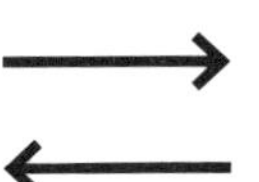 With no effort to improve,
I'll make nothing move. _______________________

Name ______________________

Mail Matchup

Which pieces of mail belong together? Match the correct "mail" syllables to make words from the box. Write the complete words on the lines.

| audible | credible | curious |
| durable | infectious | numerous |

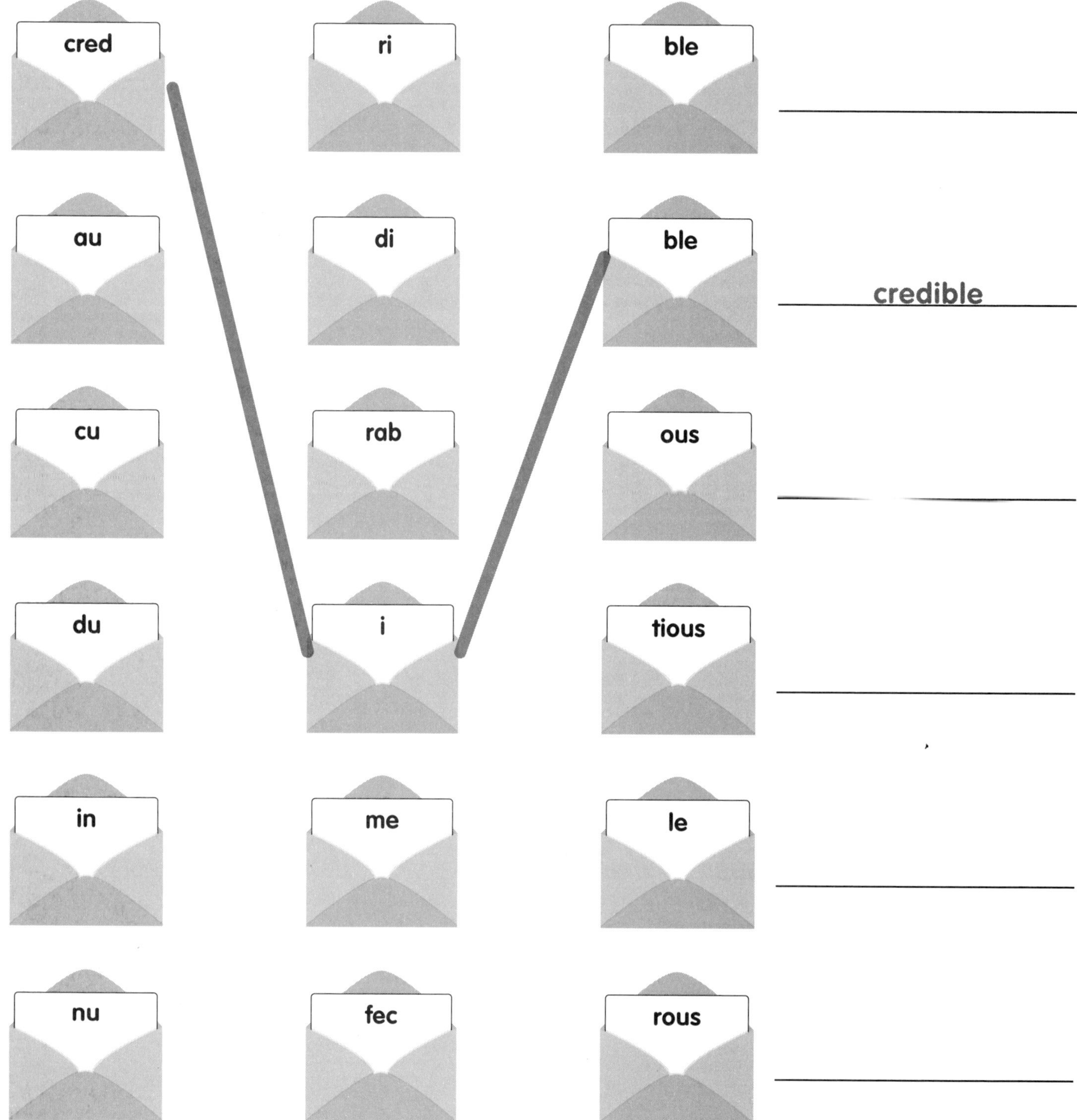

Spelling Games and Activities • EMC 8276 • © Evan-Moor Corporation

Riddle Me Right

Unscramble each word. Then write the numbered letters in the matching spaces
of the riddle to answer it.

You go at red but come to a stop at green. What am I?

___ W ___ ___ ___ ___ ___ ___ ___ ___
1   2   3   4   5   6   7   8   9   10

1. nliebilde   ___ ___ ___ ___ ___ ___ ___ ___ ___
                   10

2. eablopicmt   ___ ___ ___ ___ ___ ___ ___ ___ ___ ___
                    6

3. aapletccbe   ___ ___ ___ ___ ___ ___ ___ ___ ___ ___
                                 3

4. lleovab   ___ ___ ___ ___ ___ ___
             9

5. souecrpi   ___ ___ ___ ___ ___ ___ ___ ___
               7

6. eislensb   ___ ___ ___ ___ ___ ___ ___ ___
                          8

7. lfeptraoib   ___ ___ ___ ___ ___ ___ ___ ___ ___ ___
                      1

8. eacahglnbe   ___ ___ ___ ___ ___ ___ ___ ___ ___ ___
                    4

9. rbtcdileeap   ___ ___ ___ ___ ___ ___ ___ ___ ___ ___ ___
              5

10. uaosuitc   ___ ___ ___ ___ ___ ___ ___ ___
               2

Word Box:
- acceptable
- cautious
- changeable
- compatible
- indelible
- lovable
- precious
- predictable
- profitable
- sensible

© Evan-Moor Corporation • EMC 8276 • Spelling Games and Activities

Single Slice or Whole Pizza?

Some sentences need a singular noun. Other sentences need a plural noun. Look at the chart of spelling words. Write a word to finish each sentence. Then circle the correct amount of pizza to show what kind of noun each sentence needs.

belief   boundary   instrument   journey   mosquito   schedule   tomato   variety

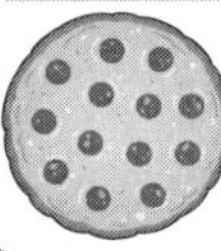

beliefs   boundaries   instruments   journeys   mosquitoes   schedules   tomatoes   varieties

Let's look at the school ___________________ to plan the rehearsals.

My deepest ___________________ is in treating people with kindness.

There are distinct ___________________ between countries.

My mom picked a fresh ___________________ from her garden.

There are many ___________________ of jam at the farmers' market.

Jaime plays several musical ___________________ .

We ran from the lake when we saw the swarm of ___________________ .

The ___________________ to our grandparents' home takes two days by car.

Name ___________________________

Vegetable Letters

The plural words below are missing their ending letters! Luckily, there are letters growing on vegetables nearby. Finish the words using the letters on the vegetables. Cross off each letter after you use it.

1. thie__________ __________ __________

2. ech__________ __________ __________

3. grievan__________ __________ __________

4. sergean__________ __________

5. passer__________

6. substan__________ __________ __________

7. hal__________ __________ __________

8. orchestr__________ __________

9. pharmac__________ __________

10. encycloped__________ __________ __________

Puzzling Anagrams

You can change the silly phrases below to spell the words in the box.
After you unscramble each phrase, write the spelling word on the line.

> careful   colorless   effortless   experiment   grateful
>
> painless   powerless   thoughtful   tireless

1. sir steel ______________________

2. next empire ______________________

3. sleep rows ______________________

4. pin sales ______________________

5. cells or so ______________________

6. hot gulf hut ______________________

7. flu race ______________________

8. frost feels ______________________

9. glue raft ______________________

   Spelling Games and Activities • EMC 8276 • © Evan-Moor Corporation

Swimming Lanes

These words want to go swimming. But they need to swim in the correct lane. Use a suffix with each word to make a new word. Write the new word in the lane that matches the suffix.

amaze   cheer   develop   doubt

effort   enjoy   govern   humor

judge   success   tire

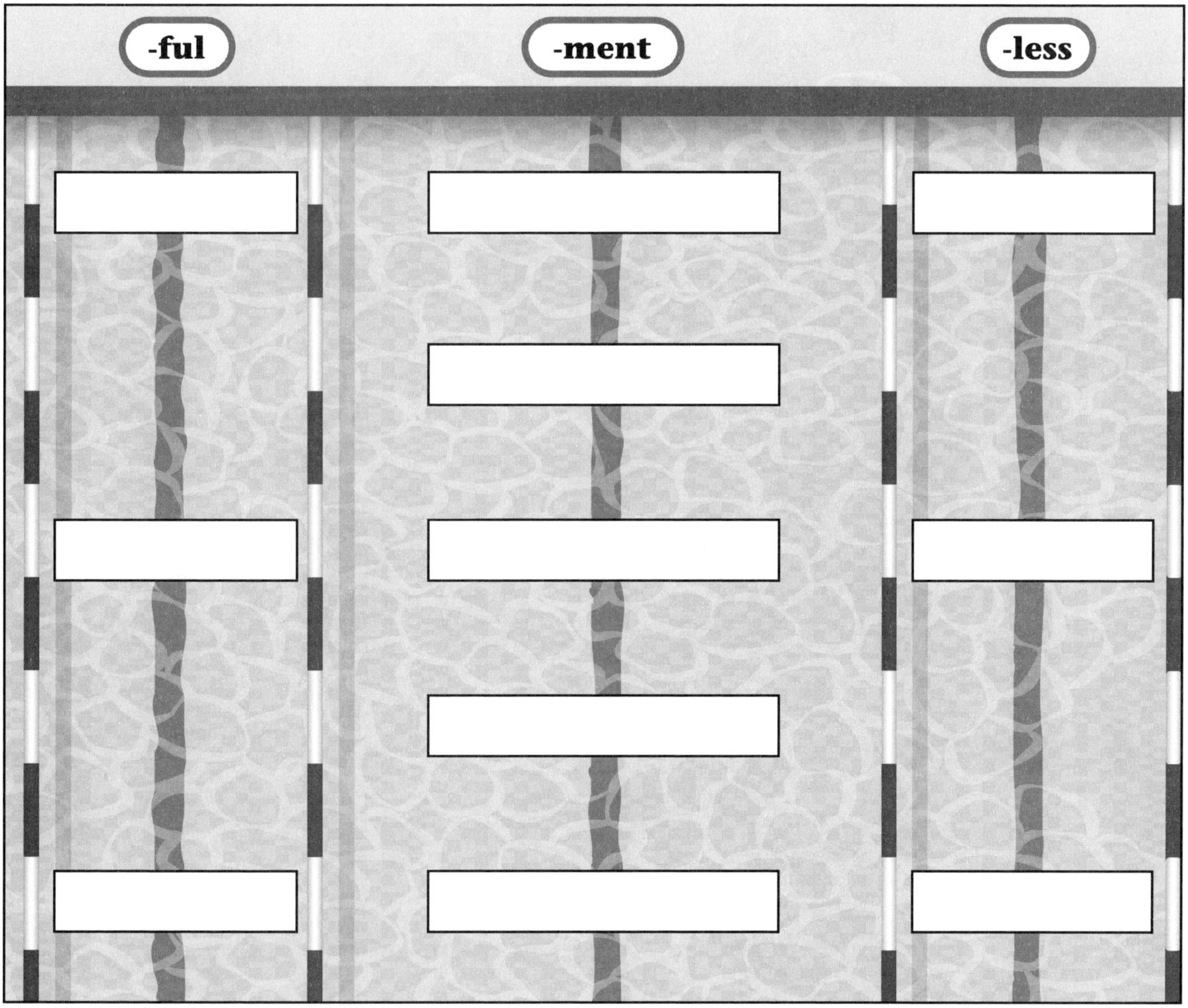

-ful	**-ment**	**-less**

Name _______________________________

Prefix Pies

Look at the base words. Each word can take one of these prefixes: **un-**, **im-**, **in-**, or **under-**. Add the correct prefix to each word and write it in the matching prefix pie.

Base Words

ability	age	animate	cautious	certain	convenient
cover	dependent	estimate	likely	mature	mobile
mortal	perfect	reliable	sure		

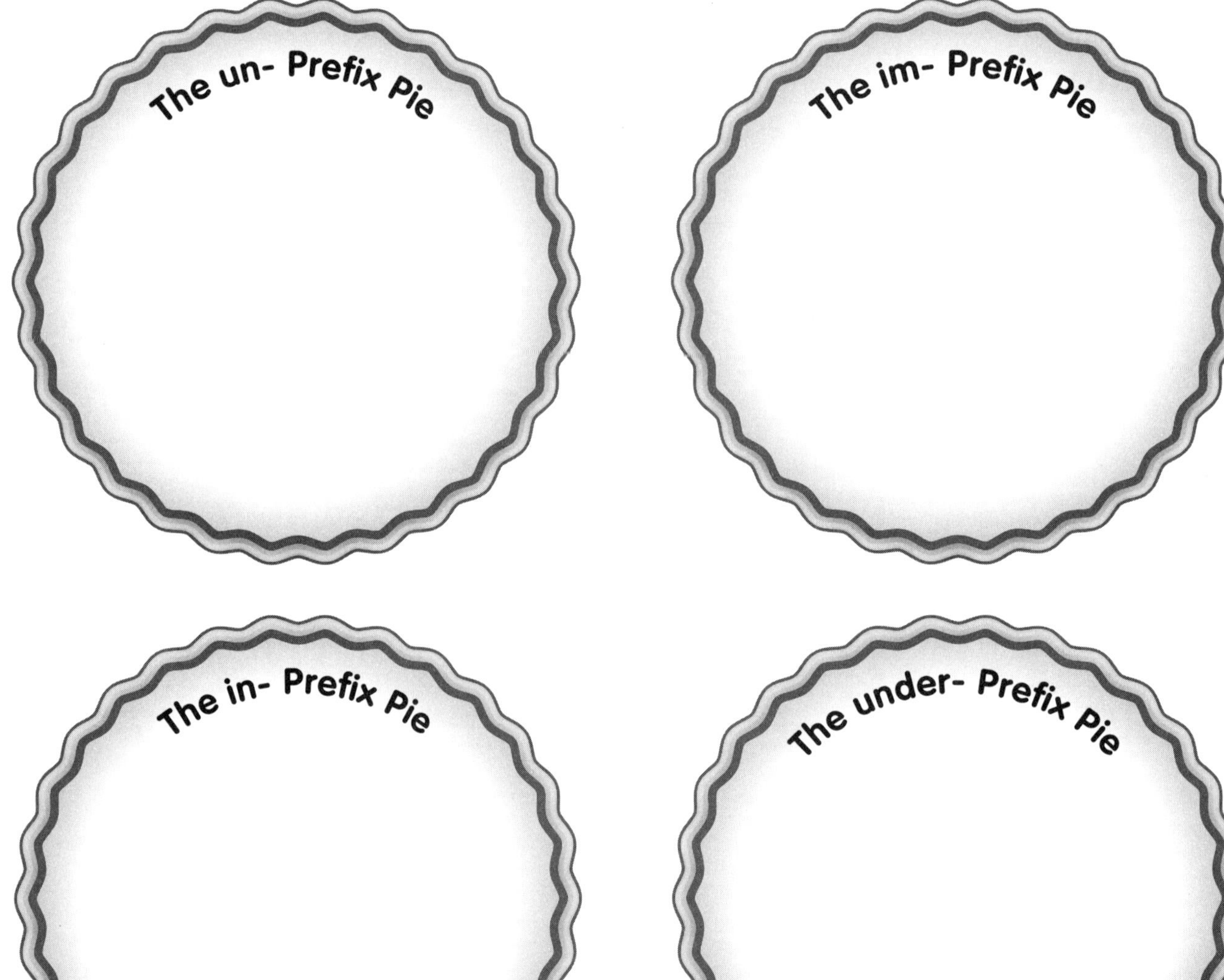

Name ______________________

Use Your Clues

Look closely at the starting, ending, and vowel sounds of the clue words in the example. They describe a mystery word in the box. The mystery word will have the same sounds, but the spelling may be different from the clue words.

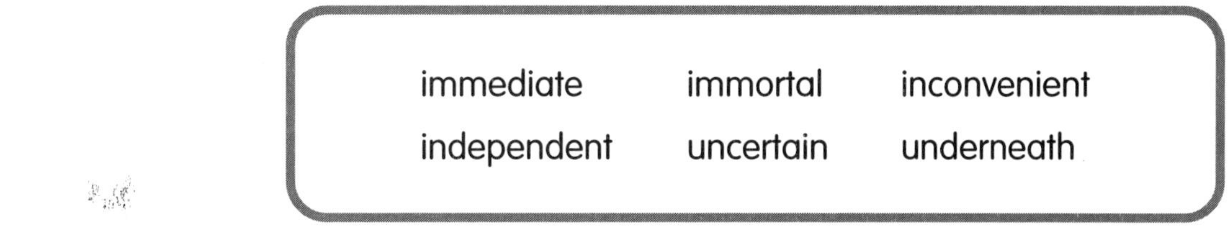

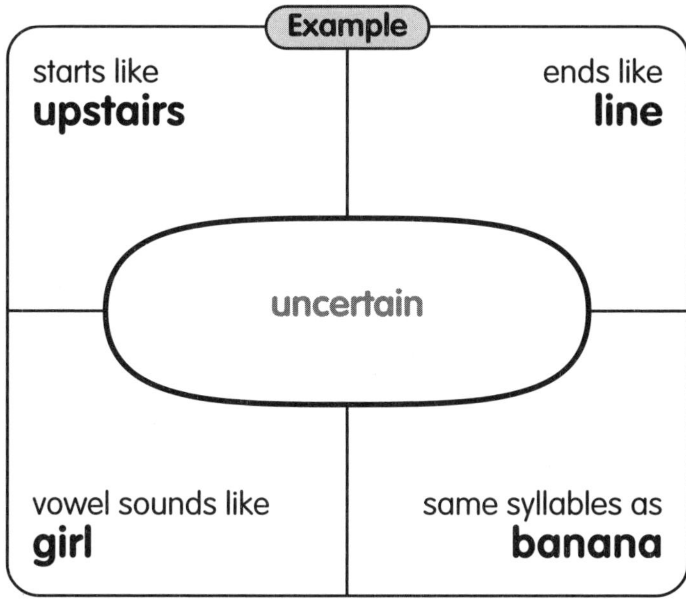

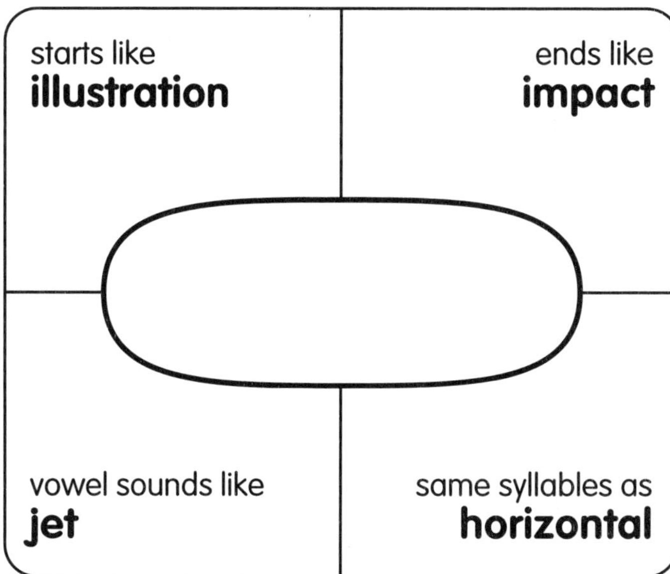

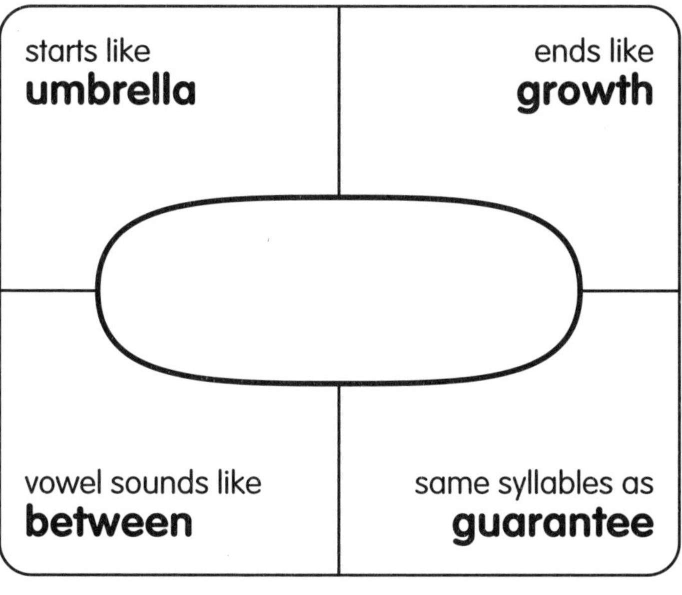

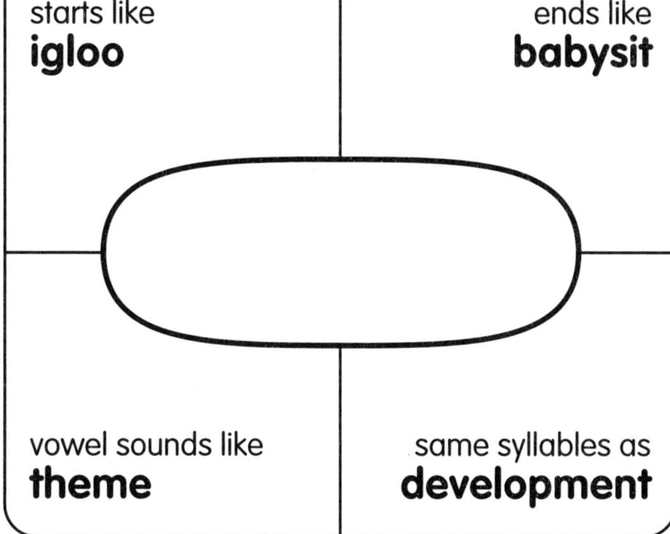

Name ___________________________

Wetland Walk

Buana is carefully making her way through a wetland to a lookout. Wetlands are areas of land that are very wet, such as swamps or marshes, in which plants, birds, fish, and other animals live. Buana will go through words that have **geo** (earth) or **bio** (life). Draw a line to show Buana's path to the lookout.

START	biosphere	geology	enact	transact
graphite	export	biopsy	transport	portable
autograph	react	geologist	import	photograph
biology	biography	geography	transport	react
geology	photograph	enact	actor	export
geography	biology	biography	autograph	import
portable	graphite	geologist	biosphere	END

Spelling Games and Activities • EMC 8276 • © Evan-Moor Corporation

Name _______________________________

Secret Tongue Twister

Find 11 words in the word search that have base words **act**, **bio**, **port**, or **graph**. Words may go forward, backward, up, down, or diagonally.

G	I	R	E	P	O	R	T	A	B	L	E
H	M	A	E	R	A	T	T	G	E	O	L
O	P	G	C	I	E	C	S	T	T	G	L
E	O	A	N	T	A	H	R	D	A	A	G
A	R	T	R	S	O	A	P	H	U	E	R
E	T	D	N	G	N	R	G	S	T	L	I
T	T	A	E	S	O	E	X	P	O	R	T
G	R	A	P	H	I	T	E	R	G	I	Y
T	G	O	E	M	S	C	O	T	R	H	B
B	R	J	M	Y	M	A	Y	H	A	H	U
T	T	U	H	H	R	N	M	E	P	V	I
R	O	V	K	O	I	E	J	S	H	Q	U

actor

autograph

biosphere

enact

export

graphite

import

photograph

portable

transact

transport

Now write the unused letters in the blank spaces below, starting in the top left corner. You will find a secret tongue twister!

__ __ __ __ __ __ __   __ __ __ __ __ __ __ __ __ __

__ __ __ __ __ __   __ __ __ __ __ __ __ __

__ __ __ __ __ __ __   __ __ __ __ __ __

© Evan-Moor Corporation • EMC 8276 • Spelling Games and Activities

Disappearing Dialogue

The speech bubbles are missing some letters!
Finish the synonyms for **said** using the letters
in the box. Cross off each letter after you use it.

a	a	a	e	h	i
i	i	i	i	i	i
i	l	m	n	o	o
q	r	r	s	s	s
s	t	u	u	u	w

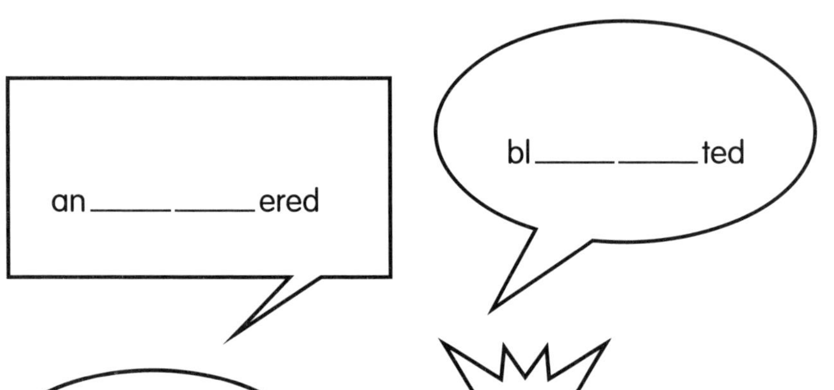

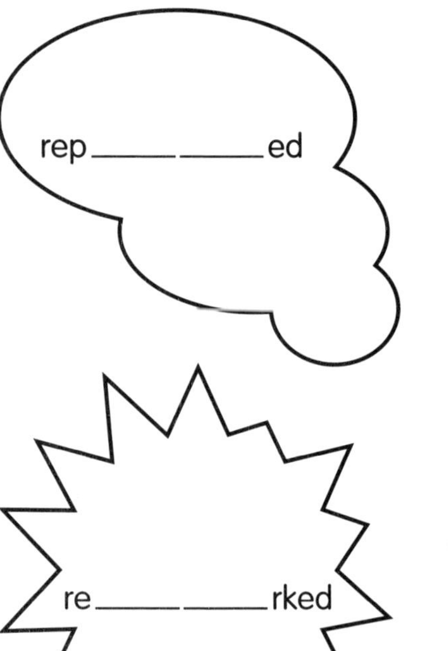

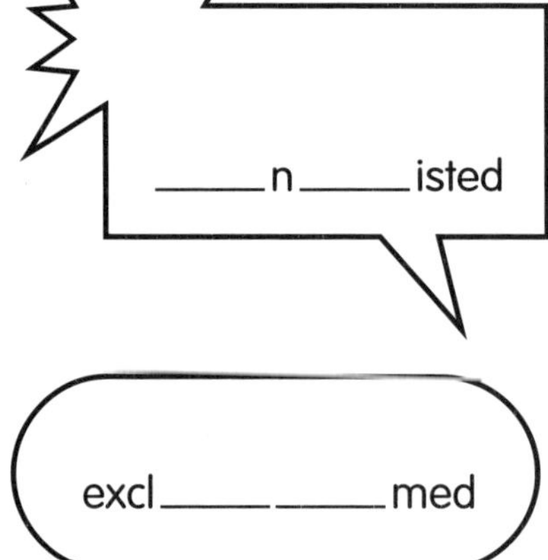

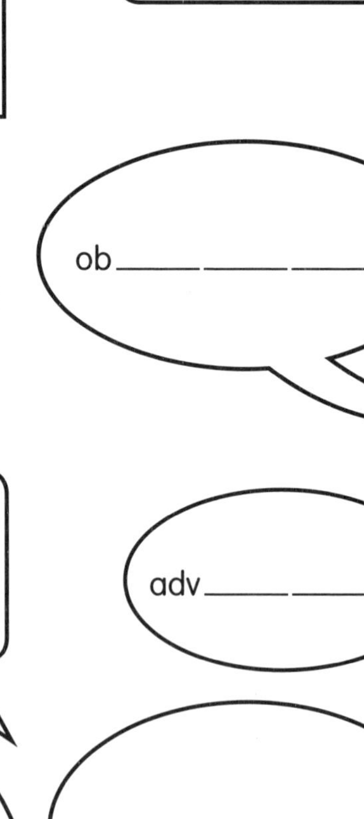

re_____rked

c_____ncl_____ded

adv_____ed

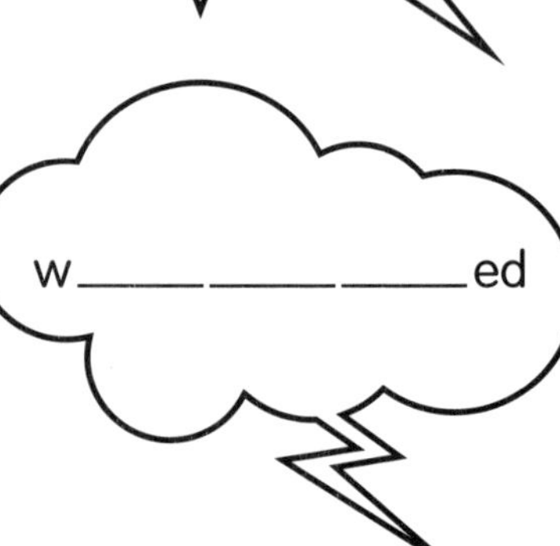

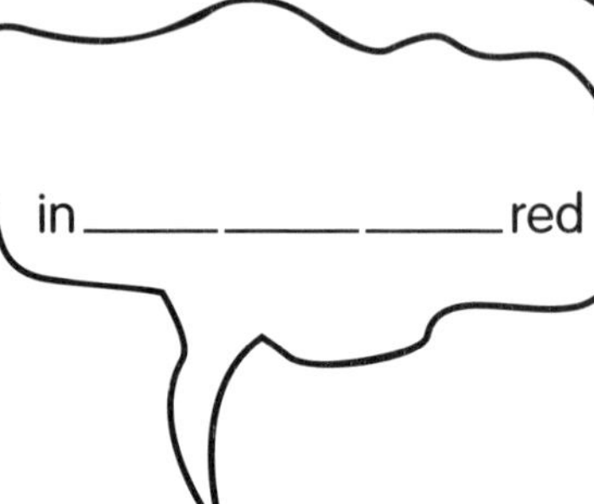

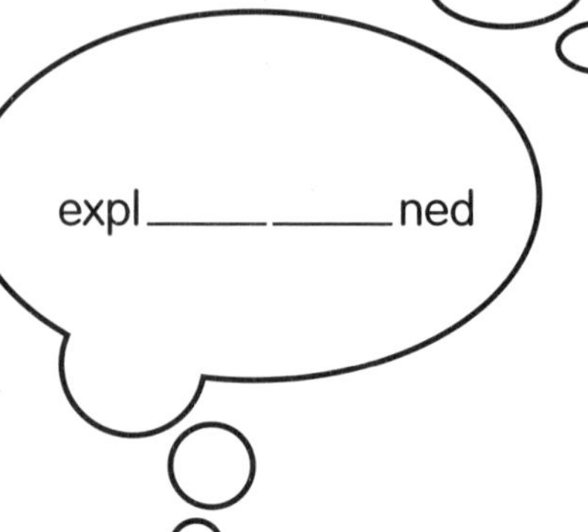

Spelling Games and Activities • EMC 8276 • © Evan-Moor Corporation

What's for Lunch?

Circle the word in each row that is spelled correctly.

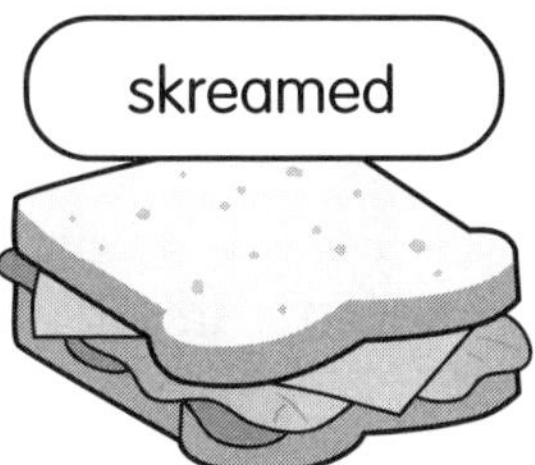

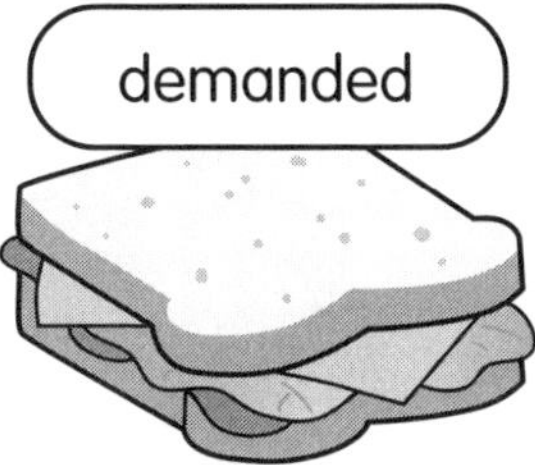

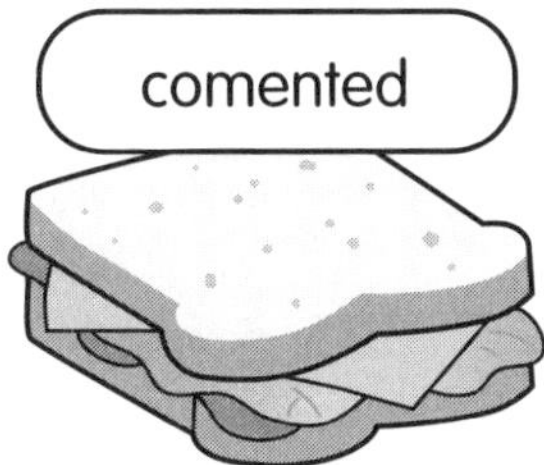

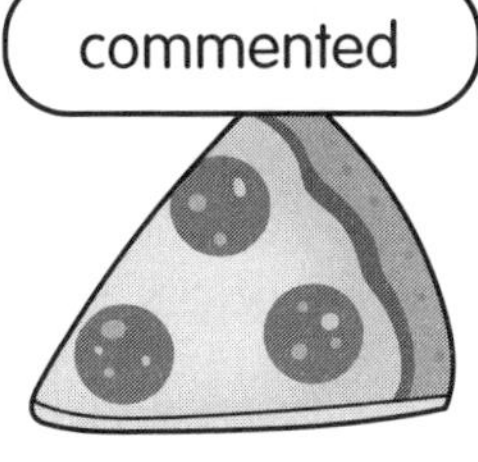

Which lunch item had the most correct spellings? ___________________________

Riddle Me Right

Unscramble each word. Then write the numbered letters in the matching spaces of the riddle to answer it.

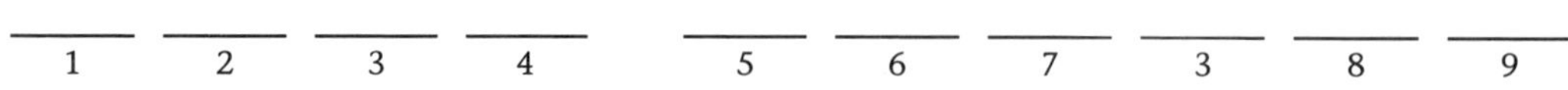

1. safnte   ___ ___ ___ ___ ___ ___
            5

2. gnehltne   ___ ___ ___ ___ ___ ___ ___
              9

3. ctauyrn   ___ ___ ___ ___ ___ ___
             6

4. ylepcfter   ___ ___ ___ ___ ___ ___ ___ ___ ___
               7

5. esmibhmepr   ___ ___ ___ ___ ___ ___ ___ ___ ___ ___
                8

6. ocynuayb   ___ ___ ___ ___ ___ ___ ___ ___
              3

7. yemaitloprr   ___ ___ ___ ___ ___ ___ ___ ___ ___ ___ ___
                 2

8. iprrpenatsh   ___ ___ ___ ___ ___ ___ ___ ___ ___ ___ ___
                 4

9. nrpyenlmaet   ___ ___ ___ ___ ___ ___ ___ ___ ___ ___ ___
                                                         1

Word Box:
- buoyancy
- fasten
- lengthen
- membership
- partnership
- perfectly
- permanently
- temporarily
- truancy

Red Light, Green Light

Some of the sentences below have words that are misspelled. Read each sentence. If the sentence is correct, **color the traffic light green**. If you find a misspelling, **color the traffic light red**. Then write the word correctly in the last column.

1. Read the sentence.	**2.** Is there a **misspelled word** in this sentence?	**3.** Write the word correctly.
The movie might **friten** me!	● ○ ○	frighten
The volleyball team is going to win its fifth straight **champeonship**.	○ ○ ○	
"You look wonderful tonight," he said **sinceerly**.	○ ○ ○	
She has complete **ownership** of the company.	○ ○ ○	
They have **citisenship** in both the U.S. and Germany.	○ ○ ○	
There is a **vacantsy** at the local bed-and-breakfast.	○ ○ ○	
Dad said we should come home **imedietly**.	○ ○ ○	
Sharing experiences together helps **strenkthin** a friendship.	○ ○ ○	
I like playing soccer, **especially** when I play with friends.	○ ○ ○	

Name _______________________

Under the Microscope

Look at the letters in each spelling word. Use them to make other words.
Write them on each microscope slide.

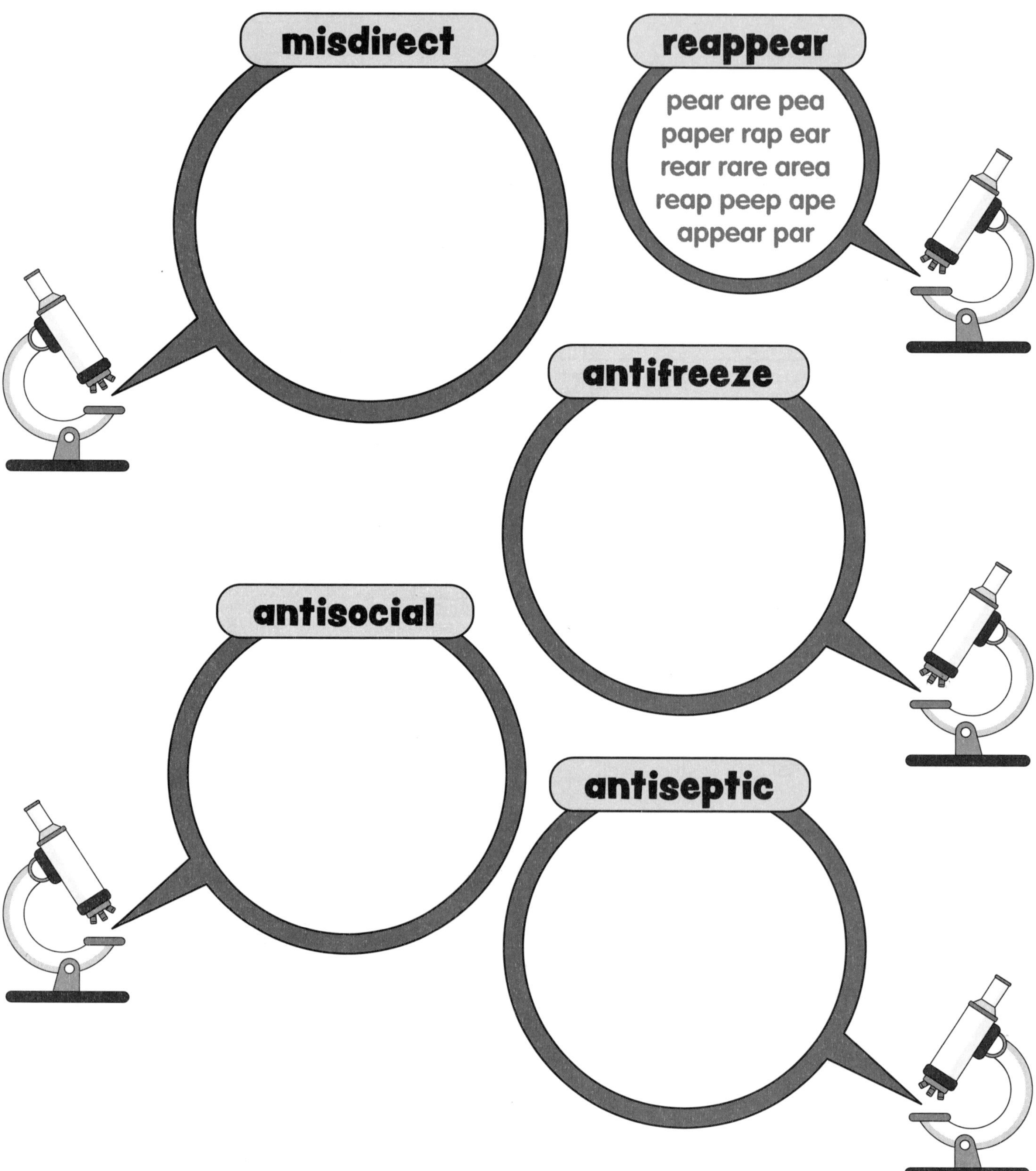

Spelling Games and Activities • EMC 8276 • © Evan-Moor Corporation

Prefix Pancakes

Look at the base words. Each word can take one of these prefixes: **re-**, **dis-**, **mis-**, or **non-**.
Add the correct prefix to each word and write it in the matching prefix pancake stack.

Base Words

agree	behave	cede	conformist	courage	existent	fiction
fortune	grace	honest	sense	spell	write	

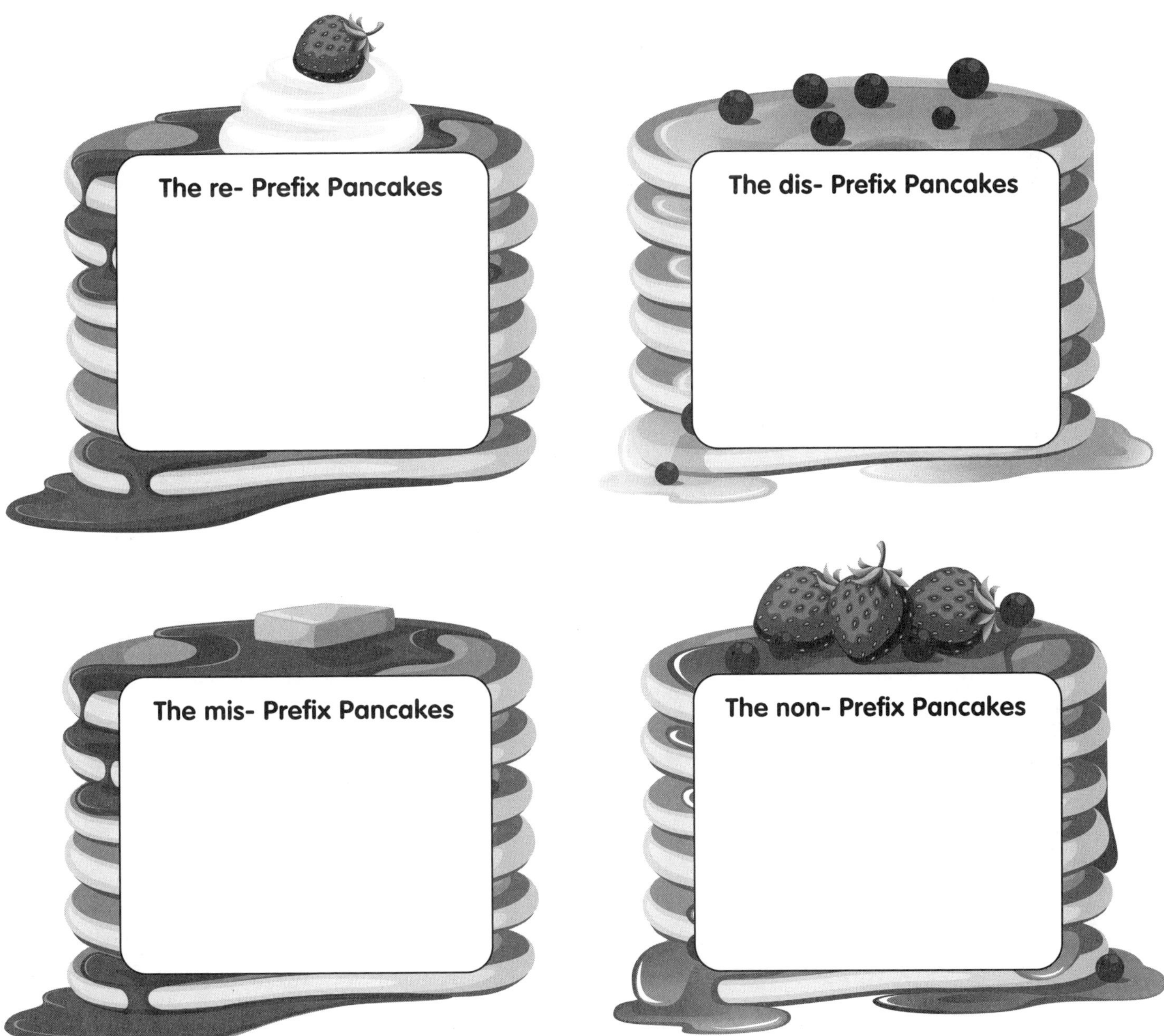

Name ______________________________

Kind Texts

Vincent and Adisa are texting each other. Circle any misspelled words. Write them correctly below.

______________   ______________   ______________   ______________

______________   ______________   ______________   ______________

Name ___________________

Violet Vowels

The words below are missing their vowels! Luckily, there are vowels growing on the violet petals. Finish the words using the vowels on the violets. Cross off each vowel after you use it.

1. p____th____t____c

2. m__________g____r

3. m____n__________t____r____

4. z__________l________s

5. ____b____nd____nt

6. sp______rs____

7. ____pt____m____st____c

8. r____d____c____l________s

9. ____bn____x__________s

10. ____nq__________s____t____v____

Riddle by the Numbers

Write the answer to each clue using the words in the box. Then use the letters to answer the riddle below.

bicentennial	bilingual	binocular	centennial
semiannual	semicircle	semicolon	triad
triceps	unify	union	unique

1. the **first letter** in the name of a punctuation mark ______

2. the **fourth letter** in a word that means **people coming together** ______

3. the **third letter** in a word that means **happening every half year** ______

4. the **last letter** in a word that means **one of a kind** ______

5. the **first letter** in a word for a celebration of 200 years ______

6. the **fourth letter** in a word that means **using both eyes** ______

7. the **last letter** in a word that means **a group of three** ______

8. the **last letter** in a word that means **making one group** ______

9. the **first letter** in a word for half of a shape ______

10. the **ninth letter** in a word for a celebration of 100 years ______

11. the **sixth letter** in a word that means **knowing two languages** ______

12. the **fifth letter** in a word naming a muscle with three parts ______

What number only keeps getting higher? ___________________________________

Spelling Games and Activities • EMC 8276 • © Evan-Moor Corporation

Name ______________________

Mail Matchup

Which pieces of mail belong together? Match the correct "mail" syllables to make words from the box. Write the complete words on the lines.

> bipedal   centipede   century
> triathlon   triplicate   unicorn

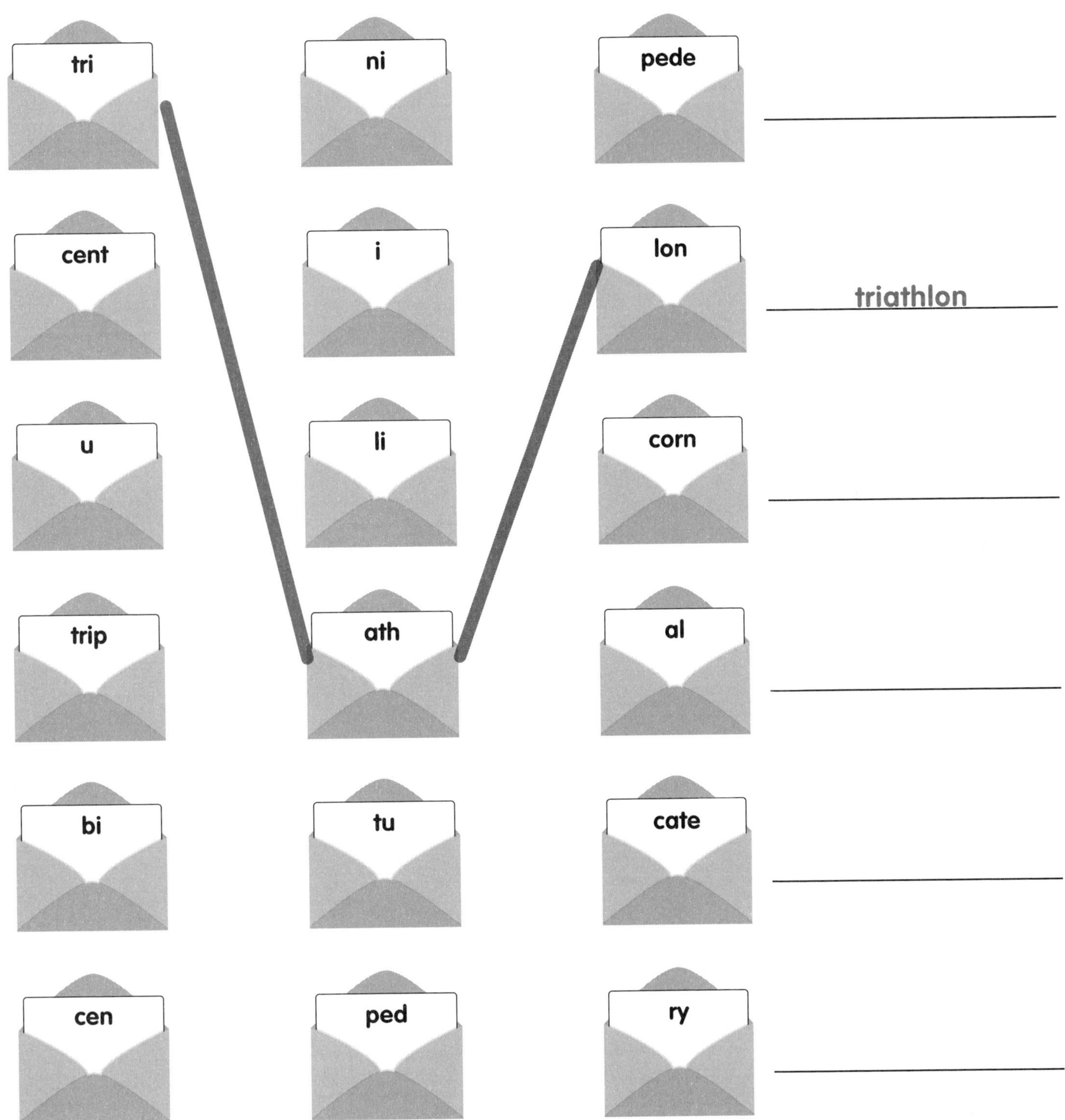

Puzzling Anagrams

You can change the silly phrases below to spell the words in the box.
After you unscramble each phrase, write the spelling word on the line.

> bankrupt   eruption   interrupt   reformat   respect
>
> rupture   spectator   suspect   transform

1. set cups   __________________________

2. rams front   __________________________

3. tip return   __________________________

4. Rome raft   __________________________

5. state crop   __________________________

6. ruin poet   __________________________

7. trap bunk   __________________________

8. Peru rut   __________________________

9. step rec   __________________________

Spelling Games and Activities • EMC 8276 • © Evan-Moor Corporation

Name ________________________

Spot the Schwa

Most words with more than one syllable have a **schwa** sound. Read each word in the box and decide which vowels are making each schwa sound. Circle the vowels. Then write each word in its Schwa Zone. If a word has more than one schwa, write the word in each zone. Use a different color for each zone.

formal	insignia	microscope	signal	signature
spectacle	stethoscope	telescope	uniform	

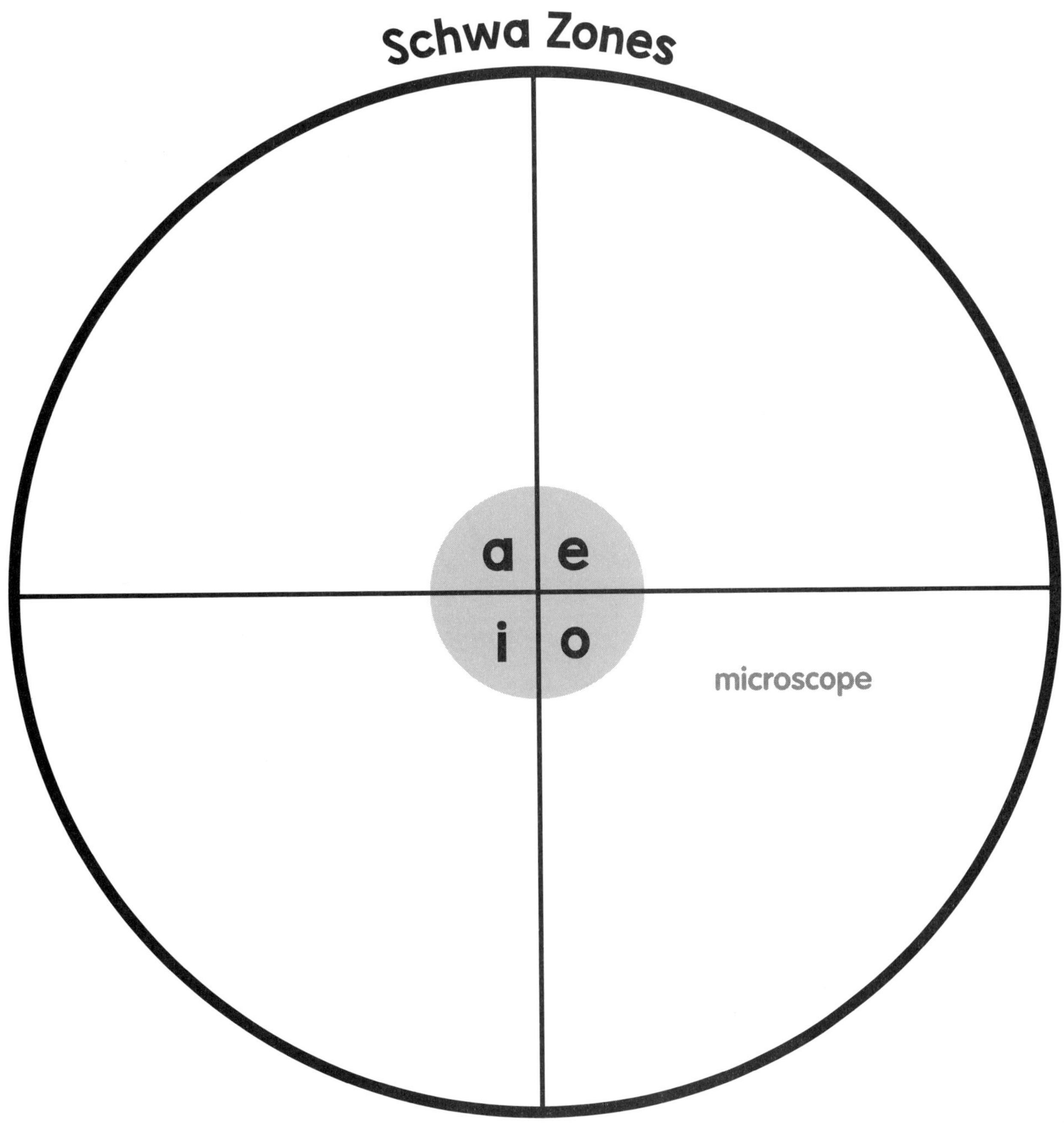

Name ______________________________

Time for "R" Break

Look at each word below. Write the **r**-controlled vowel that is missing.
Then write each word in the correct smoothie jar or jars.

Ant______rctica   b______reaucracy   p______rallelogram   c______rtograph______r

______rcheology   co______rdinates   env______ronment   p______rpendicul______r

hemisph______re   atmosph______ric   int______rnational   c______rcumf______rence

Syllable Socks

Say the syllables in each word in the box to yourself, one at a time. Figure out which syllable is accented the most. Write the complete word in the correct syllable sock.

Antarctica	bureaucracy	constitutional	environment	parallelogram
patriotism	peninsula	polyhedron	rhombus	theorem

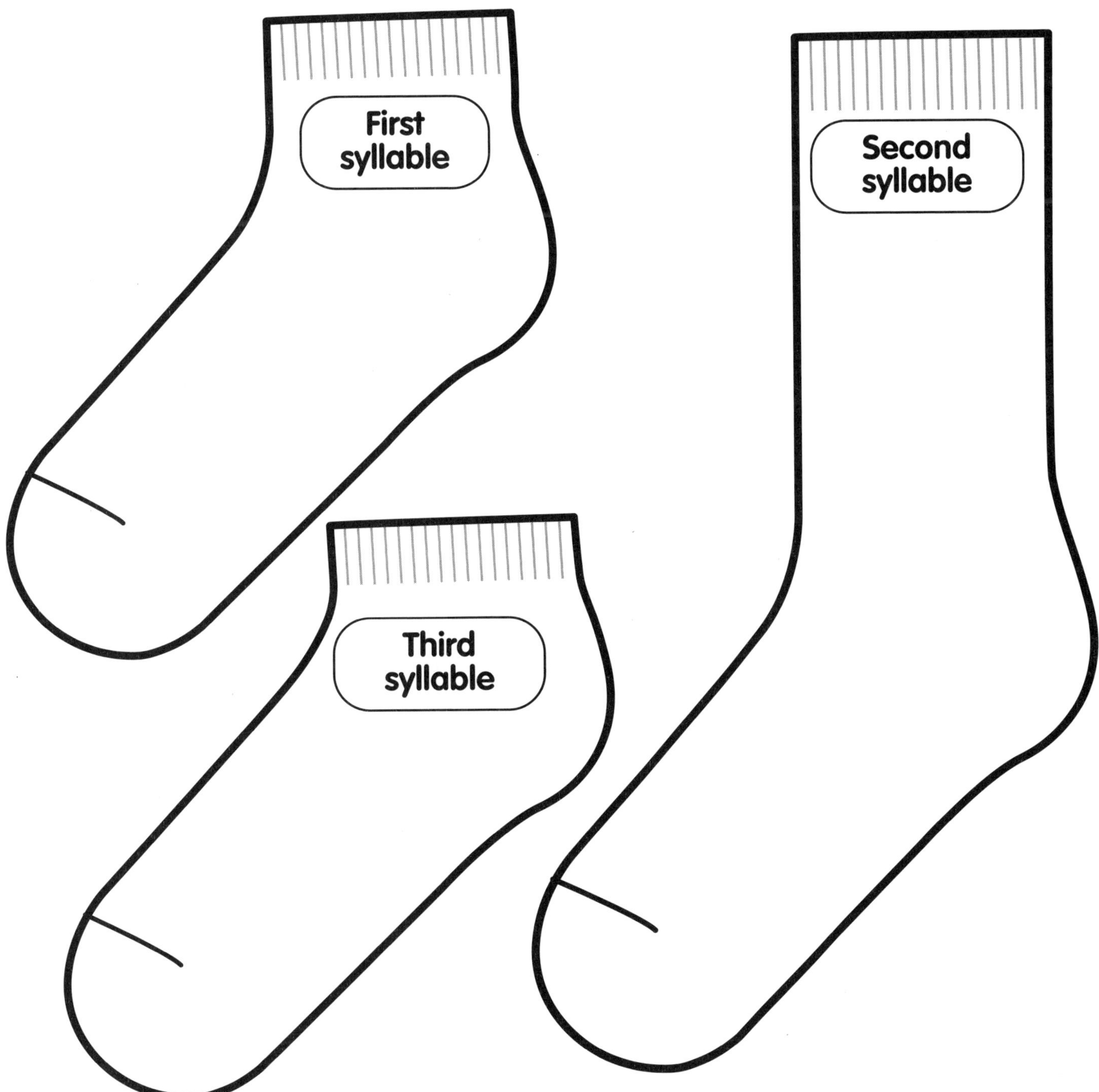

Spelling Strategies

How to Spell Hard Words

There are so many words that it would be hard to memorize them all!
It helps to have a plan when you are writing. Here are ways to figure out
how to spell words that you don't know.

	Say the word. Listen to the sounds and syllables. (Ask yourself) What do I hear? What do I know?
i before e except after c	**Think about rules or patterns** using the sounds you heard. (Ask yourself) Is there a rule or pattern I can follow?
-ight family might right bright tight knight slight tonight eyesight	**Think about similar words** that you know how to spell. (Ask yourself) Does it rhyme with another word? Is it part of a word family?
un|ex|pect|ed	**Divide the word.** Break compound words into two parts. Divide between prefix, base word, and suffix. Divide it into syllables. (Ask yourself) How can I divide it into smaller pieces?
success sŭk sĕs´ to do well	**Try to spell the word.** You can try different ways. (Ask yourself) Does it look right? Is it in the dictionary?

    Spelling Games and Activities • EMC 8276 • © Evan-Moor Corporation

Spelling Vowel Sounds

Every word has a vowel sound. There are different kinds of vowel sounds.
Look at the chart to find the kind you hear in a word.

I hear a short vowel sound.

Write the letter you hear:

gr**a**ph, h**e**lp, dr**i**nk, s**o**ng, m**u**ch, s**y**mphony

Or try a digraph:

h**ea**d, fr**ie**nd, t**ou**ch, **aw**ful

I hear a long vowel sound.

Write the letter you hear and a silent **e** after the consonant:

s**a**ve, th**e**se, pr**i**ce, cl**o**se, c**u**be

Or try a digraph:

br**ea**k, afr**ai**d, tod**ay**, w**ei**gh, pr**ey**, rec**ei**ve, n**ie**ce, **ea**sy, c**oa**st, thr**ou**gh, s**ui**t, r**oo**m

I hear a schwa sound.

Any vowel can have a schwa sound:

alive, happ**e**n, tenn**i**s, **o**'clock, min**u**te

Make a guess and write the word:

- See if it looks right.
- Check the dictionary.
- Make up a memory clue.

I hear something else.

R-controlled vowels are not short or long. Write the vowel that sounds closest.

h**ar**d, pref**er**, b**ir**d, doct**or**, t**ur**n

Diphthongs are letter pairs that make two sounds together:

v**oi**ce, l**oy**al, h**ou**se, t**ow**n

Other sounds:

c**oo**k, c**ou**ld, p**u**sh, w**a**tch

Spelling Strategies
Spelling Consonant Sounds

Every word has a consonant sound. Some consonants have two sounds. Look at the chart to find the sound you hear in a word.

 **J** I hear a **j** sound.

Write a **j** most of the time:

> en**j**oy, **j**ury

Write a **g** if the next sound is an **e** or **i** sound or if it is the last sound in the word:

> dan**g**er, **gi**ant, chan**g**e

 **S** I hear an **s** sound.

Write an **s** most of the time:

> **s**ave, al**so**, **s**urprise, a**s**k, **s**low, **sm**ile, **sn**ap

Write a **c** if the next sound is an **e** or **i** sound:

> **ce**nter, re**ci**tal, accura**c**y

 **K** I hear a **k** sound.

Write a **c** most of the time:

> **ca**rry, be**co**me, **cu**te, **cl**ean, **cr**uise, do**c**tor

Write a **k** if the next sound is an **e** or **i** sound or if it is the last sound in the word:

> poc**k**et, **ki**te, ali**k**e

F I hear an **f** sound.

Write an **f** or **ph** at the beginning:

> **f**ollow, **ph**one

Write an **f**, **ff**, or **ph** in the middle:

> li**f**e, di**ff**erent, al**ph**abet

Write an **f**, **ff**, **ph**, or **gh** at the end:

> proo**f**, o**ff**, gra**ph**, cou**gh**

 **?** I hear **something else.**

Digraphs are letter pairs that make a new sound together:

> tea**ch**er, **sh**ort, nor**th**, **wh**ere

 **?** What am I **not hearing?**

Many words have **silent letters.** Some are in word families. Memorize them:

> com**b**, colum**n**, **g**nat, is**l**and, **l**isten, hal**f**, **h**our, **k**now, **w**rap

Spelling Strategies
Breaking Down Words

It is easier to spell long words when you break them into smaller pieces.

Divide compound words.
Compound words are made of two shorter words put together.

1. Say the word.

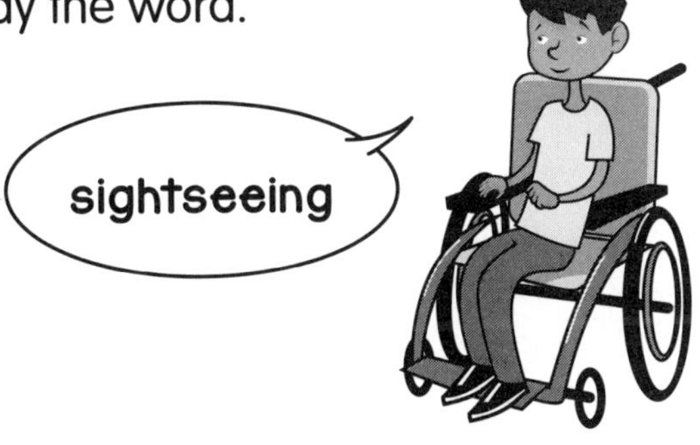

2. Figure out the two words that make up the compound word.

sight

seeing

3. Spell the smaller words.

sightseeing

Divide words between syllables.
Syllables are short pieces of a word. Each syllable has a vowel sound in it. Every time you say a syllable, your chin moves.

1. Say the word.

2. Listen to each syllable. Figure out the sounds in each syllable.

ther – mom – e – ter

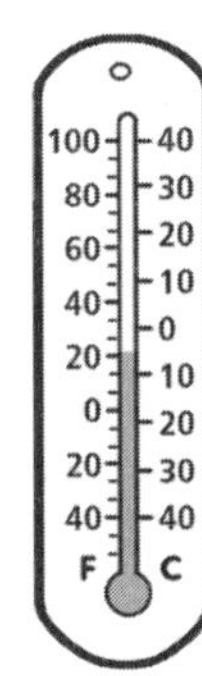

3. Spell the syllables together.

thermometer

Spelling Strategies
Using Suffixes

You can make more words by adding suffixes to the ends of words you know.

Make plural words.

Most nouns: add **s**	Nouns ending in **s**, **ss**, **sh**, **ch**, **x**, or **z**: add **es**	Nouns ending in a consonant + **y**: drop the **y**, add **ies**
shoe**s**, insect**s**, turkey**s**	bus**es**, guess**es**, wish**es**, watch**es**, box**es**, waltz**es**	cherr**ies**, stor**ies**

Make describing words.

Most words: add **er**, **est**, **ly**, **ful**, **ness**, **less**	Words ending in **y**: change **y** to **i** and add the suffix
hard**er**, high**est**, friend**ly**, care**ful**, great**ness**, fear**less**	happ**ier**, happ**iest**, happ**ily**, happ**iness**

Change action words.

Most verbs: add **ed** or **ing**	Verbs ending in **e**: drop the **e** and add **ed** or **ing**	Verbs ending in **y**: change **y** to **i** and add **ed**
finish**ed**, call**ing**	believ**ed**, clos**ing**	carr**ied**, suppl**ied**

Spelling Strategies

Using a Dictionary

A dictionary can tell you a lot about words. It tells you how to spell them, how to say them, and what they mean.

How to find a word

"I don't know how to spell it. How can I look it up?"

First, guess at the spelling. Is it in the dictionary? If you don't see **howce** there, think of another way to write the **ow** sound. Try **houce**. If you still don't see it, think of another way to write the **soft c** sound. Try **house**.

How to say a word

"I've seen that word before, but what does it sound like?"

After the word is spelled, you'll see symbols that tell you short and long vowels and basic consonant sounds.

It also shows the syllables.

enough (ē nŭf´)

How to learn a word's meanings

"I can read the word, but how do I use it?"

After showing how to say the word, you'll see what it means. If you look up a word that sounds the same as another word, check the meaning to see if you have the right word.

kind (kīnd)

1. nice 2. a type or group

Spelling Strategies
Making Memory Clues

Even if you know every spelling rule, you just have to remember how to spell some words. Making up your own memory clue can be helpful and fun!

Write a rhyming sentence.

This memory clue helps you remember that **climb** has a **silent b** in it.

Be silent and tall as you clim**b** the wall.

Write an acrostic.

The first letter of each word spells **ocean**.

Write a silly sentence.

All the **a**'s remind you that **taught** has an **a** in it.

Annie t**a**ught **a**nts to d**a**nce.

Spelling Games and Activities • EMC 8276 • © Evan-Moor Corporation

Answer Key

Page 12

Page 13

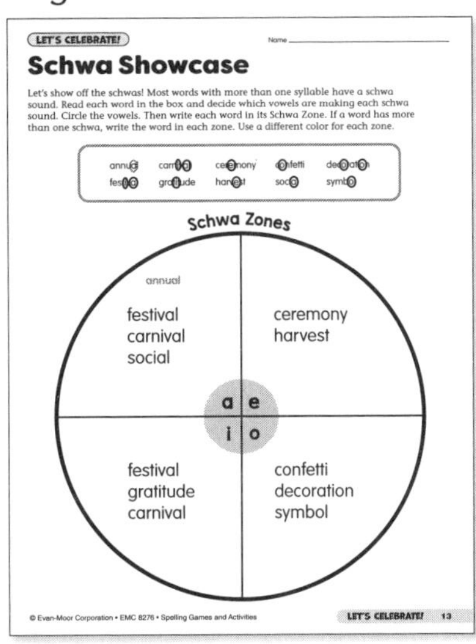

Page 14

Page 15

Page 16

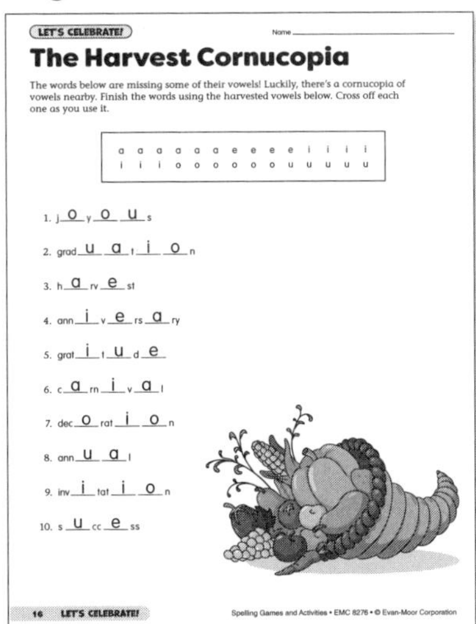

Page 17

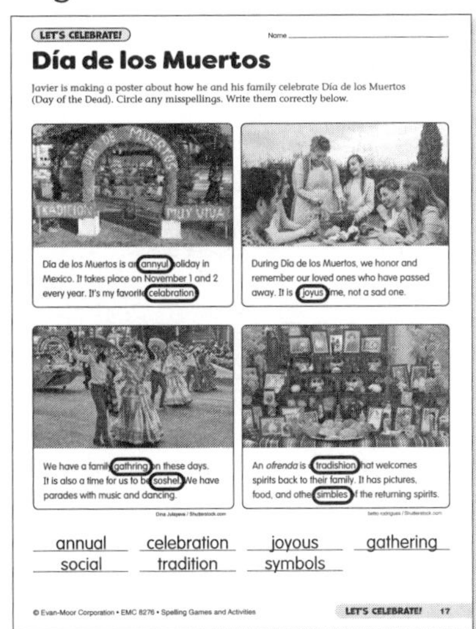

Page 22

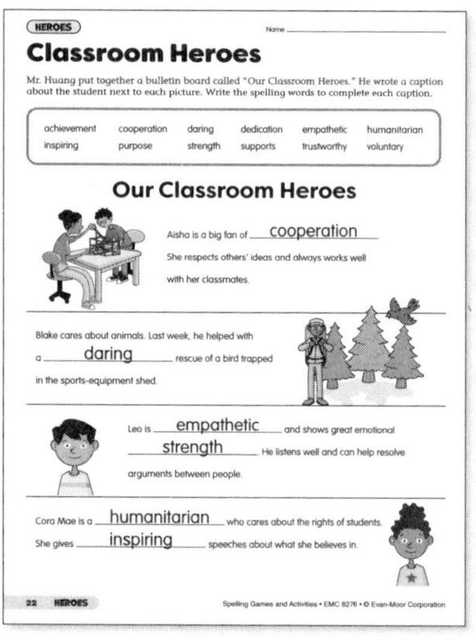

Page 23

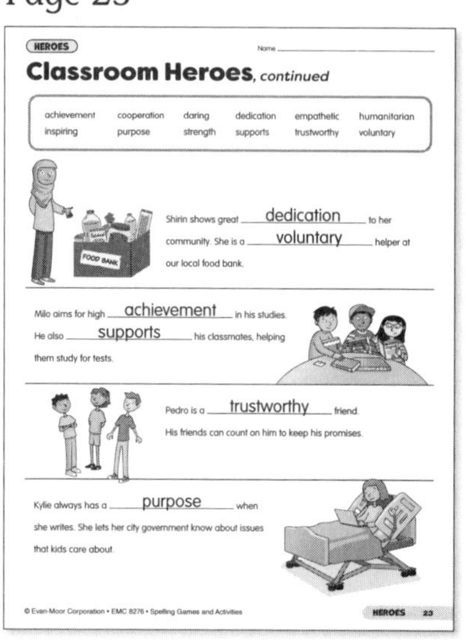

Page 24

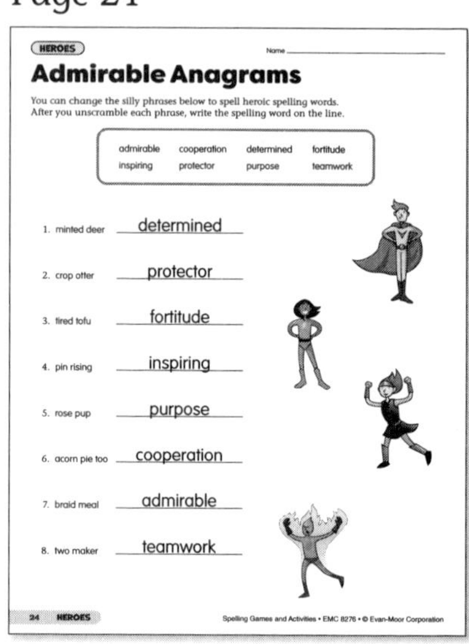

Page 25

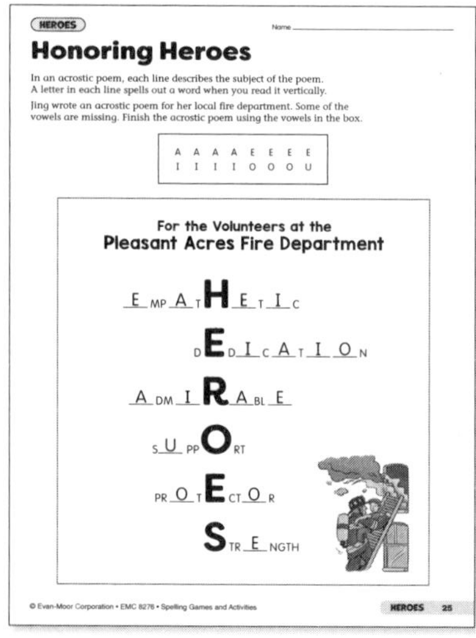

Page 26

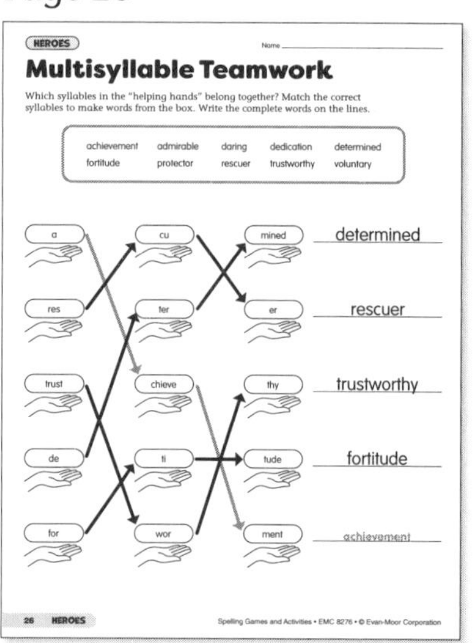

Page 27

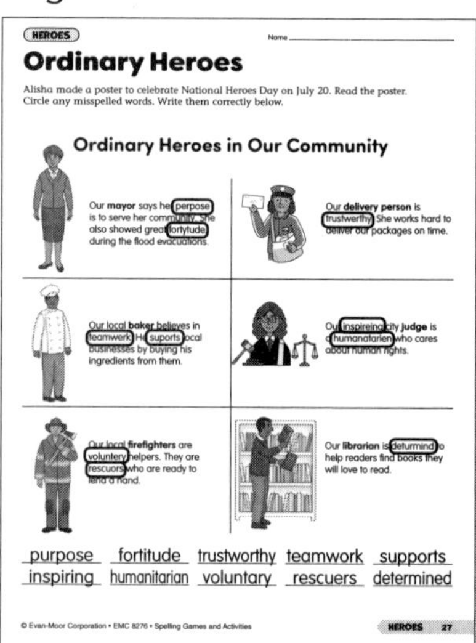

Spelling Games and Activities • EMC 8276 • © Evan-Moor Corporation

Page 32

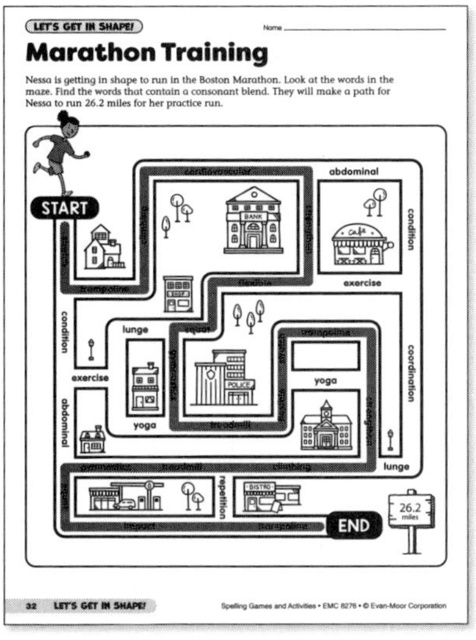

Page 33

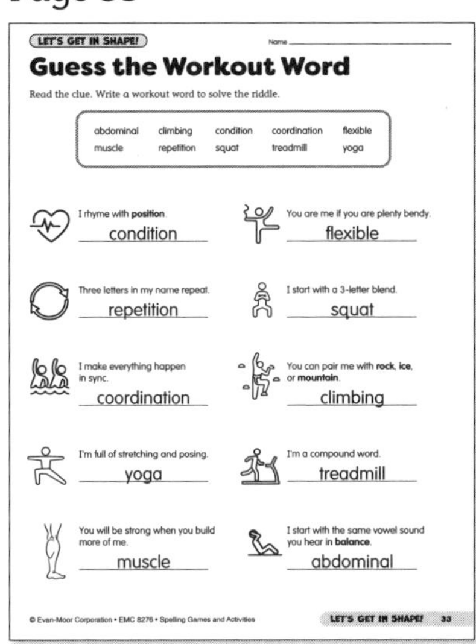

Page 34

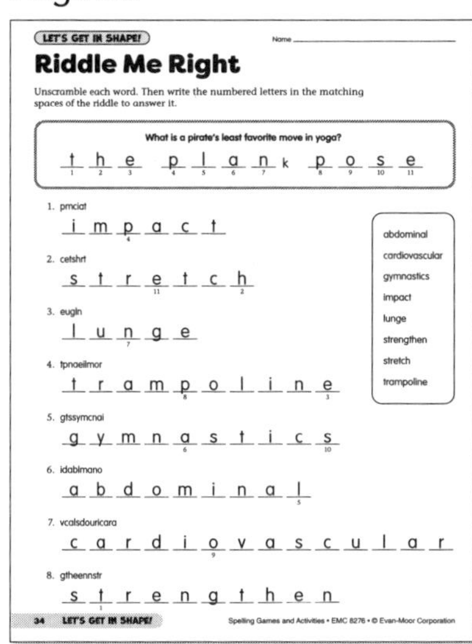

Page 35

Page 36

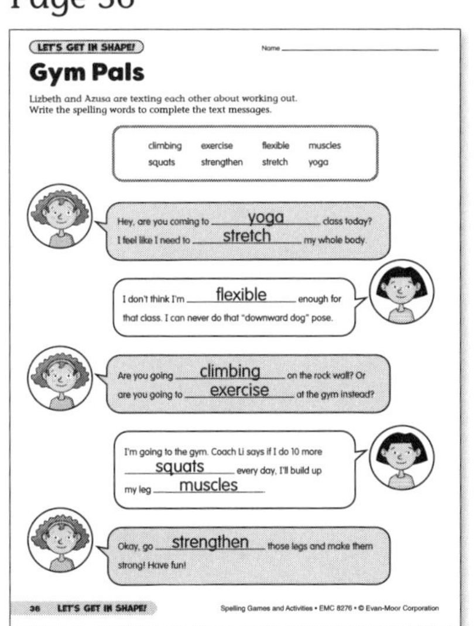

Page 37

Page 42

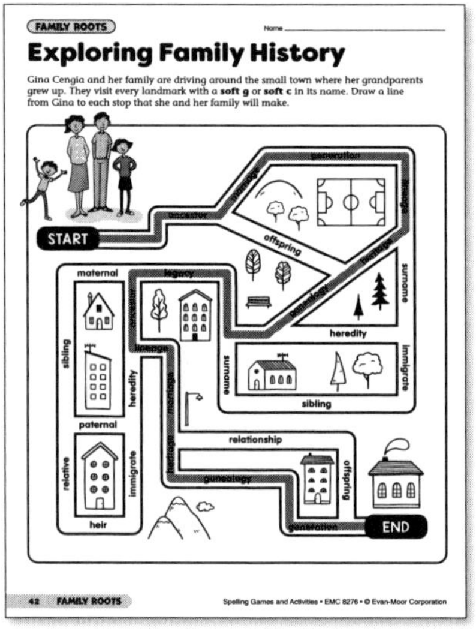

Page 43

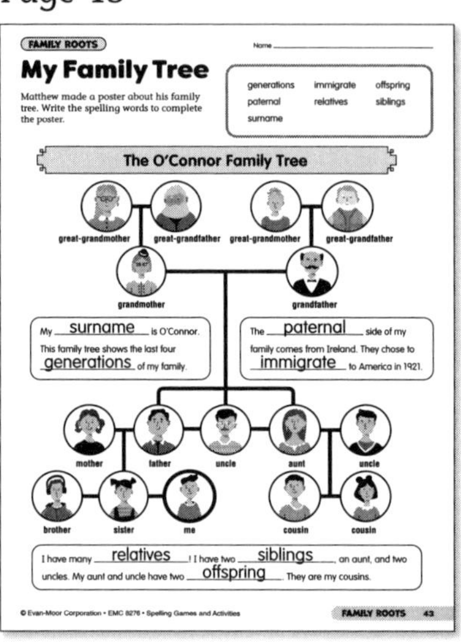

Page 44

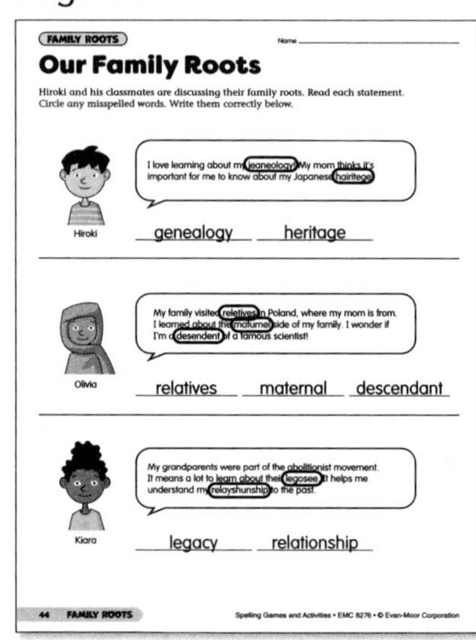

Page 45

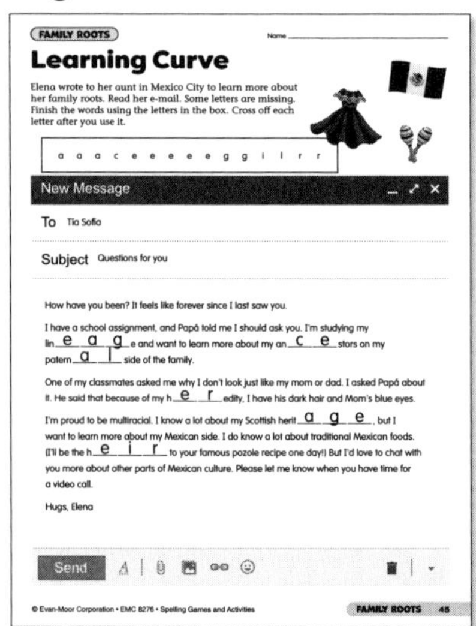

Page 46

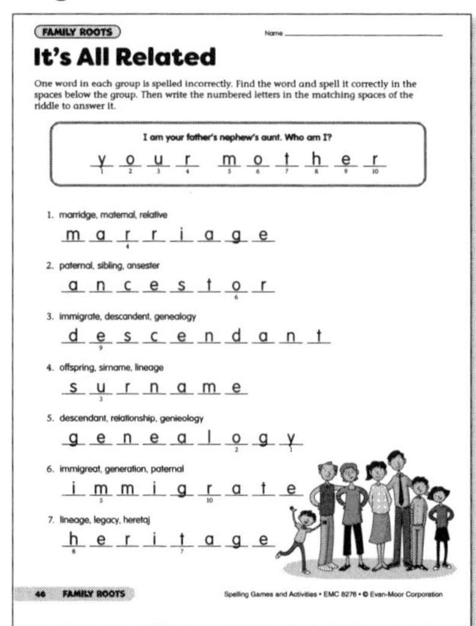

Page 47

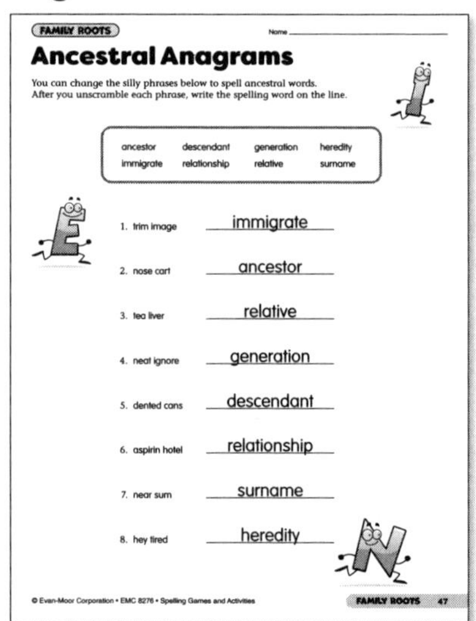

Page 52

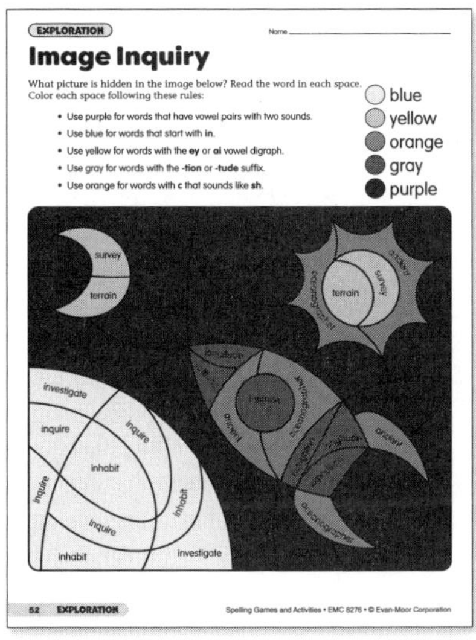

Page 53

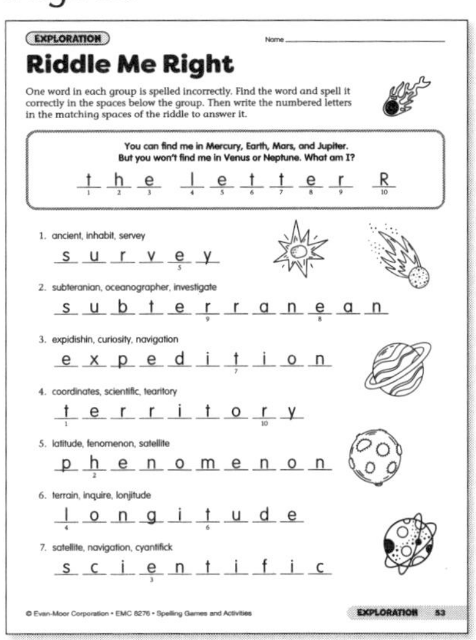

Page 54

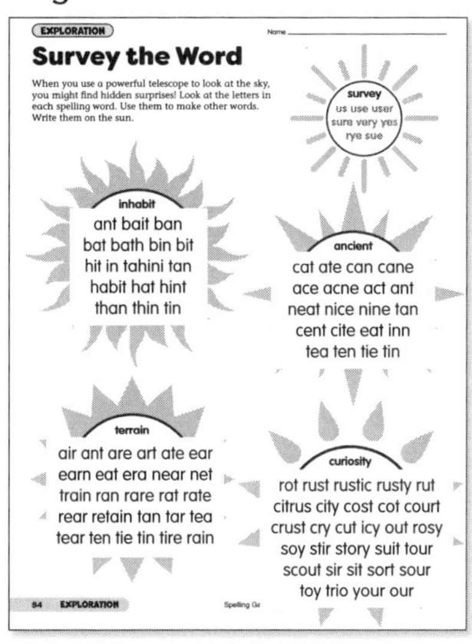

Page 55

Page 56

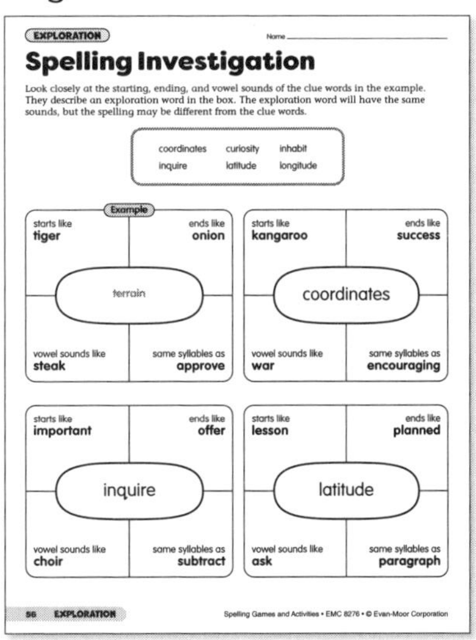

Page 57

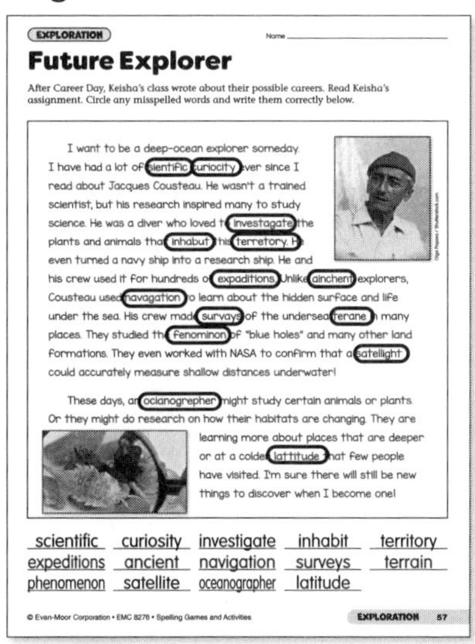

Page 62

Page 63

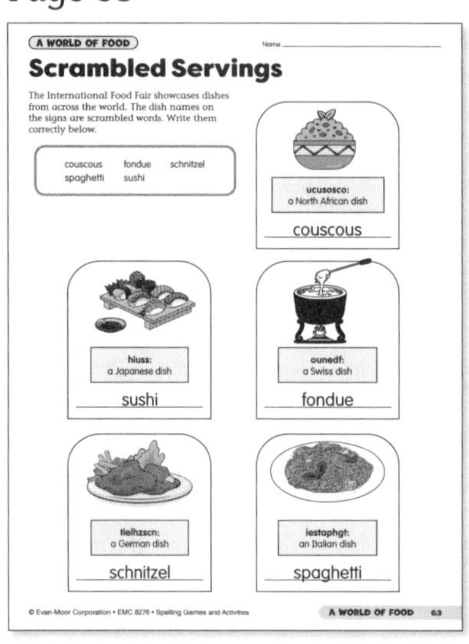

Page 64

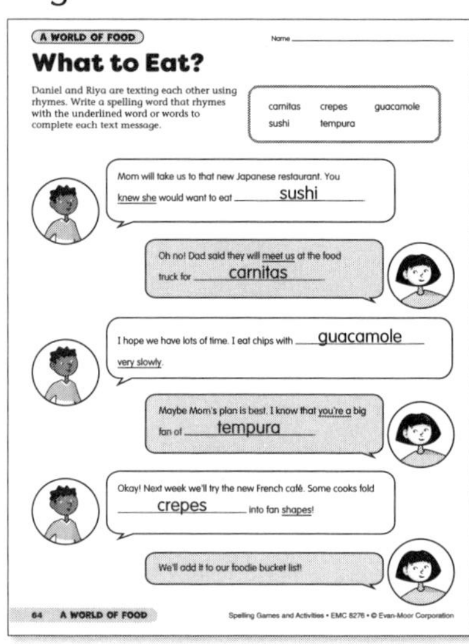

Page 65

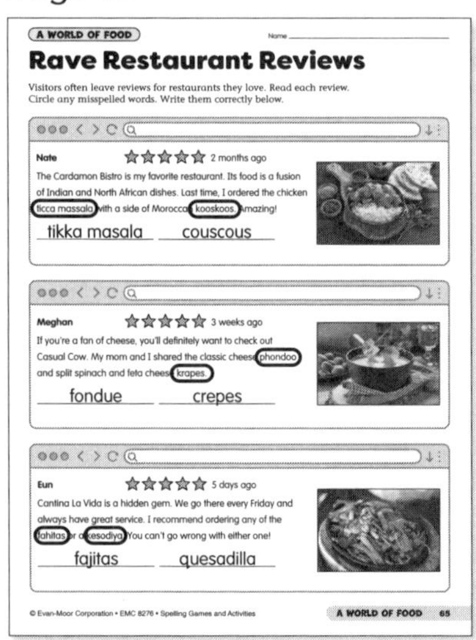

Page 66

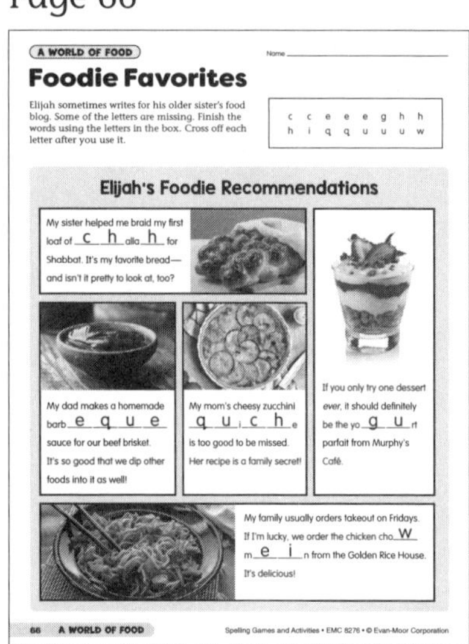

Page 67

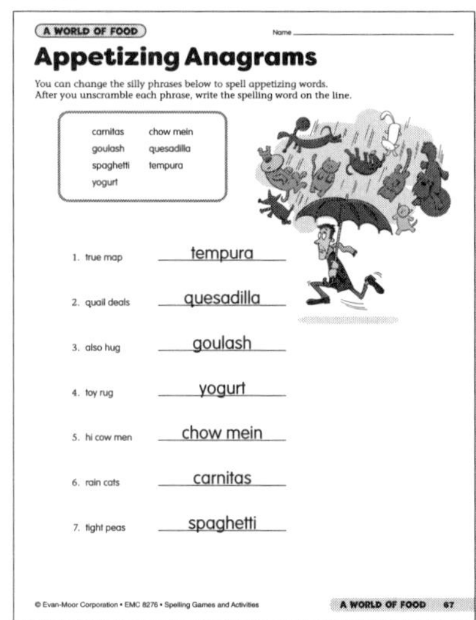

Page 72

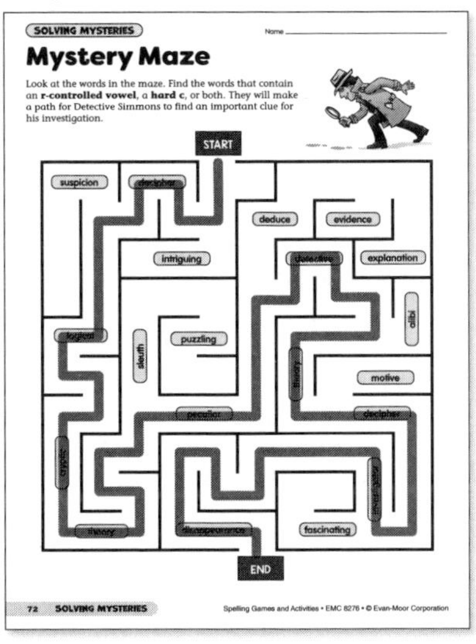

Page 73

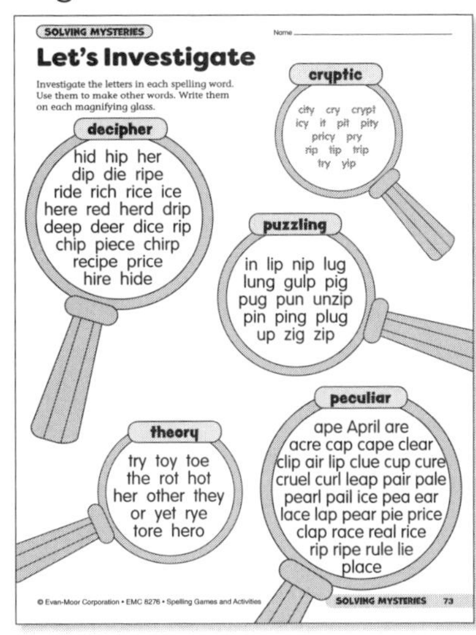

Page 74

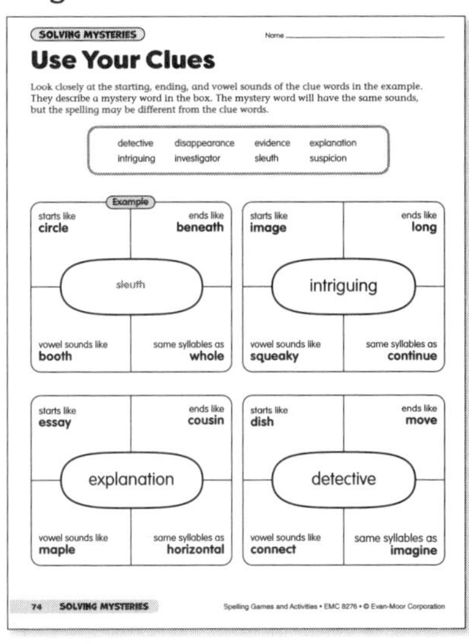

Page 75

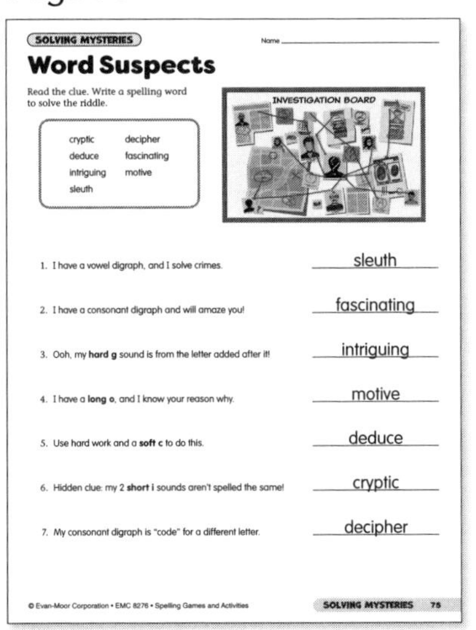

Page 76

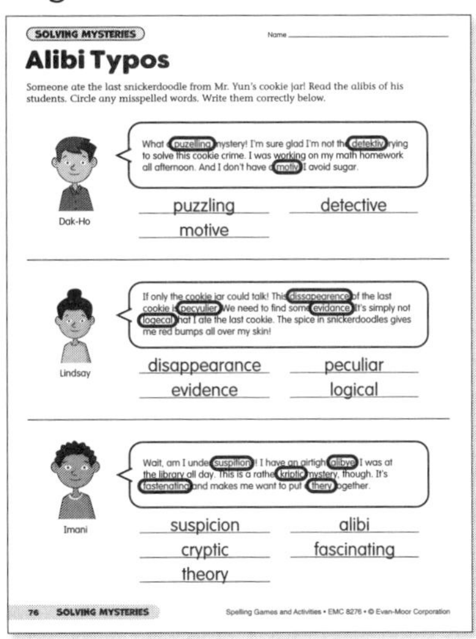

Page 77

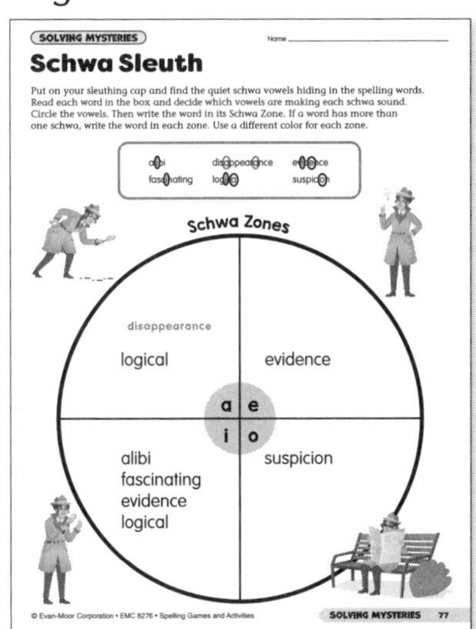

Page 82

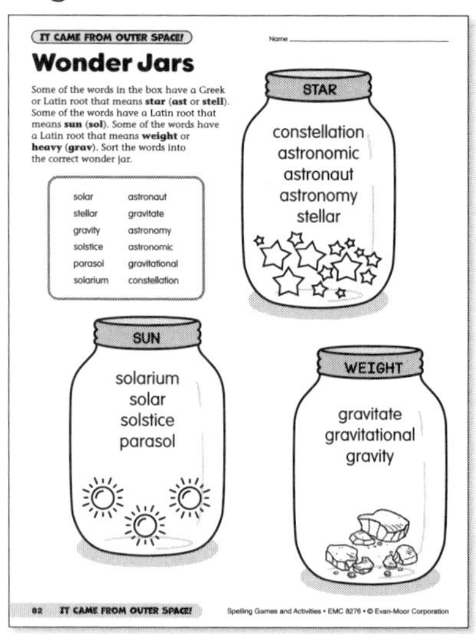

Page 83

Page 84

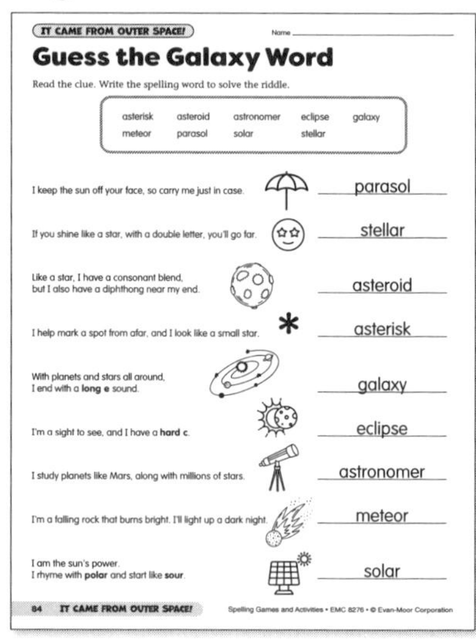

Page 85

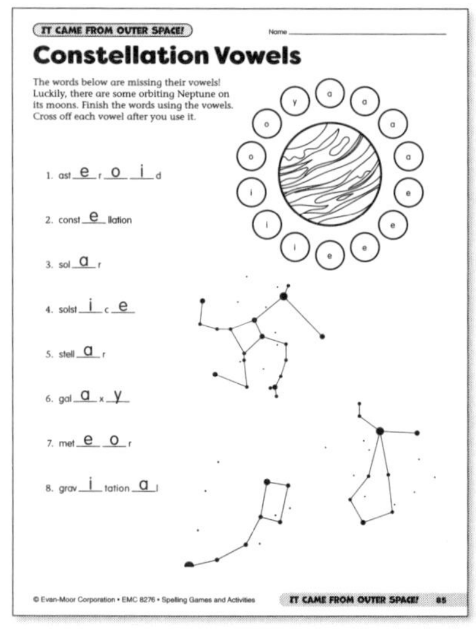

Page 86

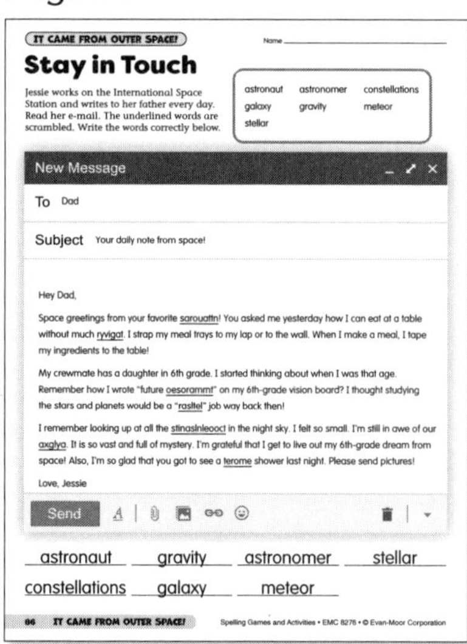

Page 87

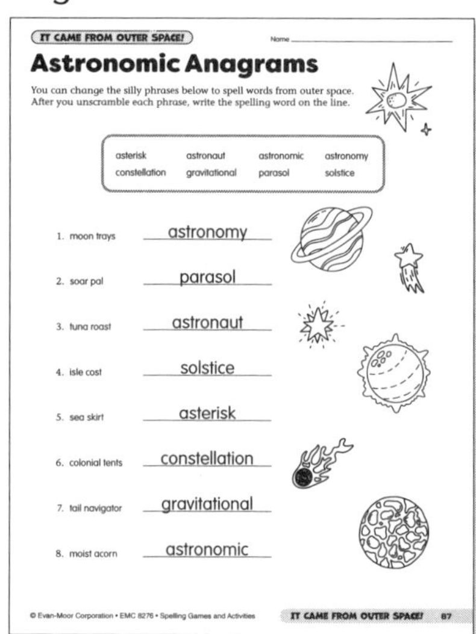

Spelling Games and Activities • EMC 8276 • © Evan-Moor Corporation

Page 92

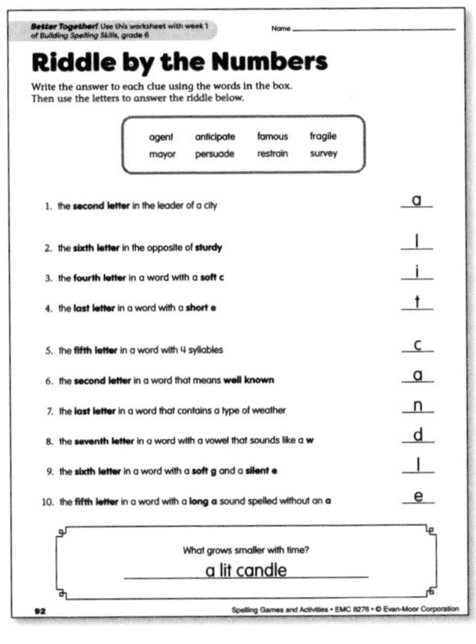

Page 93

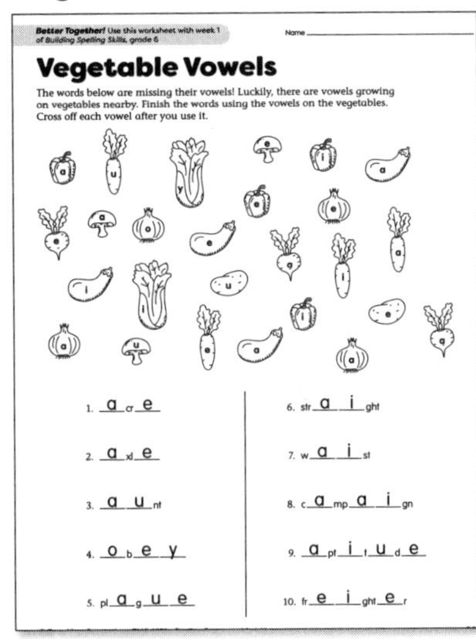

Page 94

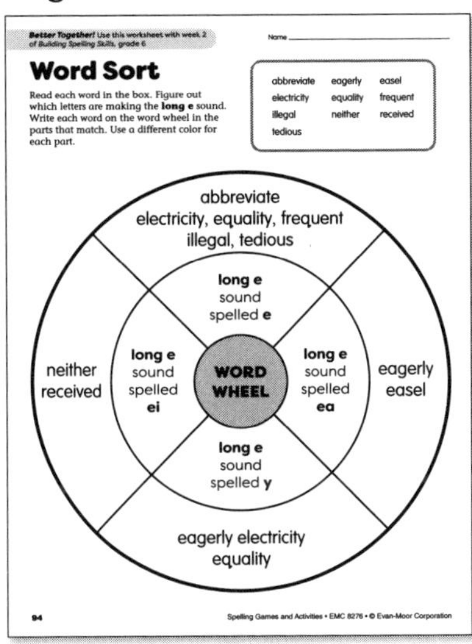

Page 95

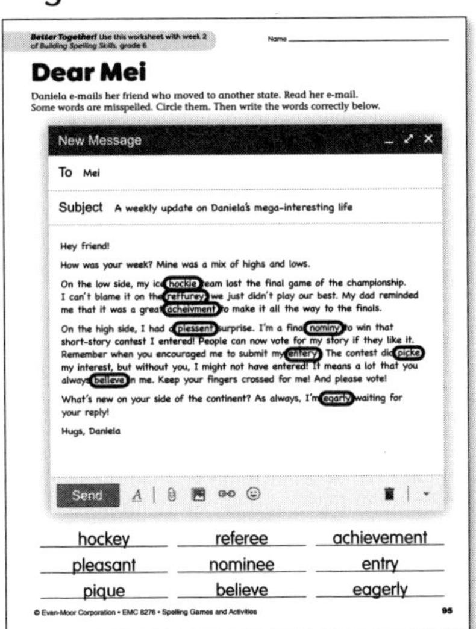

Page 96

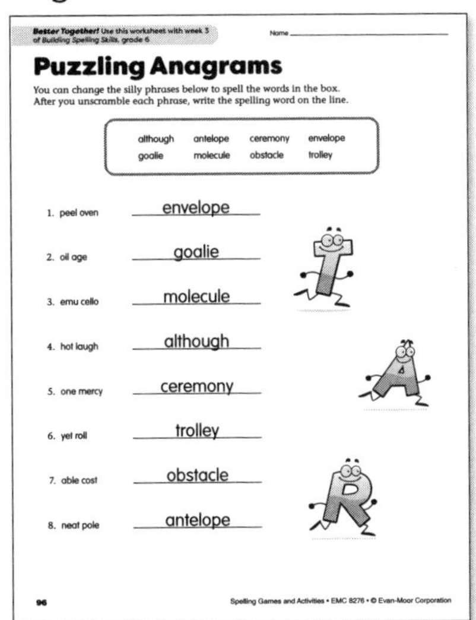

Page 97

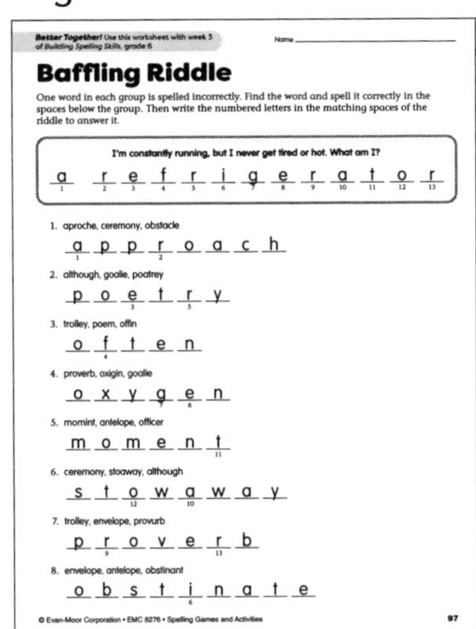

Page 98

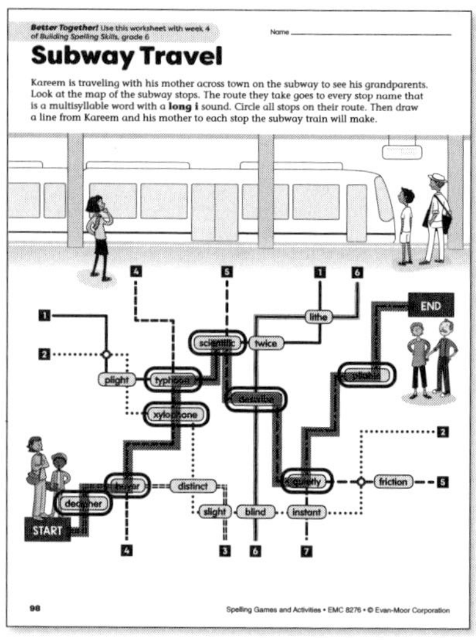

Page 99

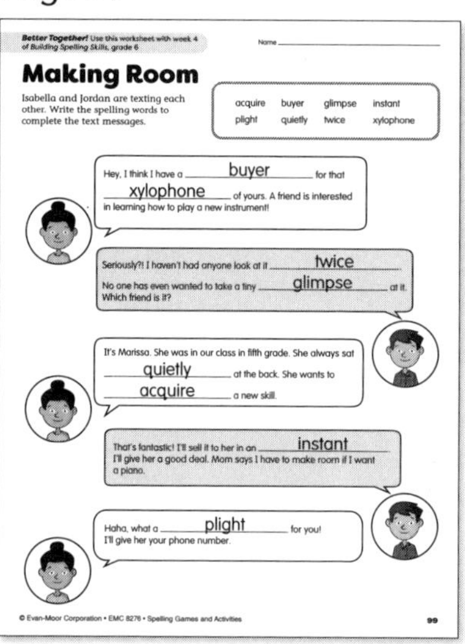

Page 100

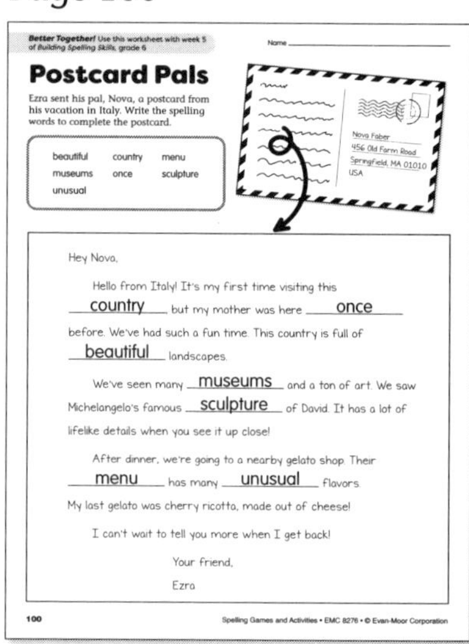

Page 101

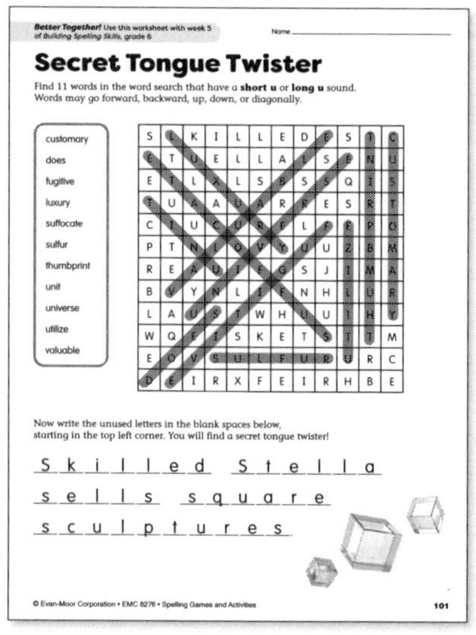

Page 102

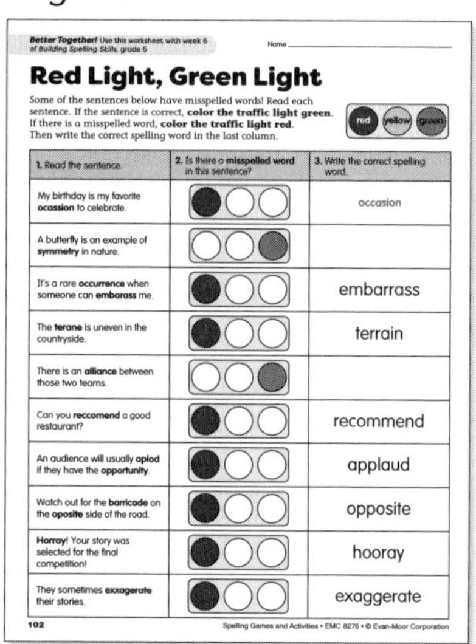

Page 103

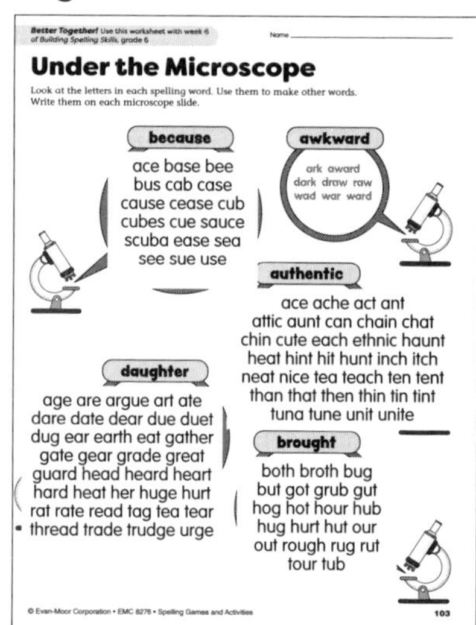

Page 104

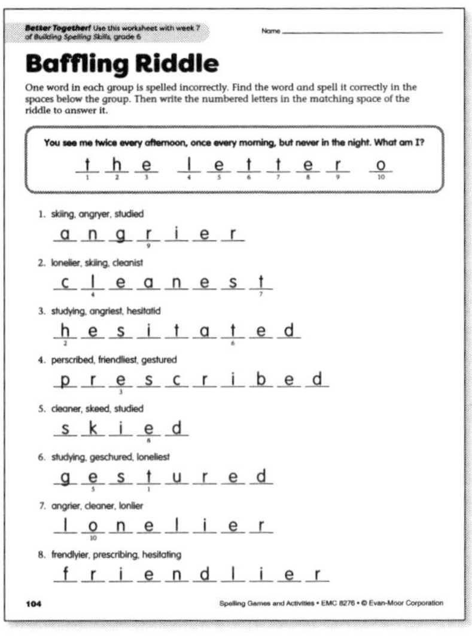

Page 105

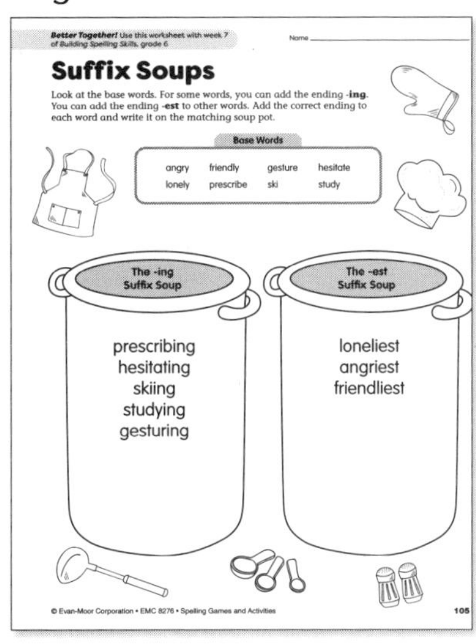

Page 106

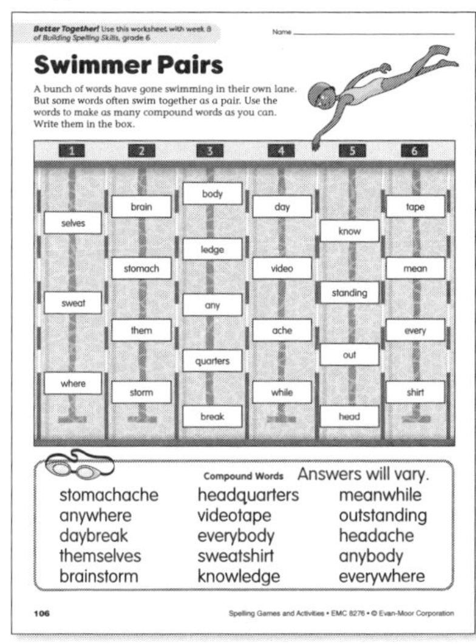

Page 107

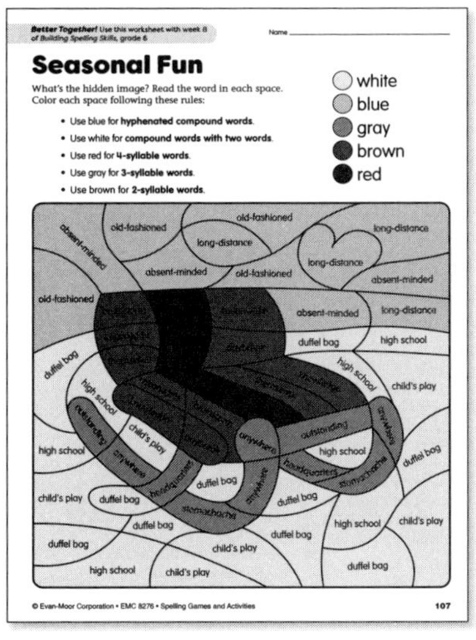

Page 108

Page 109

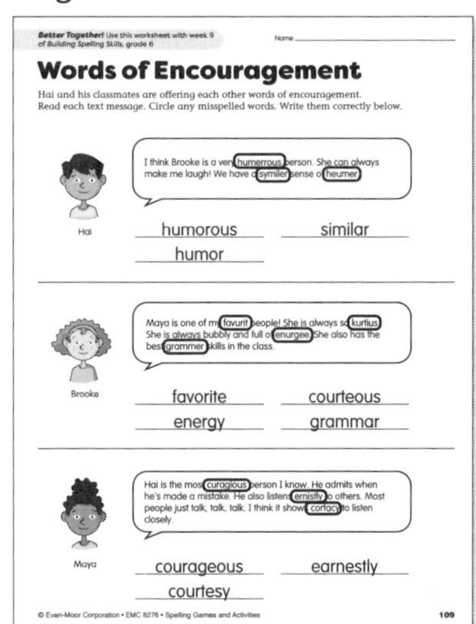

Page 110

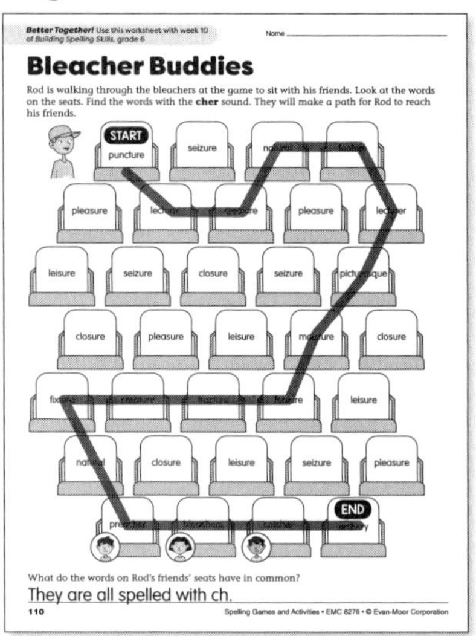

Page 111

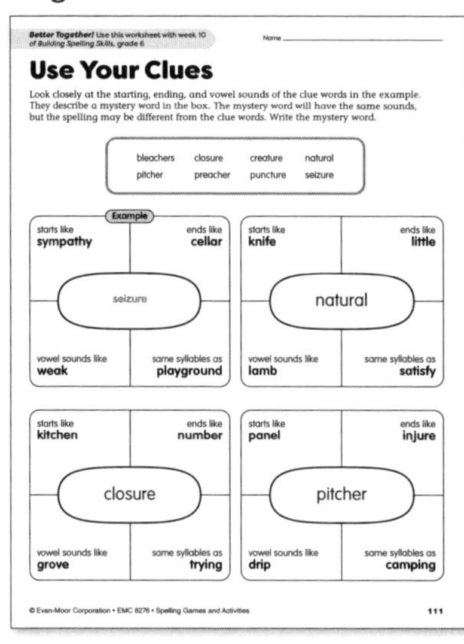

Page 112

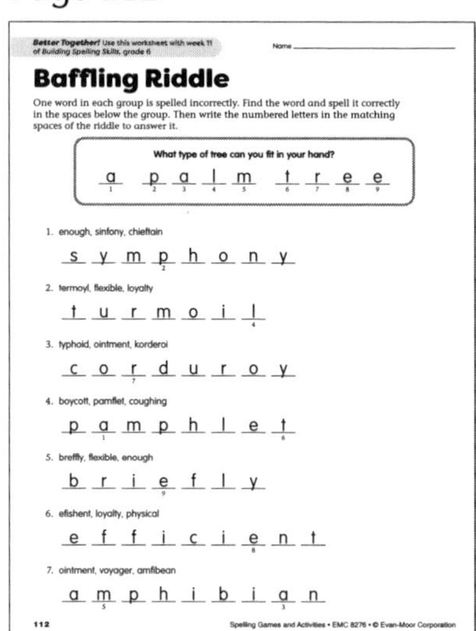

Page 113

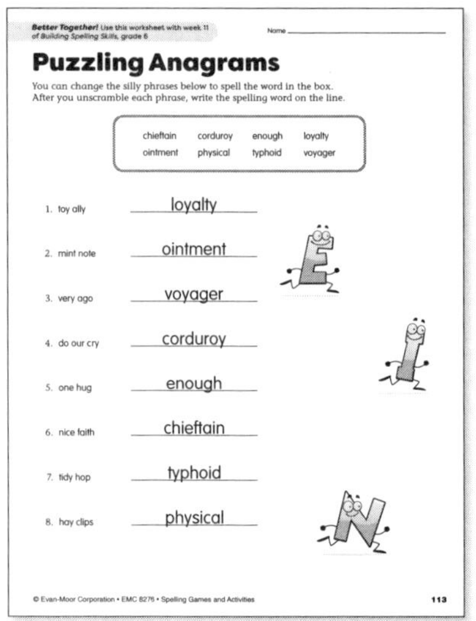

Page 114

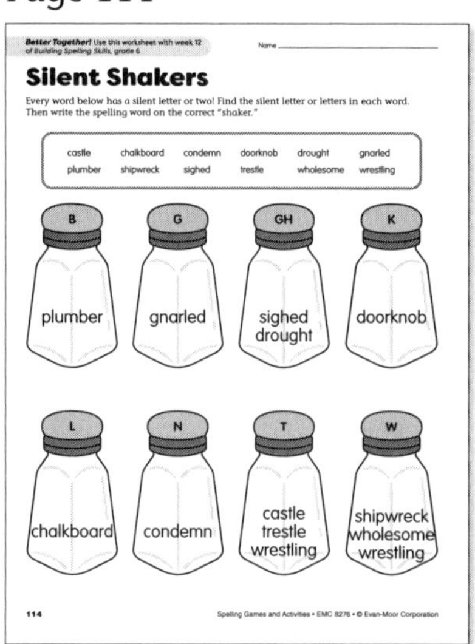

Page 115

Page 116

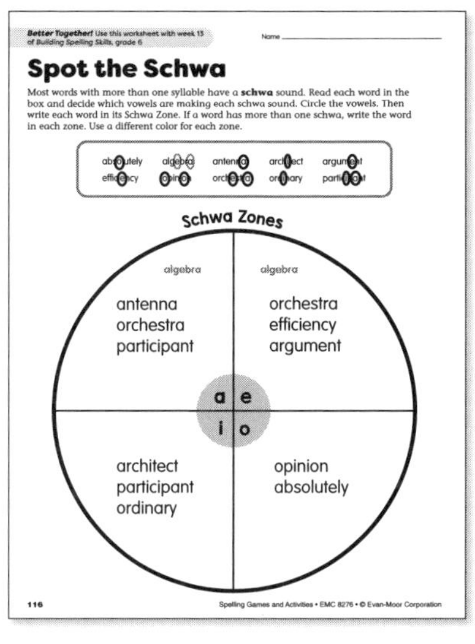

Page 117

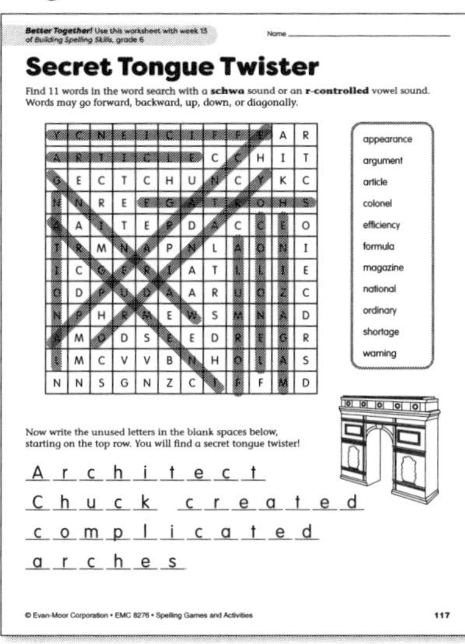

Page 118

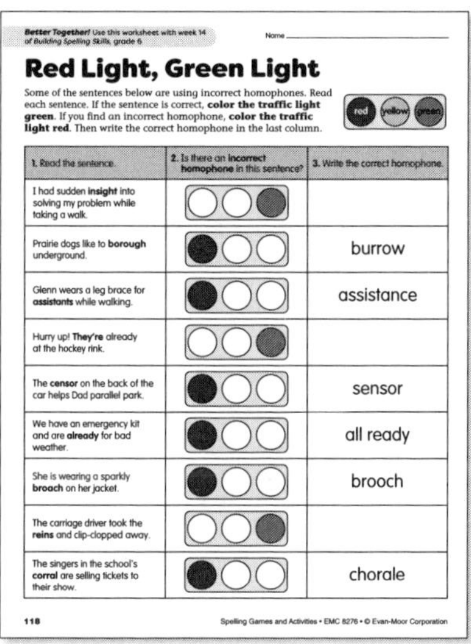

Page 119

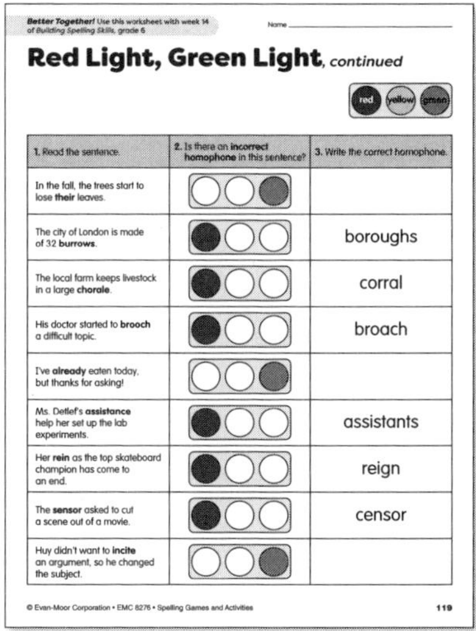

Page 120

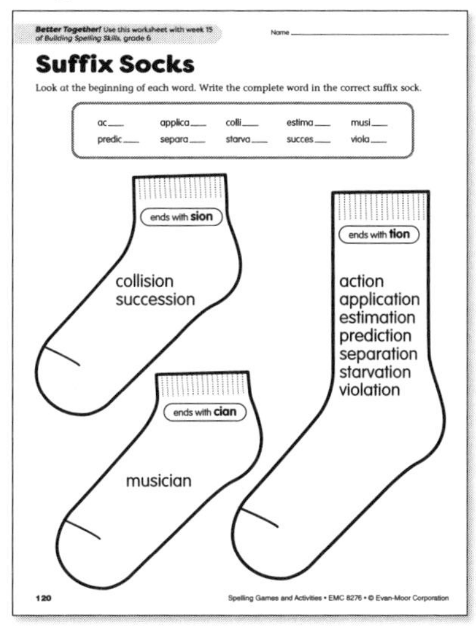

Page 121

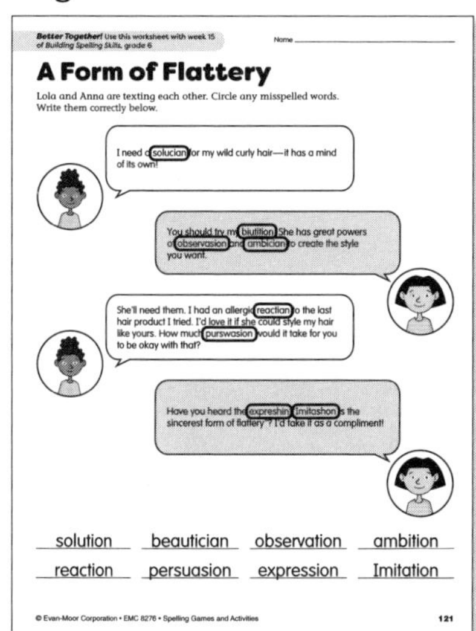

Page 122

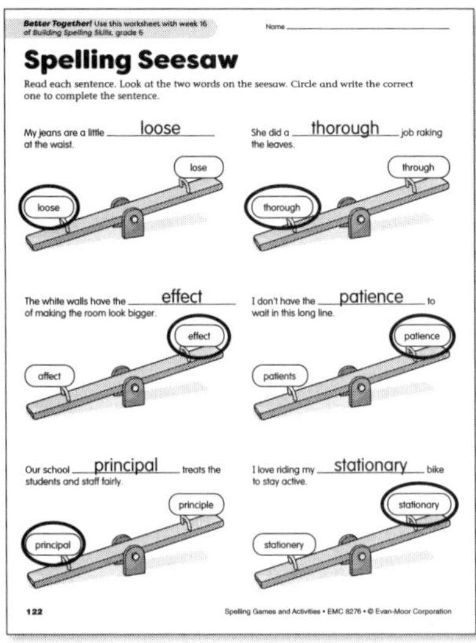

Page 123

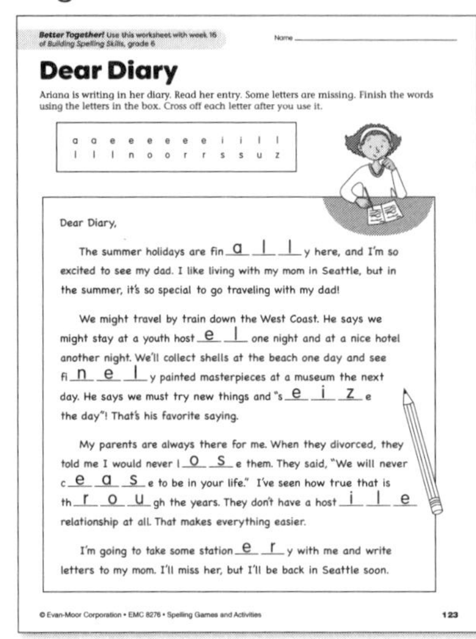

Page 124

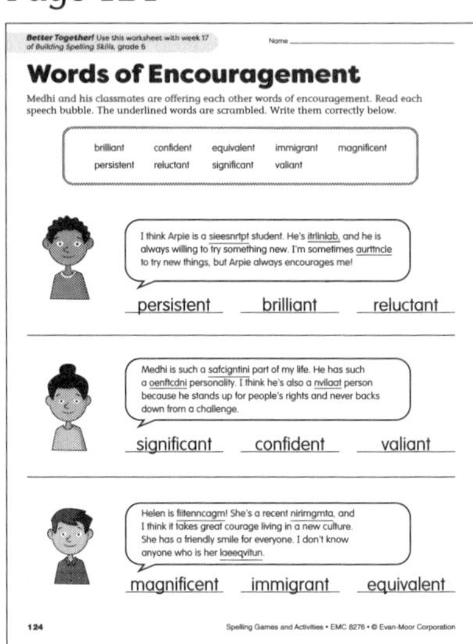

Page 125

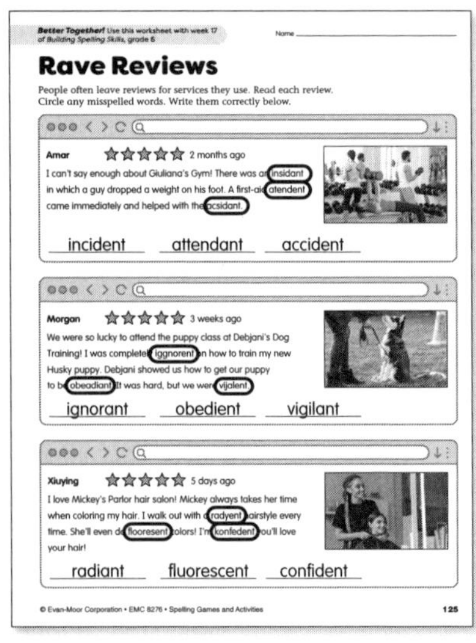

Page 126

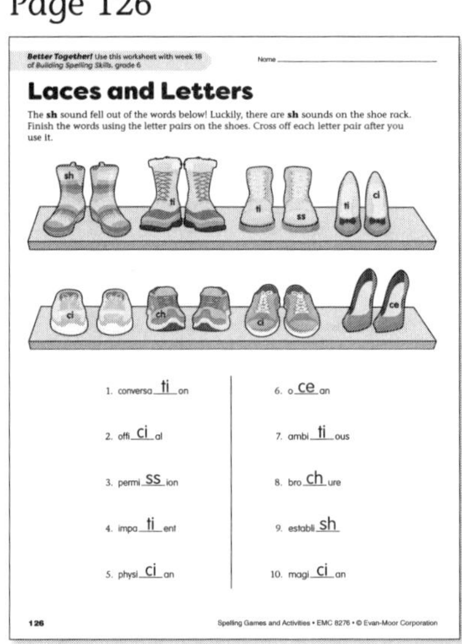

Page 127

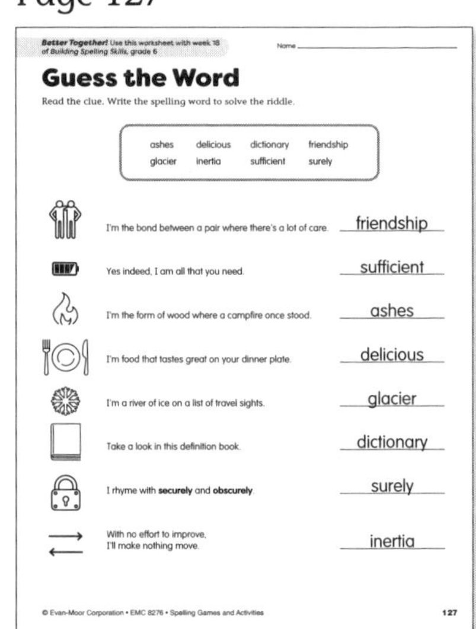

Page 128

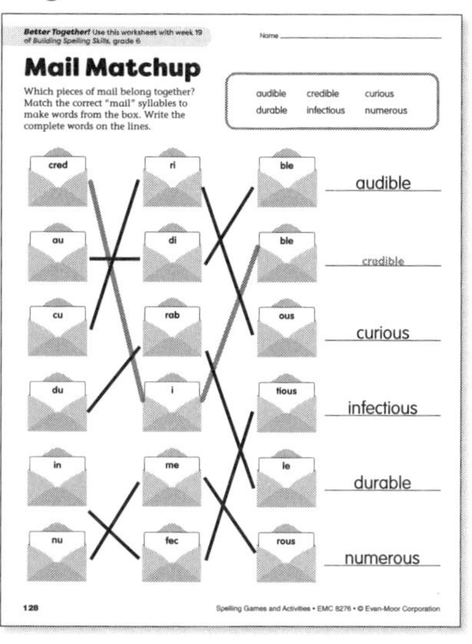

Page 129

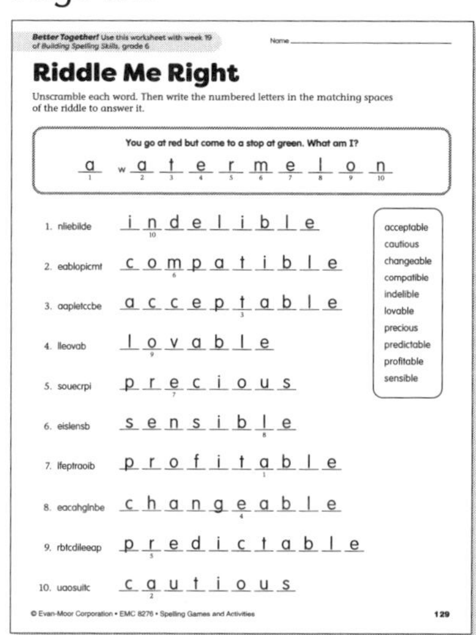

Page 130

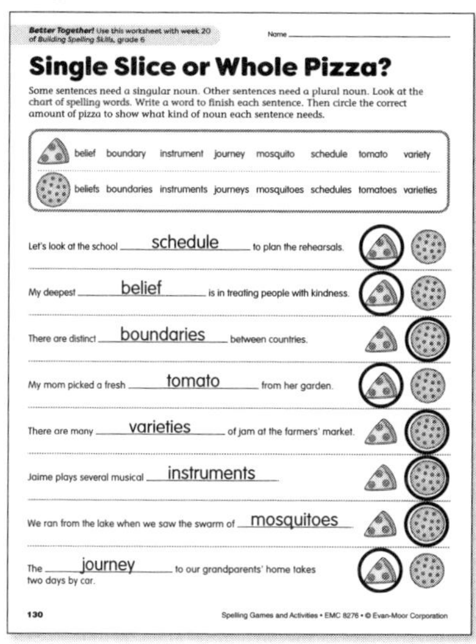

Page 131

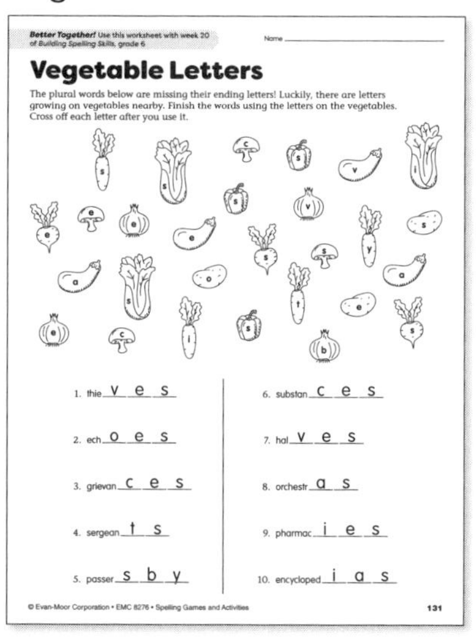

Page 132

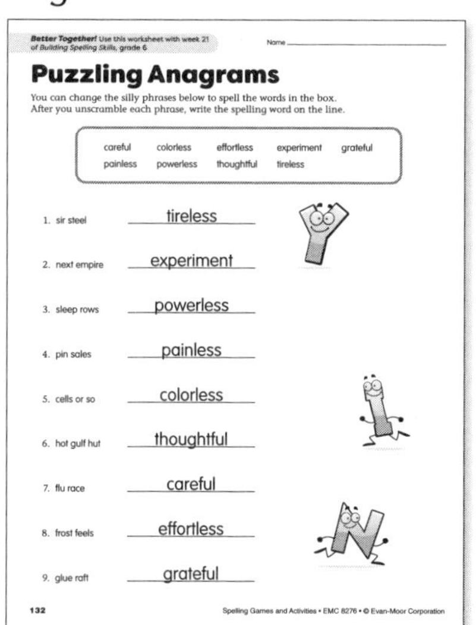

Page 133

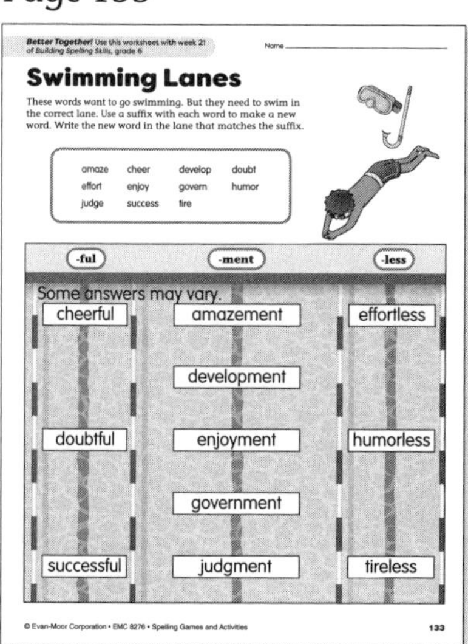

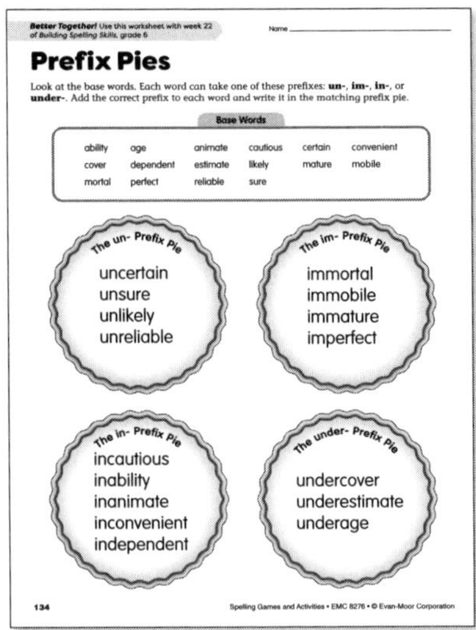

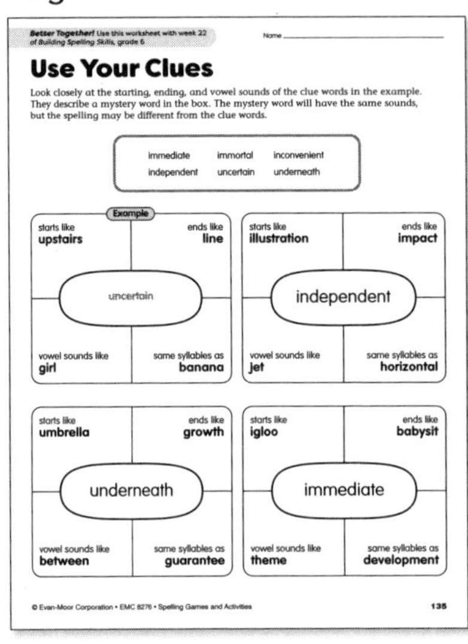

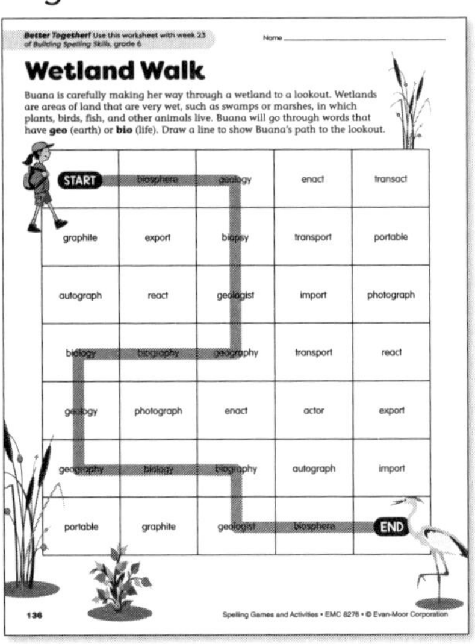

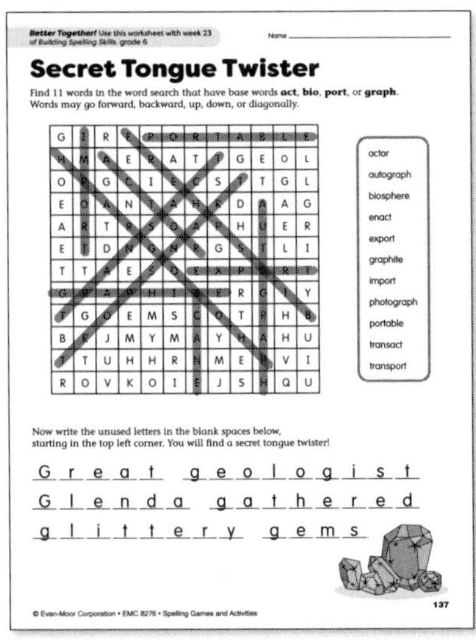

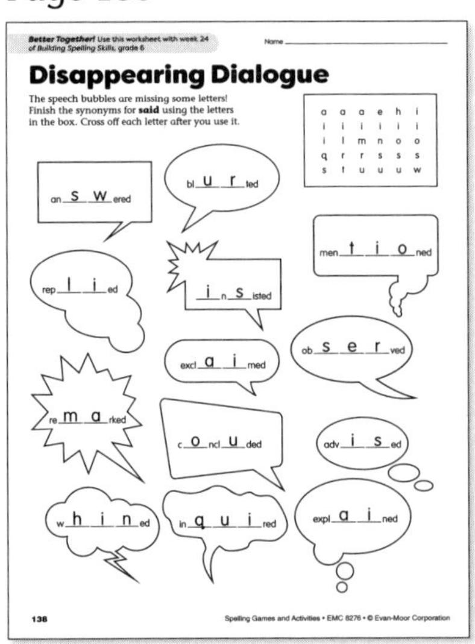

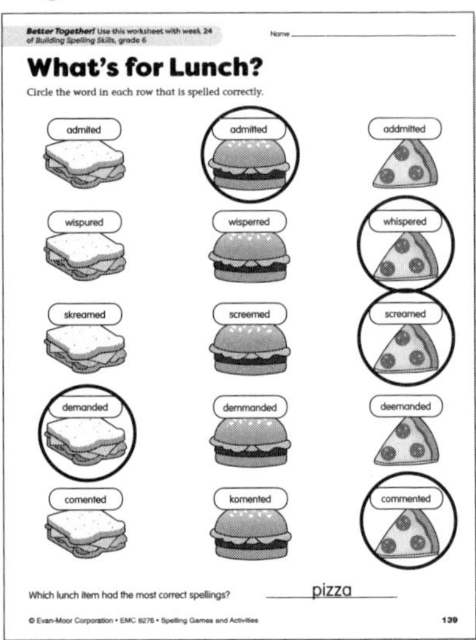

Page 140

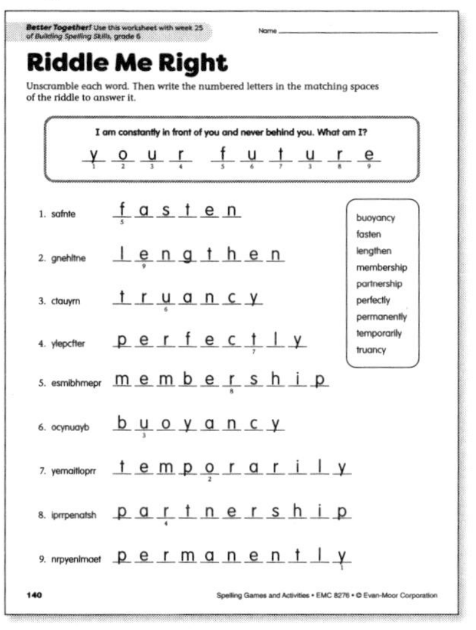

Page 141

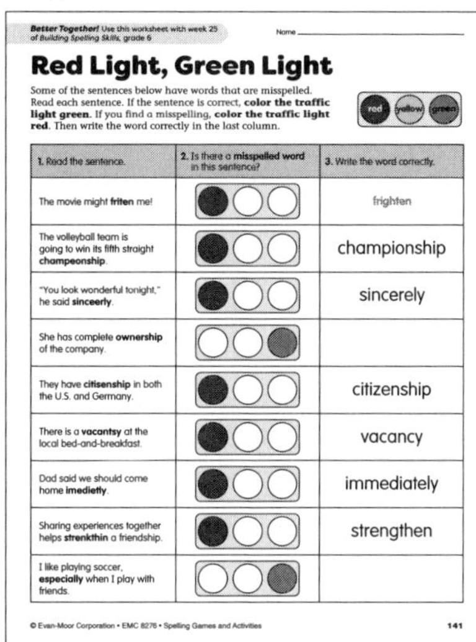

Page 142

Page 143

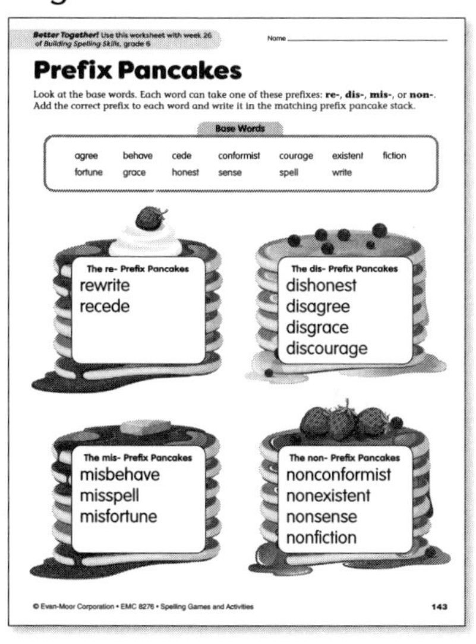

Page 144

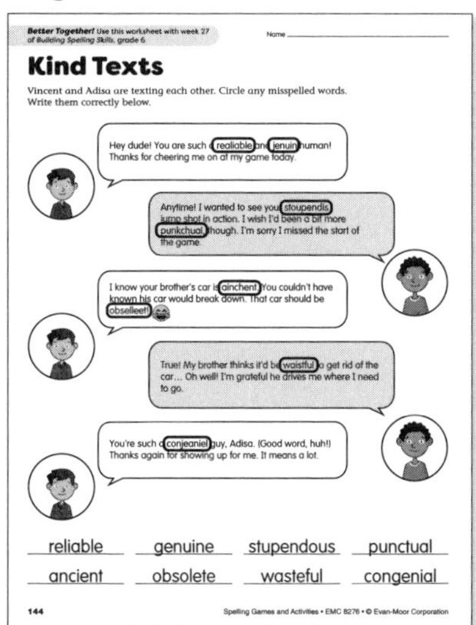

Page 145

Page 146

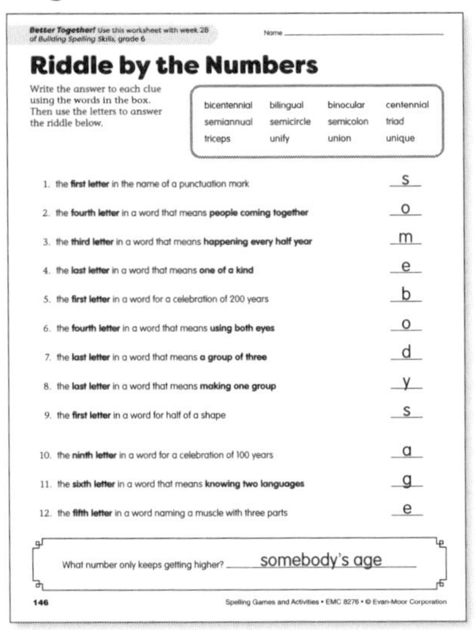

Page 147

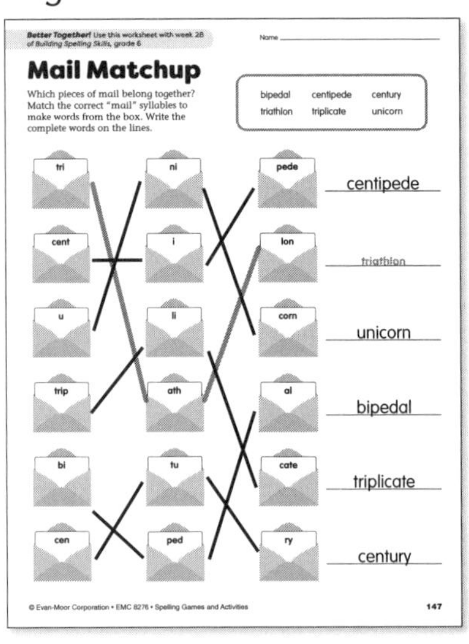

Page 148

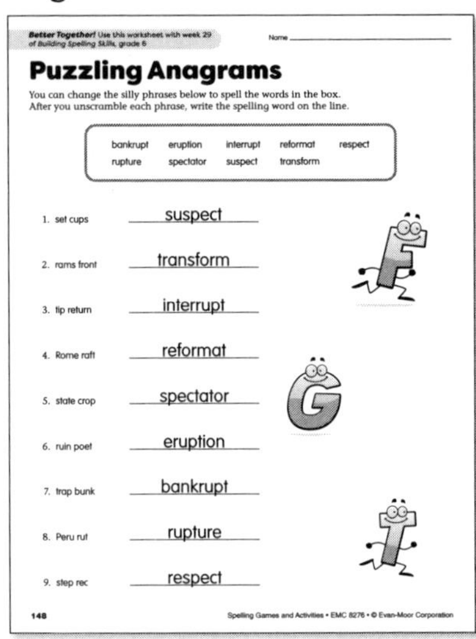

Page 149

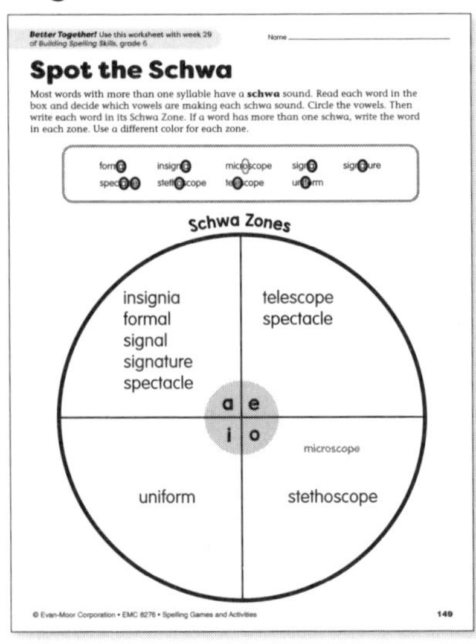

Page 150

Page 151

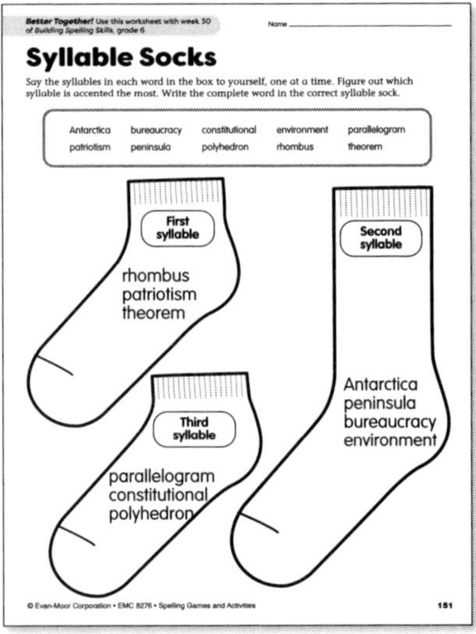